Critical Perspecti~

General Editor Ric Kno~~

2005

Aboriginal Drama and Theatre
ed. Rob Appleford
volume one
978-0-88754-792-8

African-Canadian Theatre
ed. Maureen Moynagh
volume two
978-0-88754-794-2

Judith Thompson
ed. Ric Knowles
volume three
978-0-88754-796-6

2006

Feminist Theatre and Performance
ed. Susan Bennett
volume four
978-0-88754-798-0

George F. Walker
ed. Harry Lane
volume five
978-0-88754-800-0

Theatre in British Columbia
ed. Ginny Ratsoy
volume six
978-0-88754-802-4

2007

Queer Theatre in Canada
ed. Rosalind Kerr
volume seven
978-0-88754-804-8

Environmental and Site-Specific Theatre
ed. Andrew Houston
volume eight
978-0-88754-806-2

Space and the Geographies of Theatre
ed. Michael McKinnie
volume nine
978-0-88754-808-6

2008

Sharon Pollock
ed. Sherrill Grace &
Michelle La Flamme
volume ten
978-0-88754-751-5

Theatre in Alberta
ed. Anne Nothof
volume eleven
978-0-88754-753-9

Collective Creation, Collaboration and Devising
ed. Bruce Barton
volume twelve
978-0-88754-755-3

2009

Theatre Histories
ed. Alan Filewod
volume thirteen
978-0-88754-831-4

"Ethnic," Multicultural, and Intercultural Theatre
ed. Ric Knowles & Ingrid Mündel
volume fourteen
978-0-88754-832-1

Design and Scenography
ed. Natalie Rewa
volume fifteen
978-0-88754-833-8

2010

Theatre in Atlantic Canada
ed. Linda Burnett
volume sixteen
978-0-88754-890-1

Popular Political Theatre and Performance
ed. Julie Salverson
volume seventeen
978-0-88754-891-8

Canadian Shakespeare
ed. Susan Knutson
volume eighteen
978-0-88754-893-2

2011

Community Engaged Theatre and Performance
ed. Julie Salverson
volume nineteen
978-0-88754-932-8

Solo Performance
ed. Jenn Stephenson
volume twenty
978-0-88754-933-5

Theatre and Performance in Toronto
ed. Laura Levin
volume twenty-one
978-0-88754-934-2

PLAYWRIGHTS CANADA PRESS

Community Engaged Theatre and Performance

Critical Perspectives on Canadian Theatre in English

volume nineteen

Critical Perspectives on Canadian Theatre in English
volume nineteen

Community Engaged Theatre and Performance

Edited by
Julie Salverson

Playwrights Canada Press
Toronto • Canada

Playwrights Canada Press
215 Spadina Avenue, Suite 230, Toronto, Ontario, Canada M5T 2C7
phone 416.703.0013 fax 416.408.3402
info@playwrightscanada.com • www.playwrightscanada.com

Playwrights Canada Press acknowledges the financial support of the Government
of Canada through the Canada Book Fund and the Canada Council for the Arts
and of the Province of Ontario through the Ontario Arts Council and the
Ontario Media Development Corporation for our publishing activities.

Cover image: Jin-me Yoon, between departure and arrival, 1996/1997.
Partial installation view, Art Gallery of Ontario.
Video projection, video montage on monitor, photographic mylar scroll,
clocks with 3-D lettering, audio. Dimensions variable.
Courtesy of the artist and Catriona Jeffries Gallery, Vancouver.
Typesetting/Cover Design: JLArt

Library and Archives Canada Cataloguing in Publication

Community engaged theatre and performance / edited by Julie Salverson.

(Critical perspectives on Canadian theatre in English ; v. 19)
Includes bibliographical references.
ISBN 978-0-88754-932-8

1. Canadian drama (English)--20th century--History and criticism.
2. Canadian drama (English)--21st century--History and criticism.
3. Community theater--Canada. 4. Theater and society--Canada.
5. Drama--Social aspects--Canada. I. Salverson, Julie II. Series: Critical
perspectives on Canadian theatre in English ; v. 19

PS8169.C64C64 2011   C812'.5409355   C2011-901763-6

First edition: May 2011
Printed and bound in Canada by Hignell Book Printing, Winnipeg

For Peter and Joan Oliver, original engineers of the imagination.

Table of Contents

General Editor's Preface

Canadian Theatre Studies, as a formal discipline, is barely thirty years old, yet already it has moved through empiricist, nationalist, regionalist, particularist, materialist, and postmodernist phases, each of which has made significant contributions to the almost simultaneous construction and deconstruction of the field's histories. This series, *Critical Perspectives on Canadian Theatre in English*, was founded in order to trace these histories in volumes focusing on specific topics of significance to the still emerging discipline.

The series was launched in 2005 with the intention of making the best critical and scholarly work in the field readily available to teachers, students, and scholars of Canadian drama and theatre. It set out, in individual volumes, chronologically to trace the histories of scholarship and criticism on individual playwrights, geographical regions, theatrical genres, themes, and cultural communities. Over its first seven years the series has published twenty-one volumes, collecting work on *Aboriginal Drama and Theatre*; *African-Canadian Theatre*; and *"Ethnic," Multicultural, and Intercultural Theatre*; on playwrights *Sharon Pollock, Judith Thompson*, and *George F. Walker*; on *Feminist Theatre and Performance* and *Queer Theatre in Canada*; on *Theatre in British Columbia, Theatre in Alberta, Theatre in Atlantic Canada*, and *Theatre and Performance in Toronto*; on *Environmental and Site-Specific Theatre*; *Collective Creation, Collaboration, and Devised Theatre*; *Space and the Geographies of Theatre*; *Theatre Histories*; *Design and Scenography, Popular Political Theatre and Performance, Community Engaged Theatre and Performance, Canadian Shakespeare*, and *Solo Performance*. I am very proud of this achievement, proud that these volumes have already been widely cited in subsequent scholarship, and proud that, although this is primarily a reprint series, essays newly commissioned for individual volumes have been nominated for and have won scholarly awards.

The series has had several objectives. Each volume has been edited and introduced by an expert in the field who has selected a representative sampling of the most important critical work on her or his subject since the 1970s, ordered chronologically according to the original dates of publication. Each volume has also included an introduction by the volume editor, surveying the field and its criticism, and a list of suggested further readings which recommends good work that could not otherwise be included. Where appropriate, the volume editors have commissioned new essays on their subjects, particularly when these new essays fill in gaps in representation and attempt to correct historical injustices and imbalances, particularly those concerning marginalized communities. The volume topics have also been chosen to shed light on historically marginalized communities and work, while individual volumes have resisted the ghettoization of such work by relegating it to special topic volumes alone.

Volumes 19 to 21 bring the series to its conclusion. They continue to address specific geographical regions, in this case the "region" of Toronto, and particular genres, including community engaged theatre and the Canadian phenomenon of solo performance. As this series comes to its conclusion with the launch of its final volumes in the spring of 2011, they will be succeeded by a new series, *New Essays on Canadian Theatre*, which will make its own contributions to the development of the discipline. Already in the planning stages are volumes of new essays on Asian Canadian theatre, on new Canadian realisms, on Latino/a Canadian theatre, and on "Affect."

It is my hope that these series, in conjunction with the publications of Playwrights Canada Press, Talonbooks, and other Canadian play publishers, will facilitate the teaching of Canadian drama and theatre in schools and universities for years to come. I hope that, by making available and accessible comprehensive introductions to some of the field's most provocative figures and issues, that they will contribute to the flourishing of courses on a variety of aspects of Canadian drama and theatre in classrooms across the country. And I hope they will honour the work of some of the scholar/pioneers of a field that is still, excitingly, young.

Ric Knowles

Acknowledgements

I would like to thank Ric Knowles for imagining this series, making it happen, and offering me this volume. His editorial support was invaluable. Also thanks to Bill Penner for the painstaking job of research assistant.

Don Bouzek's "In The Neighbourhood of My Heart" was first published in *Canadian Theatre Review* 53 (1987): 20–25; Sarah B. Hood's "Shadowy Existence: Shadowlands Creative Design Community" first appeared in *Theatrum* Issue #11 (1988): 21–25; Sarah Stanley's "Permission Granted: Romeo & Juliet" first appeared in *Canadian Theatre Review* 84 (1995): 29–31; Edward Little and Richard Paul Knowles's "*The Spirit of Shivaree* and the Community Play in Canada; or, The Unity in Community" first appeared in *Contemporary Issues in Canadian Drama*, edited by Per Brask. Winnipeg: Blizzard (1995): 68–85; Denyse Lynde's "Wabana: A Native Word Meaning 'Place of First Light'" first appeared in *Canadian Theatre Review* 93 (1997): 32–37; Sherene H. Razack's "The Gaze from the Other Side: Storytelling for Social Change" was first published in *Looking White People in the Eye*. Toronto: University of Toronto Press (1998) 36–55; Alan Filewod's "The Working Body/The Working Gaze" was first published in *Canadian Theatre Review* 99 (1999): 31–35; Richard Bruce Kirkley's "Caravan Farm Theatre: Orchestrated Anarchy and the Creative Process" was first published in *Canadian Theatre Review* 101 (2000): 35–39; Richard Payne's "Theatre Inside-Out: An Educational Monograph: Alternative Theatre in Prisons" was first self-published as a Monograph (2000) 1–22; Honor Ford-Smith's "Whose Community? Whose Art? The Politics of Reformulating Community Art" was first published in *No Frame Around It: Process and Outcome of the A Space Community Art Biennale*, edited by Melanie Fernandez and funded by the Laidlaw Foundation. Toronto: A Space Gallery (2001): 11–27; Edward Little and Rachael Van Fossen's "Pedagogies, Politics and Practices in Working with Youth" was first published in *Canadian Theatre Review* 106 (2001): 5–10; David Fancy's "The MarshFire Guild System: Mobilizing Community Resources" was first published in *alt.theatre* 2.1 (2001) 12–13; Nisha Sajnani's "Strategic Narratives: The Embodiment of Minority Discourses in Biographical Performance" was first published in *Canadian Theatre Review* 117 (2004): 33–37; Julie Salverson's "Imagination and Art in Community Arts" was first published in *alt theatre* 3.2 (2004): 2–4; Savannah Walling's "Practicing Responsible Arts: *The Downtown Eastside Community Play*" was first published in *alt.theatre* 3.4 (2005): 12–15; Ruth Howard's "The Cultural Equivalent of Daycare Workers?" was first published online in *Dramatic Action*, produced by Dale Hamilton (2006) www.communityengagedtheatre.ca: 12–15; Clarke Mackey's "The Politics of

Play: Welfare State's Swan Song" was first published in *alt.theatre* 5.1 (2007): 21–23; Kirsty Johnston's "Performing an Asylum: *Tripping Through Time* and *La Pazzia*" was first published in *Theatre Topics* 18:1 (2008): 55–67; David S. Craig's "They Don't Get Us and We Don't Get Them" was first published in *CANPLAY* 24:1 (2008): 12–13; Yvette Nolan's "Of, For, By" and Kelley Aitken's "The Give-Back of the Giving Profession" were commissioned for this volume and appear here for the first time.

Introduction: Deep and Difficult Eyes

by Julie Salverson

Editing a book of essays is a bit like throwing a large dinner party. You try your best to arrange the seating in an engaging not combative manner; you provide enough wine to encourage a scattering of lively, even intense conversation, no awkward moments. But perhaps the image of an orderly gathering isn't the best analogy for a collection of writings that engage a field of artistic and social endeavour that manages with maddening consistency to be vibrant with possibility, riddled with contradiction, and a messy quagmire of political and personal challenges—usually all at the same time.

This collection of new and previously published writing is intended as a companion to volume seventeen in this series, *Popular Political Theatre and Performance*. Although there are distinctions I am making between the two books—the first explicitly addresses companies and people where the politics and desire to provoke social change is front and centre, the second concerns projects where the primary goal is to engage community voices—the worlds of each are intimately connected. Both collections grapple with problems puzzled over and sweated through; explain strategies attempted and refined; reveal "ah-ah" moments and questions left unanswered; honour personal and communal victories and defeats, private and public gains and losses. Neither group of writings attempts to be a definitive list; many excellent pieces had to be left out. Taken together, however, these two books present a wide range of artists and scholars in English Canada who engage people not usually involved in theatre or in the project of performing stories.

The title of this introduction comes from the writer Jeanette Winterson. In her essay "Art Objects," Winterson is killing time in Amsterdam when she is stopped in her tracks by the power of a painting. After a fitful night she postpones her flight and spends an intense few days wandering through galleries, reading, gazing, eating, and sleeping art. Winterson has realized with a shock that "all art, not just painting, is a foreign city, and we deceive ourselves when we think it familiar" (4). She is reminded of an animal trainer she knows who has written of the "acute awkwardness and embarrassment of those who work with magnificent animals, and find themselves at a moment of reckoning, summed up in those deep and difficult eyes.... Better to pretend that art is dumb, or at least has nothing to say that makes sense to us" (11–12).

This discovery, profoundly affirming to anyone who spends his or her life engaged with an artistic practice, has particular resonance for the work of community art. She is indeed a foreign city, a most misunderstood animal. Her territory is not amateur theatrics, although the love of the thing that accompanies the word amateur is certainly applicable. Nor does she prowl the world of hobbies, or badly mounted feel-good classics, or even the grand fun of an enthusiastically offered neighbourhood play. Community engaged theatre throws professional artists together with people who have stories to tell and something to say, and who, just this once (unlike professionals or dedicated amateurs) choose performance as the best way to say it.

The essays appear in the order in which they were first published. Although in this introduction I categorize them according to content and focus, there is as much crossover of subject areas in these writings as there is in the work itself. Honor Ford-Smith's 2001 essay, "Whose Community? Whose Art? The Politics of Reformulating Community Art," establishes a history and context for the aspects of this work that have evolved from participatory and popular education practices and social movements associated with Latin America and the educational strategies of Brazil's Paulo Freire. She brings theory and her experience as an artist to bear on an interrogation of critical encounters with community cultural expression "in the current context of the enormous expansion of global capitalism—an expansion which is commodifying almost everything, transforming both the potential of cultural production [and] how we think of communities, nations, and the state." While endorsing the support of community art by public and private institutions, Ford-Smith challenges artists and participants of these projects to lead the way in scrutinizing the institutions that fund and sometimes claim them. "Without this, community art is in danger of becoming a process which can be used both as a brightly packaged form of welfare and as a means for the manufacture of the myths which justify traditional narratives of Canadianess and the status quo."

The challenge of writing a history of community arts and understanding local projects not as isolated endeavours but, rather, as informed and informing the culture they operate within and through, is taken up by a number of other authors. Edward Little and Richard Paul Knowles's "*The Spirit of Shivaree* and the Community Play in Canada; or, The Unity in Community" addresses Canada's first community play to use the Colway Theatre Trust Process developed in Britain in the late seventies and made famous in Ann Jellicoe's 1987 book *Community Plays: How To Put Them On.* Knowles and Little pose key questions to Dale Hamilton's pioneering project near Rockwood, Ontario, questions which orient critical discussion of community engaged theatre and thus reappear throughout this volume: What constitutes power, belonging, stability or participation in a community play? What is the continuum between cultural affirmation and intervention? How can community be understood as a process rather than a stable entity? How does this model of project, with its emphasis on celebration, broad involvement, and the tendency to engender solidarity, employ both processes and historical icons that "tend to function as conservative, affirmative, and stabilizing forces in the production of value and meaning"?

Another direct source of inspiration to community engaged theatre in Canada is the celebratory arts company Welfare State International. Founded in the late sixties by visual artists and prankster/renegades John and Sue Fox, their exuberant, fanciful, yet carefully crafted and planned outdoor extravaganzas helped birth longstanding Canadian companies like Public Dreams in Vancouver and Shadowlands on Wards Island, Toronto. Clarke Mackey's moving tribute to the final swan song under the Fox's directorship both articulates his vision of vernacular culture—which Mackey finds in unofficial homemade activities that tap the bred in the bone impulse to create and imagine—and acknowledges the formative link between much Canadian celebratory art (lantern processions, musical walks), Welfare State International, and Bread and Puppet Theatre in Vermont. Sarah B. Hood explores collective design in the work of Shadowland, one of the longest lasting celebratory companies in Canada. Hood reminds us that this rich aspect of our theatre tradition is rooted across arts practices as diverse as graphic design, visual art, music, and landscape architecture. Here also we get a good taste of the aesthetics and style these artists and projects embrace: "The two words 'oversize' and 'grotesque' keep popping up whenever people speak of Shadowland's work. 'We don't like to duplicate reality,' says [company member Kathleen] Doody. 'Shows where we have done that have been dismal.… We prefer the outsize, the zany, the beyond-the-real.'"

The range of aesthetics, practices, and institutional relationships called upon to address marginalized voices are examined in a number of ways in this volume. The late Richard Payne takes us through his high-wire act in Matsqui Institution, a high-medium security federal prison in Abbotsford, British Columbia. I am grateful to Steven Bush for editing this essay and honouring Payne's contribution to our field. Payne describes mounting an absurd political clown play in a program run in partnership with Langara College Theatre Department. At a time when the Canadian government is increasing the numbers of incarcerated and "corrected" citizens, this essay describes an initiative that I hope will inspire people working in schools and prisons around the country. In a CBC Radio review in 1981, John Lazarus called this event "a gleefully defiant bellow" from within the prison walls. At the time of writing this introduction, the only performance program I can find in a Canadian penal institution is run by SNAFU Dance Theatre and William Head Prison, again in British Columbia.

I have included a letter from Richard Keating in this collection. At the time of Richard Payne's project, Keating was an inmate at Matsqui; he is now an actor in Vancouver. I realize putting something like this in a volume of essays is a bit unusual, but it seems to me that participants are the bloodstream of this work and in no other place are they able to speak directly. Keating is eloquent in his testimony to the power of theatre, and startling in what he reveals:

> One day Richard came into the classroom decked in full clown regalia and started doing his clown turns and I remember thinking there is no way this clown is going make me crack a smile. Trust was, and I imagine still is, a scarce commodity in a Federal Penitentiary. But he persisted and eventually got that smile and a couple more. How could you not be taken with a man who was willing to come into a high security penitentiary and try to teach murderers, drug traffickers and bank robbers the

Laban theory of flick and dab in preparation for a clown show. He even came through the front gate in full clown and let the Guards search him. They did their job, shook their heads, and said "Might as well come in, the place is full of fucking clowns." The production went up and it was a huge success. I put off my release date just so that I could stay and finish the course and the show.

Stories that don't get told in most of the places Canadians go for entertainment or refuge—theatres, television, concert halls, galleries, cinemas—take centre stage in articles by Nisha Sajnani, Kirsty Johnston, and Don Bouzek. Sajnani's "Strategic Narratives: The Embodiment of Minority Discourses in Biographical Performance" documents the process of five close friends exploring "personal and collective memories of immigration, integration, and assimilation into Canada's multicultural mosaic." As they "theorized, positioned and imposed [themselves] in relation to each other, [they] became aware of the willingness necessary to attend to the many questions that arose as [they] transgressed the familiar and ended up, often, on unfamiliar terrain." Johnston's *Tripping Through Time* and *La Pazzia* brings us two productions that address mental illness and stigma, one speaking to the broader community, one to medical professionals; one greeted with praise, the other protest and challenge. Her essay theorizes the complex relationship between audience and performer when lines between fiction and reality challenge our most basic assumptions about who we are and how we define ourselves. In Don Bouzek's work with homeless people "In The Neighbourhood of My Heart"—including collaboration with another key figure in community engaged theatre in Canada, the late Rhonda Payne—he addresses the sometimes crazy-making juggle of funding challenges (which part of your project meets which part of our mandate; which language matters to who and why; what are opportunities and what are exploitations) as well as the fascinating challenge of how what's real, what's true, is best told. Talking about the dramatic and the documentary impulse, Bouzek says: "In my experience this tension between fact and fiction is one of the toughest issues in the work, but at the same time it's what gives a real power when you get it working for you."

One complicated issue in community-engaged theatre is the tendency to oppose historical and imaginary discourses, privileging the documentary at the expense of the fictional. This presents two particular difficulties. First, what Alan Filewod has called the tendency in Canadian collective creation/documentary tradition to valorize experience at the cost of inquiry or analysis. What happens when a moment in a community's history is considered significant simply because it has been presented on a stage, as art, without any effort to address who it means what to, and why? In the complex negotiation between reception, perception, and what can be counted as truth, what does it mean to call something "authentic" (183)? Second, why does framing something as historical assume it is any less a constructed narrative than if it were a deliberately shaped fiction? Ernst Van Alphen has pointed out how "documentary realism has become the mode of representation that novelists and artists must adopt if they are to persuade their audience of their moral integrity" (20). In this volume, imaginative and documentary vocabularies offer different strategies for tackling risky stories and situations, but it is still true, I think, that within community engaged practice in English Canada we are hobbled by the idea of "the authentic" and the belief that a "rhetoric of fact"¹—use of testimonial fragments or the witness as final arbiter of "what really happened"—gives a (false) sense of authoritative finality to a community based performance.

Messy questions are tackled head-on in Sherene Razack's "The Gaze From The Other Side: Storytelling for Social Change," an in-depth examination of what it means to solicit, tell, and receive stories. This essay is not explicitly about theatre practice, but it is one of the most articulate and thorough discussions of the transaction of embodied storytelling to have emerged in several decades. Razack, a professor of sociology and equity studies at the Ontario Institute for Studies in Education, considers how personal narratives are mobilized in law and critical pedagogy. She reminds us that these practices aren't straightforward, and they can't be seamlessly transplanted from, say, Paulo Freire's Brazil to inner city Winnipeg. Furthermore, lives and the stories of lives are always more than meets the eye: "I have been drawn to the poetry and to the stories because they are layered, because more than one truth is represented, because there is ambiguity and paradox."²

"Partnerships" is a loose and easy term, usually found on grant application these days. It may appear as a simple category to answer "yes" to, but working across organizations is often fraught with difficulty. In David Craig's "They Don't Get Us, and We Don't Get Them," an award-winning performance and the creator's desire to engage young people in a discussion on risk makes school boards and educators nervous: the show is refused and the encounter never happens. "They wanted theatre, but they didn't want this theatre." Craig's essay asks, "How did this happen?" He addresses the power ceded by school boards to parents and the danger of presenting unambiguous "message" plays that try to address rigidly defined learning outcomes while trying to please everyone. David Fancy describes how "The MarshFire Guild System" in Sackville, New Brunswick, resurrected the concept of Guilds to help them avoid corporate branding and write their own design content, still bringing together a wide spectrum of players and funders. Savannah Walling's account of the challenges to a community play and a marriage describes the working relationship between Vancouver Moving Theatre and their co-producer when their stance as a company is to not take sides on divisive issues, in part because "the community's problems have been sensationalized in the Canadian media." Alan Filewod theorizes working class theatre as a relational practice in "The Working Body/The Working Gaze," while the multiplicity of interests people bring to having their stories told is evident in Yvette Nolan's commissioned essay "Of, For and By," which discusses Native Earth's Made to Order program of community-commissioned performances. Faced with an always changing roster of invitations and challenges—"the Canadian Aboriginal Minerals Association; how do you make consultation active and theatrical?"—Nolan remarks that, after many years, "popular theatre is insinuating itself back into my life, cleverly disguised as community engagement".

One of the reasons these two volumes belong together is the increasingly permeable territory between what's termed "community engaged theatre" and "popular theatre." What were once posed as mutually exclusive political divides—activist goals striving for social change, community building practices stressing celebration and affirmation—are now more likely to exist side by side. Is this because it is harder to find explicitly political theatre companies, or because politics itself is being reshaped and redefined so that either everyone—or no one—considers his or herself political anymore? I asked Ruth Howard about this and her reply was interesting:

> If "community" is something you create as well as engage, I think there is a distinction between activism as subject matter to be expressed, and as form or social context to experience. Most of us who come under the umbrella of "community arts"—whether there is any other affinity between our work or not—would consider and call ourselves political. It's very much present in all the conversations, whether said earnestly or dogmatically or with more complexity of thought. Other than the fact that terminology gets changed from time to time by funders and critics, I think the difference has to do with a relative focus on experience versus message, or form versus content—not just dramatic form but social and relational form. Is that a less or more optimistic kind of political activism? I often wonder. (Howard)

While even the term "popular theatre" is hard to find these days, community projects are all the rage. But the surge in institutional support for community engaged theatre does not necessarily translate into arts councils or artists championing fights for social justice. However we might answer this question from one historical moment to the next, Ford-Smith reminds us that if cultural institutions are not scrutinized, "community art is in danger of becoming a process which can be used both as a brightly packaged form of welfare and as a means for the manufacture of the myths which justify traditional narratives of Canadianness and the Canadian status quo." This is something to pay attention to, particularly if Simon Critchley is correct when he writes that "institutions of secular democracy simply do not sufficiently motivate their citizenry [and] there is a motivational deficit at the heart of liberal democratic life" (7).

What can motivate engagement at this juncture in the relationship between Canada, its breadth of communities, and its multiplicity of artists? What does looking back at over two decades of explicitly community-engaged arts practice offer? Is there power and possibility in the "orchestrated anarchy" described by Caravan Farm Theatre member Ken Smedley in Richard Bruce Kirkley's rich discussion of the tension between individuality and collectivity "central to the practical pursuit of anarchism"? Or in Denyse Lynde's whirlwind tour that takes an audience from the ferry docks at Portugal Cove, Newfoundland, across the icy waters to Bell Island and then deep into an abandoned mine shaft for an "exciting, moving theatrical feast"? Is it enough to revisit the many moments of engagement witnessed in these encounters with the imagination, and to remember—as I do in my plea for art and the imagination in this volume—to "trust the artists and the [participants], let them dig deeply and play with their world, and they will surprise you and themselves."

Many of the writers in this collection have found ways to be mentors and teachers, to nurture community engaged theatre and performance in emerging artists. Edward Little and Rachael Van Fossen describe Concordia University's Drama for Human Development program and not only the processes but also the aesthetic forms that emerge from their work with young people. Ruth Howard's Jumblies Theatre provides mentorship and training through an inter-disciplinary and flexible studio program that invites and encourages idiosyncratic artistic visions, even as her article humorously asks if artists in this practice are all "The Cultural Equivalent of Daycare Workers." Howard marvels at the curious relationship between the desires and intentions of the artist and the participant, at the end of the day satisfied, I think, by a woman who has wandered into Davenport Perth Community Centre, where Jumblies is working. Asked by Howard why she keeps coming, the woman replies, "Because it's art, because people need to learn everything, I think. I like to learn everything because it's better I think for life, for mind—for everything!"

This seems to be the bottom line for Sarah Gartner Stanley. In her adventure with *Romeo and Juliet* under the Bathurst Street Bridge in Toronto (1995) permission is not simply granted, but taken. It is a permission that allows Stanley to let herself be changed by her encounter with this project and its people. The teenagers in Stanley's re-imagining of Shakespeare's timeless story are "still dying for love, but more importantly are dying for their courage to believe in something." In this remarkable essay Stanley claims a place for that kind of courage. And so I think, at this dinner party that is these twenty-three essays, I would seat Stanley with Kelley Aitken at an end of the table where they could put their heads together and compare notes.

It is Aitken who has the last word in the volume, a writer and visual artist for whom performance is only a small part of her practice, but who speaks eloquently about why she loves this hard to explain kind of art-making that happens twice a week in a Toronto women's centre. In "The Give-Back of the Giving Profession" Aitken says that when she visits this foreign city that Jeanettte Winterson tells us takes time to get to know, she finds "a sense of myself offering something real, and that has less to do with art—although that's the reason we're all there in the same place, with me giving my dorky little demonstrations—than with showing up as myself." She continues: "If art is essentially a reflection of belonging or identity, then the craving to be involved in artistic practice could be described as a psychic 'going home.'"

It is my hope that there is something of this sense of recognition or return for the readers of this collection.

Notes

¹ Cited on pg. 20, Van Alphen, and first used by James Young in *Writing and Rewriting the Holocaust: Narrative and the Consequences of Interpretation.*

² Razack is citing Aptheker 254.

Works Cited

Aptheker, Bettina. *Tapestries of Life.* San Fransisco: Spinsters/Aunt Lute Foundation Books, 1987.

Critchley, Simon. *Infinitely Demanding: Ethics of Commitment, Politics of Resistance.* London: Verso, 2007.

Filewod, Alan. *Collective Encounters: Documentary Theatre in English Canada.* Toronto: U of Toronto P, 1987.

Howard, Ruth. Email to the author, 20 January 2011.

Van Alphen, Ernst. *Caught By History: Holocaust Effects in Contemporary Art, Literature, and Theory.* Stanford, California: Stanford UP, 1997.

Winterson, Jeanette. *Art Objects: Essays on Ecstasy and Effrontery.* New York: Knopf, 1996.

Young, James. *Writing and Rewriting the Holocaust: Narrative and the Consequences of Interpretation.* Bloomington: Indiana UP, 1993.

In the Neighbourhood of My Heart

by Don Bouzek

1. Shudell Avenue, Toronto, 4 September 1985

I'm writing these notes part way through a process. I don't claim it's a model. It's another group of people trying to make a change—socially, theatrically. We're aiming for September 18. At an alternative event, organized by homeless people, we'll produce a show combining Ground Zero's work with a performance by residents from Homes First, a Toronto project to house single people. We'll also be setting up a booth to videotape the event. It will be a community celebration on several levels.

This project is the most extensive Ground Zero has undertaken to date. Our labour union work has not had the same scope—it has isolated theatre from video, solidarity from analysis. Also, having Rhonda Payne's ten years of experience in popular theatre on the project has given it a greater degree of self-analysis.

There's no way to count the homeless. Some say, 100,000 in Canada. But if you combine the United Nations definition that includes "affordability" with the usual guidelines that rent shouldn't exceed 30 per cent of income, then I'd say there are millions. Of course, I live in Toronto where a one-bedroom apartment downtown goes for $900 a month. If you can find one.

2. Project design: May to December 1986

Lina Chartrand and I started talking about a show on housing when she first came to work at Ground Zero. Lina's background is in tenants' organizing and co-ops. She found out that 1987 was the International Year of Shelter for the Homeless (IYSH), and that there was to be a special Ontario government department under the Ministry of Housing. We applied to them for an integrated theatre/video project.

As usual video appeared sexier. The Ministry was prepared to support a half-hour docudrama tape. No money for the live work. Fortunately the Canada Council and the Ontario Arts Council came through with project grants (although the OAC jury at first turned us down, calling the project "sociology not art"). From the beginning we had seen two eventual "product" objectives—a tape and a live show. We wanted the latter to be available for tours to co-ops and community groups. The process of developing the live material would, we hoped, form the basis of the video scripts. However the split in the funding bases underlined the tensions between the two components, between the dramatic and the documentary impulses. In my experience this tension between fact and fiction is one of the toughest issues in the work, but at the same time, it's what gives a real power when you get it working for you.

3. *"Gimme Shelter" Forum, Harbourfront, 26 February 1987*

Within a few days of officially being told we had no money from the Ministry of Housing for a video, we were told the Minister would speak at a meeting at Harbourfront. Would we tape it? We did. After the presentations, all questions were directed at the Minister. It was politely "hot," with queries that ranged from a woman applying for project funds, to roomers and boarders asking about the fate of a task force report on their issues. Obviously we were in an interesting position—paid by the Ministry but sympathetic to the questioners. The project was going to be a tightrope.

4. *"Homelessness and Health" Inquiry, Central Neighbourhood House, 28 March 1987*

The meeting was organized by local NDP alderman Jack Layton and the Union of Unemployed. One hundred fifty people crammed into a small basement room. The video lighting made it even less comfortable. The first four hours was informative but unexciting, with two exceptions. Arlene Mantle got a group of women together who read a "script" of their issues and sang a song they had written. Later a young woman recounted her experiences in a hostel. Her attitude showed that she hated the inquiry format that turned her into a specimen. Interestingly, she worked as an outreach worker at a place called Homes First. The name kept coming up.

Then in late afternoon, the meeting changed. Person after person came up to the microphone to make cogent, angry remarks. Suddenly, for an hour, the meeting was great theatre. It was moving, funny, and directly relevant. These people weren't talking about the issue, they were living it.

A woman in Public Housing: If you put rats in an overcrowded situation they will eat each other. That's what people do. The husband comes home and beats the wife and the wife turns around and kicks the child. You become an angry woman. Hey, one of the things you're not allowed if you're a woman is your anger. If you fight back, that makes you suspect—psychologically.

I went home and looked at the tapes. We'd caught a remarkable moment. These were no longer "the homeless." They were intelligent, witty, passionate human beings who couldn't afford a place to live. I hoped our work could do them justice.

5. *Carlos Bulosan workshop, Hugh Garner Housing Co-op, April 1987*

Voltaire de Leon has asked me to do a popular theatre workshop on the issue with the Filipino community group, the Carlos Bulosan Cultural Workshop. Because I didn't know who from the Filipino community would come, I decided on a general approach rather than one that emphasized theatrical skills. Rhonda suggested that the popular education technique of drawing pictures and explaining them to the group has worked for her in a variety of cross-cultural contexts.

As it turned out, the workshop participants ranged from members of the group through community activists on the issue to our own project members—Lina, Allan Merovitz and Rhonda. The drawings of where people want to live brought out some interesting cross-cultural similarities and differences. We all seemed to want private space, peace and a proximity to natural elements like trees and water. However, while we North Americans drew variants on the single-family dwelling, Voltaire created an environment that combined personal space and gardens, with housing for his whole extended family. His idea was more familial, more social and more co-operative than ours.

In the second part of the workshop we did improvs. In all workshops, the trauma of renting a place to live always came up. Here this was compounded by racism. In the scenes the participants created we saw every variety of racism from subtle deferral to overt insult. It was an object lesson in the Canadian "multicultural" reality.

6. *Toronto Homeless Workshop, 5 May 1987*

We played the first workshop presentation of the live show under what might best be called trying conditions. We were part of "the entertainment" at the official Toronto IYSH (International Year of Shelter for the Homeless) workshop. That meant we were scheduled over lunch hour. Now, early in my career I worked out the fact that faced with a choice between fried chicken and theatre, most people will pay attention to the chicken every time.

We had only been working for about a week prior to the conference. The thing about project grants is that they only allow you enough money to get people together for short periods. We started from the videotapes and everybody's own experience with the issue. By the end of the week we had about an hour of improvised and written material for a twenty-minute show. It was a real mixed bag of comic sketches, songs, character monologues and even an adaptation of a story by Japanese writer Kobo Abe. A line from that story gave the show its title: *In the Neighbourhood of My Heart*. It was a rough and ready piece of theatre that made its point clearly. We managed to hold down the room and pull off a standing ovation from some participants.

I look at this kind of event as an exact parallel to workshopping a script in a place like Factory Theatre. The difference is in the feedback process. The work is created to address certain issues, so you are checking for the response of a community concerned with that issue. First you want to know that the script has included the right stuff. Then, since you're representing people with a community of interest to others in that community, you want to know that they consider your portrayal of them accurate.

7. Hamilton Homeless workshop, Steelworkers' Hall, May 1987

We were simply videotaping the day's events. The Hamilton meeting had a very different feel from the meetings we'd been to in Toronto. This was largely a group of social workers and community development people. There were very few of the homeless in attendance.

Because I'd left the *Standin' the Gaff* festival in Sydney the day before, this difference in meetings started me thinking about a major issue in popular theatre. There was much discussion in Sydney whether popular theatre workers should be animateurs engaged in leading a community to create a particular analysis of a problem, or whether our job is merely to reflect and chronicle. What Hamilton brought home to me is that even that argument is subject to an analysis of the particular situation in which you are working. If I worked in Hamilton, I think there would have been a valuable role to play in organizing a group of homeless people to make their presence known at this meeting.

That was completely unnecessary in Toronto. There, not only were the groups up and at the meetings, they were presenting an analysis that was far more sophisticated and radical than any we had yet evolved. Groups like the Roomers and Boarders Association are clearly working on a strategy of applying political pressure to lobby for their issues. They didn't need us to do any of that work. What was needed was the documentation and a sharing of the ideas and feelings they had invested a lot of energy in articulating.

8. Homes First workshop, July 1987

Ground Zero hired Rhonda Payne to design a series of popular theatre workshops with Homes First. After two sessions in June, she and I made an evaluation tape. This excerpt from that tape talks about an exercise, originally developed by Jan Selman at Catalyst Theatre, that we used in the first session:

> Rhonda: I asked people to think about a personal situation in which they had a problem to solve, and then in a small group to share those stories with each other. They were then to agree on a story the group wanted to portray, and to tell the story through a series of five snapshots. The final snapshot was to present the problem, and the preceding four, the stages leading up to it.

> Don: We chose to show the story of a young female resident—where she was first (which was a home for young women), then her interview, her concern, her worry about being accepted into Homes First. The process was a fairly arduous one, from her point of view. She was interviewed and then people wouldn't confirm whether or not she was accepted for a period of time.

Rhonda: We went through picture by picture, and tried to do an analysis of "what's happening here?" "Is there anything that this individual could have done to change the situation?" But in fact the pictures that were being shown really were not such that we could offer suggestions as to how that individual could alter her own situation, how she could take more control of her own situation.

Don: Catalyst work is predicated on the concept that people have choices in a situation. In the particular scenario that we were presenting, this woman didn't have a lot of choices.

Rhonda: I think the key to this kind of work, as animators, is to try and find the ways to make people understand what's happening in that situation, where they fit, and that they do in fact have choices. The real trick to a whole process of empowerment for people is for them to be able to find the resources to say "yes, I do have choices and my life is not necessarily being controlled by others."

As an animator with theatrical skills, you are limited in the impact that you have in a situation like that. What you need is a broader range of skills than just theatrical. I think that's one of the areas that we, you and I, have a slightly different approach to the work, in that at this point I see this as an educational process. I see in you a tendency to want to create material—you are looking for the nice little scene that can be put into a performance somewhere.

Don: In fact, I'm very hesitant to affect people's lives, in so far as I do feel a lack of skills on basic social-psychological levels. Also, my own questions around one's right to make assumptions that I should or could affect these people's lives… I have certain other skills, mainly theatrical, which I can offer. My own background makes me jump-cut more quickly to a theatrical solution than a purely development solution.

9. Writing workshop, Ground Zero rehearsal hall, July 1988

One of the things about doing theatre in Toronto is that it's next to impossible to get everyone together. When we all sat down with our datebooks, we discovered that there was only one week all summer when we could all work together. We agreed that we now had to create material about housing alternatives. Further, we wanted these to be all within the possibilities included under the current slogan "Housing for people, not profits." From there we narrowed our solutions to tenants' associations, co-ops and non-profit projects. We invited spokespeople from each to come and talk to us.

Fresh from a screenwriting course in Ottawa with Hanif Kureishi (author of *My Beautiful Laundrette*), I pushed to orient the show around three characters and their stories. Each would draw on certain elements of the material we'd already created but then go further into one of the housing options we were looking at. Over the course of the week, three characters emerged.

Reg was created as a person whose father had been involved in steelworker organizing in Cape Breton. He'd travelled to Sudbury, been laid off, and ended up in a Toronto hostel. Evicted as a roomer, he begins organizing Homes First.

Diane is a woman who starts well-off, but loses her house and security when the only company in town leaves. She goes from the hostels to sharing with another woman, who introduces her to co-ops. Eventually she becomes part of a newly established co-op.

Denise is from Grenada. She worked in literacy under the Bishop government and came to Canada to upgrade her qualifications. Married here, she finds that she can't go back after the Americans invade. She faces the racism of looking for an apartment here, and eventually settles into a place. Then the landlord threatens to convert to condos. She forms a tenants association.

We've tried to avoid the stereotypes of the homeless—the Woody Guthrie hoboes or the bag people. Most homeless people today are young women. We've also created people whose homelessness is not the result of personal problems. By the end of the week we have an outline and a long list of scenes to be written.

10. *Homes First workshop, 15 July 1988*

Tonight I'm running the workshop because Rhonda has a CIDA briefing in Ottawa. We decide to explore why people become homeless. Because this is emotionally "hot" territory for the people in the workshop, I'm quite careful. I don't want the session to be therapy, but rather a way of getting at some of the real causes of homelessness instead of myths and labels. I ask the people to work in pairs, each telling her story to the other. Then the receiver of the story tells it to the group. In this way I hope to get a bit of distance from the material. These excerpts give a sense of the many stories that were told:

> I was put in a series of foster homes. I had a roof over my head, food in my mouth and clothes on my back. But to me, I felt that was a kind of homelessness, because I never felt it was a home. It wasn't my house, I was put there, I was a property of the state.
>
> My mother and father were not together, and he remarried and had kids, um, we didn't get along very well. She didn't like me. I didn't like the kids, I didn't like her. And my father … my father, because he didn't raise me, he started making passes at me. So that's when I knew I couldn't stay. So, I came to the city.
>
> I grew up in a family where my father was an alcoholic who was abusive and my mother was verbally abusive. By the time I was seven, I'd gotten to the point where I would take all the abuse so that my brother

and sister wouldn't have to take it. I don't remember things clearly. I think I was destroying all my stuff and the next thing I know they put me in the nuthouse and from there it was just growing up in and out of hospitals.

The stories were more poignant than anything we could make up. But all the people were clear. They did not want their stories used to make the homeless seem victims of tragic circumstance. Their clarity was a forceful reminder not to get so caught up in the personal pain that you lose sight of its social and political context.

11. Documentary video. Trinity Square Video, August 1988

Like working in theatre, you really only get a feel for what you're creating when you're actually in the middle of working on it. I've decided that the video component of the project needs two tapes. The first, which we're currently editing, will be essentially documentary. Right now I'm watching a young Native man tell his story for what seems like the hundredth time.

I'm seeing clearly that the documentary tape can cover a broad cross-section of the problem. We hear from the people in hostels, the disabled, refugees, the under housed, ex-psychiatrics. In the fifteen minutes we've finished so far, we have deliberately paralleled the theatrical process. We've stated the problem, just the way we did on May 5th. Now we need to look at what people are doing about it. We have just realized that, in fact, there are so many issues raised in the first half of the tape that we need to do more interviews.

Watching the tapes I find the effect powerful, but it is a cumulative result of a lot of different stories—there simply isn't time in a half-hour tape to stop for long with any one person. But it makes it clearer to me that drama works in the opposite direction. You gain power by gradually coming to know a lot about particular individuals. You come to care about them because of the details you're shown. It's a slower process, but I think it goes deeper.

12. Homes First reading, 26 August 1988

We set up in a second floor room and by show time the place is a maze of video lights, cables, chairs, actors and residents. The Homes First crowd are a noisier audience than the polite co-op folks. But they also laugh out loud, clap, and yell "right on!" more often.

They're quite excited about having their story on stage, and feel good about how it is told. One objects to a line that goes, "hard to house, hard to handle." She feels it puts them down. The irony is that it was said by a resident during one of the workshops. It goes to show that what you're willing to say internally about a situation may not be what you want others to hear. Still, it'll probably be out of the script by the next reading.

The big discussion, though, centres around two things. First, they feel we left a lot of people out. We don't show all the forms of homelessness. Second, they think the piece is too optimistic because all three characters find a place to live. It doesn't work out that well in real life. Our choices were deliberate: in the first case, we chose three people who had gone from being all right to the edge because we didn't want the audiences to feel that homeless people are a breed apart.

> Diane: Now, I know what most of you people out there are thinking. You're thinking, those people up there—up here, I mean—us—you're thinking those people are the losers, right?
>
> Being on the street, homeless, they're the ones who don't quite know how to take care of themselves. You're thinking, hey, I'm all right, I got my job, I got my house, that couldn't happen to me, right? You know that's exactly what I used to think, I used to think, my God, that couldn't happen to me.

In the end the people at Homes First decide they will focus the material they are creating around the people we didn't cover.

The second point is tougher. We chose to have three people who make it because we didn't want to leave viewers in the powerless situation of thinking, "Oh, another social problem, what can I do?" We also wanted to reinforce the not-for-profit alternatives. However the point, that we make it seem as if the problem is actually getting better, is a serious one. After all, there are only 71 units at Homes First and 10,000 people on the street. Not good odds. Right now, we're working on whether it will be enough to have one of the characters more aware that the "solutions" are only partial. Or should there be another character, one who doesn't make it?

13. Songwriting workshop, 90 Shuter St., 29 August 1988

The roof of 90 Shuter is a kind of open patio eleven storeys in the air. From the top you can see the mass of office towers pyramiding toward the CN Tower. From the other side you can see the area around Dundas East that many of the homeless frequent. You can see the next Homes First project, a new building with single units for each person. When this building was planned, a lot of people said they wanted everyone to have their own space. But the government wouldn't fund it. So things are getting better. Homes First has also just been told that they've been funded for a project at Larry's Hideaway. Because it was a notorious boarding house, it'll provide a really symbolic victory, if it can be turned around to provide good housing based on principles of resident management.

Allan and I and about eight residents are trying to compose a song. We're actually having a really good time. The whole group is jamming ideas and lyrics as the sun shines. They've created a hard rock rhythm.

Medication, inebriation
Too many frustrations
I can't think straight
They put too much in my head.

My only mistake
Is not having the rent
But who gives a damn
When you don't got a cent?

What about me?
What about you?
What we gonna do?
Together

Various unofficial housing groups have decided to stage an event on September 18 in Allen Gardens, a park famed for its street population. It's meant as an antidote to all the official IYSH (International Year of Shelter for the Homeless) events. This song is going to be part of a Homes First presentation. They're going to intersperse verses with short stories of people that we don't include in our show. So far the characters include a runaway teenager, a native woman forced off her reserve, a person living on minimum wage in a rooming house, and a woman who has lost everything because of a nervous breakdown.

Allan has found an immediate rapport with the people there, so I'm writing a bridge from Reg's story into the material from Homes First. We'll try tagging the show with Reg reminding us that there's still a lot to be done.

It has been very exciting working with the residents. They have an energy born of hard experience and deep conviction. They're doing what they wanted, which is getting a chance to say some of the things they want people to hear. And our show is getting stronger as a result. I feel like the disparate elements of the project are finally coalescing. There's already talk of using the work as a way of communicating in the face of the opposition Homes First is facing on the Larry's Hideaway project, from the neighbours in this recently sandblasted part of town.

Meanwhile we're having a great time singing up on the roof.

(1987)

Shadowy Existence: Shadowland's
Creative Design Community

by Sarah B. Hood

A theatrical production is necessarily a group effort, yet stage design is often the work of an individual who, with the director's consent, imposes his or her personal stamp upon the visual aspects of the show. In opposition to this tradition, Shadowland Production Company is an artists' collective that designs props, costumes, and set pieces (as well as conceiving and producing their own shows) by drawing from the creativity of their community.

Physically and artistically rooted on Ward's Island in Toronto Harbour, Shadowland's four principal artists (Kathleen Doody, Leida Englar, Sarah Miller and Brad Harley) came to know each other through living in the tight-knit island community. "Being Islanders, we're a lot more politically aware and active because of our struggle to be here,"[1] says Kathleen Doody, referring to the efforts that have been made from time to time to forbid private residences on the Islands. Despite these efforts, Ward's Island is home to many families, which include a high proportion of artists, musicians, and others with an avid interest in the arts.

Originally called Shadowland Repertory Company, the group consists of members from a wide variety of backgrounds, none of them specifically theatrical: Englar is a visual artist, Doody and Harley each hold degrees in graphic design, while Miller is an environmentalist with the Canadian Environmental Law Association. The original members of the company (which included landscape architect Jerry Englar, as well as musician and producer Whitney Smith), discovered each other through working on events around the Island. Their first big project together was *Island Follies* (1984), an outdoor production based on the history of the Toronto Islands which was scripted, designed and performed by Shadowland, with the help of about eighty volunteers from the community, including children. Their creative approach derives from the work of Welfare State International, an English theatre company with whom Shadowland members have studied and worked. Sarah Miller's introduction to their method came in 1981 when she joined Welfare State for Onstage '81, the Toronto international theatre festival. Another Welfare State project took Kathleen Doody to Togamura, Japan. "Welfare State is the opposite of what the Japanese do," she laughs: "The Japanese are understated; they like to use a lot of detail and exact craftsmanship. The backside that you don't see is as finished as the front that you do see. Our things are big, oversize, with found material."

"The staplegun is our favourite tool," adds Leida Englar. "With theatre you have to do things big, oversize." The two words "oversize" and "grotesque" keep popping up whenever people speak of Shadowland's work. "We don't like to duplicate reality," says Doody. "Shows where we have done that have been dismal," Englar ruefully confirms. Doody continues: "We prefer the outsize, the zany, the beyond-the-real."

Doody explains their method of developing ideas: "There's a design coordinator and a production coordinator for each job. We throw ideas out and narrow them down. We get the concept down—we might have worked out that we need a flying toad on a stick that lights up—and then we do sketches. The overall design coordinator has to keep checking around, to keep things looking like they belong to the same show. It's not just the one designer: the Susan Benson, the Michael Levine. I think it's the most exciting part of Shadowland, the brain bashing that goes on. It's the power of the group: the power of the collective mind."

Award-winning Toronto designer Jim Plaxton, who has worked with Shadowland, feels strongly that the collective approach to design is a sound one. "It can lead to chaos, but if it is working, it works best," he asserts. Like Shadowland, he believes in giving the people he works with as much creative autonomy as possible, and prefers to see them as craftsmen rather than as technicians. He cites a favourite quotation: "Magic is the work of many hands."

Traditional, indoor theatre is definitely not Shadowland's primary interest. "I think the theatre community, through its mainstage approach, is reaching too few people," explains Englar, "We're trained visual artists. Our roots, artistically, are not in the theatre. We're interested in the construction of the pieces." This approach has led Shadowland to work on outdoor festivals, carnival parades (in Trinidad, at Toronto's extravagant Caribana celebrations, as well as in the Popular Summit Parade, a public commentary on the Economic Summit held in Toronto in June), peace rallies, weddings and picnics. "It's the power of the street," affirms Englar. "Carnival is the true revolution. We've become a resource in the community. We energize people and give them a focus, give them a reason to be there."

Kathleen Doody draws back from a purely political interpretation of Shadowland's motives. "We like to make things," she says. She sees the company as essentially celebratory: "We like people to have a good time with it. Not only in the building, although the process is important, but the audience too. That's why we do parades. Events like the Popular Summit and the peace rally tend to be rather 'down' events that people are getting a bit bored with. If we have a bit more spectacle, people get more out of it."

Shadowland's materials, which contribute to the fantastical look of their designs, derive from their nontraditional approach to theatre and from their community orientation. As Doody says, "We like to use a lot of found materials. If something has an industrial—rather than a theatrical—use, it's cheaper." Consequently, the company searches the highways and byways for useful bits and pieces to transform into props and sets. "We've found a great source of cardboard: an old furniture factory that throws away boxes," Englar reveals, "And we're still using raffia from a hat company that threw out all this awful braid."

The exploration of materials is central to what Shadowland is about. "If you gave the same prop to all four of us you might get four different things. Sarah likes wire and papier-mâché. Brad likes wood. We like different things, I guess," muses Doody. "Last year we discovered poly-foam. It's 1/8" foam that you can cut out and glue to make instant costumes. The year we discovered glitter, it took us weeks to clean up." Englar eleborates: "We've learned a lot in the process." She pauses and smiles. "Things don't fall apart as often as they used to."

"Part of going to Trinidad was seeing how they make these enormous structures that are generally carried. We're not interested in making floats," Doody explains. Their Trinidad trips involved them in the construction of Carnival costumes for the Peter Minshall Band. Their second effort won King of Carnival. The theme was "Carnival is colour"; their king, wearing an impressive multi-coloured costume and headdress, walked between the legs of a larger (three or four times life-size) "king" figure which was painted like a mosaic. Trinidad taught them the use of body harnesses and other structural devices that were produced near the end of the millennium, depicting contemporary events.

Artistic Director of VideoCab and author of the series *History of the Village of the Small Huts*, Michael Hollingsworth, decided to work with Shadowland after seeing photographs of *Island Follies*; he also intends to stick with Shadowland over the next decade at least. "They're very much responsible for the respect and esteem that the *Village of Small Huts* plays are held in by theatre people," he says. Each show uses the theatrical idiom of the period it depicts as the starting point for its visual design. So far the series has used the styles of the Miracle Plays, Commedia dell'arte, Molière, Georgian comedy à la Comedie Française, Punch and Judy Shows, and Victorian melodrama. As Hollingsworth has said in an interview, "Since Canada has no theatrical tradition to speak of except the one it is now creating, parody becomes an ideal means of absorbing not only its own history, but also a whole range of conventions and styles of presentation which one can use for one's own purposes" (Bettis 44).

Undoubtedly, the variety of idioms and requirements of the series has given Shadowland scope to develop their talents. "For the first two we bought out the Sally Ann: the most garish bedding and upholstery material we could find," says Englar, "It was that style: brocade, the time of Molière." The early productions also allowed the group to produce what remain some of their favourite pieces: oversize Iroquois false faces; and wolf head and bear head oversize costumes made of chicken wire and papier-mâché, covered with fake fur and then painted. There was also a large mace cut out of two-inch acoustic cardboard that Englar cites as a pleasant discovery. The cardboard was light to carry, but looked solid and satisfying.

Jim Plaxton, the set and lighting designer for the first two *History of the Village* plays, calls Shadowland's work "very theatrical." Although he has some reservations about Shadowland when it comes to stage architecture, Plaxton has a high opinion of their costumes and props: "They have a very strong style. They're not afraid of using a lot of colour."

For the third *History of the Village* play, Englar explains, "We did painting and full-body padding. Shadowland made a breakthrough with rendering the costumes." The actors were made to look like enormous Punch and Judy Show puppets by padding their costumes to create big, distorted body shapes. All of the cloth patterns, ranging from plaids to enormous peonies, were painted on.

The innovation for the fourth show was two-dimensional props. Englar explains that the 2-D idea came out of the fact that the play was scheduled for a forty-show tour; everything had to fit into one truck. Doody adds: "We were interested in forced perspective. We wanted something different." The props included cutout rifles, enormous brandy glasses, and even a train consisting of about six cars, all elaborately painted. The cutout train was held up from behind by actors who were visible through the "windows" as it "carried" them across the stage—a wonderful theatrical moment.

In August, Shadowland produced one of their own creations, the *Handsome and Grusome Festival* on Ward's Island. The event consisted of a parade, games, and a series of plays written by Toronto artist Barbara Klunder to be performed over a long weekend as part of the 65th annual Ward's Island Gala Day. The plays, irreverently based on three of Grimm's fairy tales, featured a multitude of impressive props. On the Thursday before the production, the principal designers and their assistants (many of them volunteers) were finishing work on, among other things, a life-sized camel's head made of wire and papier-mâché. The eyelids were made of tennis balls cut in half, the hide from clumps of an unraveled wool rug, stuck on with glue. The jaw of the camel was functional; it was operated by a mechanism inside the head that its builders couldn't resist pulling from time to time.

The project came about because Shadowland had seen Klunder's drawings. They then approached her about collaborating on a show. She agreed, and wrote the script as well as painting props. Work was done in two large, bare buildings constructed for community events. In one building a row of sewing machines was set up, while newly painted 2-D props were set outside to dry in the sun. Many were cutouts designed to be held up against the faces of the performers. One such cut-out showed two life-sized, painted faces on either side of a hole for the performer's own face to economically give the effect of a crowd.

The shows themselves, filled with impossible puns, were essentially children's entertainments. The actors were amateurs from the Island. Their audience clearly derived a lot of pleasure from seeing their neighbours dressed up as fish, bears, witches and angels. The hilarity and outrageousness of the costumes and props was one of the main carrying points of the production. The plays were performed on and around a moveable stage, reminiscent of the wagons used in medieval mystery plays. For this stage, Shadowland converted one of four railway baggage carts that have been used on the Islands to transport goods from time immemorial. They liked the idea of tying the show in with Island history as much as possible.

The costumes, set pieces and props were, for the most part, designed with a three-day life span in mind. Not surprisingly, the staplegun was again much in evidence, but the same exuberant imagination that characterizes the *History of the Village* plays was also apparent, as was Shadowland's favourite trick of turning people into parts of the scenery. In one of the plays, two newcomers to the proverbial big city were confronted by looming buildings on legs: elaborately painted portable cut-outs worn as combination costumes/sets. One of these, a hotel, had a little registration desk built into it; when the hero knocked, a curtain was pulled back to reveal the face of the actor behind. A two-headed cow made of papier mâché and foil, and complete with water-filled rubber glove working udders, acted as ringmaster for the spectacle.

In the late fall, Shadowland plans to mount another of its own productions, entitled *Your Home is Where Your Hat Is*, which they'll work on between various contract design work. (Such past projects include the *History of the Village* series; *Cocaine the Board Game* for Tamanhous Theatre, Vancouver; and *The Last Will and Testament of Lolita* for Nightwood Theatre in Toronto.) Meanwhile, Brad Harley has plans to tour with Bread and Puppet Theatre, a group known for its daring use of enormous puppets and masks. As Kathleen Doody recognizes, "It's important to keep in touch with other artists for construction techniques and materials."

Shadowland's roots may not be in the theatre, but their images are quintessentially theatrical, simultaneously creating, and acknowledging illusion. The oversized and fantastical images force the audience to use their own imaginative powers to make the picture comprehensible. The playful quality of their stage toys is highly involving. You can't ignore a flying toad or a brandy glass the size of a bucket: you must either make the effort to "see" them in context or else laugh at their incongruity.

Shadowland's aesthetic is informed by the desire to amaze and please the audience in spite of—or perhaps because of—a small budget. Despite the use of modern materials and techniques (such as plastics and industrial cast-offs), and despite their training in fields other than the theatre, Shadowland is following several well-established theatrical traditions. Being close in every sense to their Island audience keeps them in touch with what amuses and delights the onlooker. Their own productions irresistibly remind one of medieval performances, Victorian melodrama, ancient Greek or Shakespearian theatre, in which the audience and the players had a closer, more informal relationship. Shadowland begs involvement. The spirit of their community productions carries over to their work on more mainstream plays by making the visual aspects of the show demand as much response as the script or the performance itself, without detriment to either.

(1988)

Notes

¹ All quotations are from informal personal conversations unless otherwise noted. [The source of these are unrecoverable—ed.]

Works Cited

Bettis, Paul. "Making History: Paul Bettis talks with Michael Hollingsworth about the evolution of The History of the Village of the Small Huts." *Canadian Theatre Review* 52 (1987): 36–44.

Permission Granted: Romeo & Juliet

by Sarah Stanley

The start of Die In Debt and the mounting of the show that got us going was a remarkable time in my development as an artist and has changed how I see myself and the world that surrounds me. I write about it because I know that it happened and because I long for the freedom I remember feeling at the outset of it all. The freedom to choose based on my understanding of the universe as opposed to any dominating one. It was a time when I discovered my own sense of entitlement, gave myself permission to create, to speak. Permission is very rarely granted. The notion that it is, is a lie. It must be taken.

It started on a drive back from Montreal. I wasn't driving. I almost always drive. Had I driven, things might have been different. We were on our way home. We had closed *Vision World*, a piece I adapted from Kathy Acker's *Blood and Guts in High School*. We were singing along to any frequency that caught our car and I started to wander off into the land of "what if." What if I did a version of *Romeo and Juliet*? By the time we had cleared Cornwall my mind had made that dangerous leap. The leap which turns "what ifs" into "why nots" and by the time we landed in Toronto a project, some kind of project, was born. *Romeo & Juliet*. It is difficult to find the person in me now who saw so clearly what I saw then.

I had been blocked for eight years. Just prior to Montreal I had announced, to all who would listen, my intention to leave the theatre. I had applied to law schools and *Vision World* was to be my swan song. During those eight years, I had done much, but none of it freed me up, let me sleep. In 1985 I co-founded, built, and along with my partner Eric Kaskens ran the Baby Grand Theatre in Kingston. It was a great period in my development—I didn't know all that I didn't know! After a year of great success in Kingston, I began to discover all that I didn't know and with that came a numbing sense of despair and lack of interest in pursuing the knowledge that I felt I lacked. I worked, I learned, I grew but it felt equal in proportion to a part of me that shrivelled, and I feared disappeared.

And now I knew what I wanted to do. That was enough. Patrick (Connor) would act, Troy (Hanson) would design the set, Minda (Johnson) would design the costumes and we would make a play. What began as a quirky, perhaps even whimsical look at the Bard, within days, turned into a story of its own unfolding. Why had I chosen this particular play? It felt right. A song on the radio. The relationship I had just explored in *Vision World*. The almost adolescent sense of futility in my own life. I'm still not exactly sure.

What were my influences? Many, and extremely varied. "Soylent Green," a Charlton Heston film about the imagined devastation of our collective future, both physical and spiritual. Yonge Street. The almost surreal eviction of homeless people from unused and ironically out of sight property. The unbelievably high (that summer it was 25%) vacancy rate of commercial property in the city of Toronto. The funding cuts to K.Y.T.E.S. (Kensington Youth Theatre and Employment Skills [Program]). The untimely, tragic death of my brother's lover as she rode her bike down Bloor Street. The list is as long and as unwieldy as the project itself turned out to be. Aside from that car ride there was no one determining factor, more like a couple of thousand! Something in me had opened up and *Romeo & Juliet* became the conduit.

Romeo and Juliet, the year is 2030 and teenagers are still dying for love, but more importantly, are dying for their courage to believe in something and their conviction with regard to their entitlement to do so. The environment is barren; water comes only to those with money. Everything comes to those with money. Manufacturing has ceased, nothing is new, progressive; it is the middle ages of the future meeting Shakespeare's middle ages of the past. The Capulets are a family of men, but they have one daughter, Juliet. The Montagues are a family of women, but they have one son, Romeo. Both children were mistakes, precious, but mistakes. Clearly this was not what the Bard intended. Nor, I imagine, did he anticipate a bisexual Mercutio. We did not alter the text. It remained the same, but the characters that spoke it, genetically engineered. Benvolio was played by a woman (Soo Garay) and I think to great effect. By show's closing I was aware of things that did not, probably never could, work with my rendering of the text, but my choice of Benvolio as a woman reared in a man's world was not one of them.

Back to the beginning and we needed a name. Coffee and croissants in my Kensington Market apartment, a sunny day outside and we needed a name. We couldn't apply for grants without one, we couldn't get auditionees without one. We are a group, a quartet of extremely determined individuals and, alas, without a name, we were nobody. We are embarking on an odyssey of ambition and potential foolhardiness without a foreseeable conclusion. But we still needed a name.

"I'll pay that doctrine, or else die in debt."

The last line to the first scene of *Romeo & Juliet*. Benvolio says it to Romeo in an attempt to cheer up his friend. In our production Benvolio ended up meaning it. Under the Bathurst Street Bridge, Benvolio left Verona for Mantua. There, he became an addict, who unwittingly sold Romeo the poison that forced the story to its inevitable conclusion. Benvolio was banished and Mantua is where he ended. There was no logic to Benvolio taking the blame for Tybalt and Mercutio's death. Where were the grown-ups? Why are teenagers held responsible for things beyond their ken? Our production asked a lot of questions about what adults do and why and how, after all these years of potential progress, they still get away with it. If I lost a bosom buddy and saw another man killed and then was blamed for it, I could easily imagine doing myself in with drugs. The injustice would be too much to bear. I don't think anyone got the connection. I don't think I would do it again, but it was worth a try.

A more appropriate name could not have been found. And we seized upon it. Die In Debt was born in April 1993 around a kitchen table. Since then we have incorporated and two of us have had uncomfortably long stretches of homelessness and all of us have been flat broke many times since. We have also produced two more shows, *Through Blue* and Ned Dickens' *Oedipus* (which won the Dora Award for the best production in the small theatre category). We don't wish to die in debt, but we stand by a belief that if you have something to say, lucky and wealthy is the woman or man who does, then you must say it. And often saying what one means costs dollars that the sayer doesn't have in a bank account to spend. That is what we have discovered at any rate. It is also something that glues us together philosophically as a company, that and our desire to redefine the word "future" as a concept that means something positive.

My initial concept changed and stretched with each breath I took and each exchange I had. I cast Patrick as the Nurse and many decisions flowed from that choice. And then we met K.Y.T.E.S. Actually I met Ned on the patio of a bar that burnt to the ground during our tech week for *Romeo & Juliet*. I had seen him around and we started talking. I was doing a lot of talking that spring; it was an extremely creative period. His company was in dire straits. A company that supported and encouraged homeless youth in a way no other program in the country could was having its funding cut. Their success, which was clear to our immediate community, did not sit well with the statisticians. A program which taught self-reliance and survival skills did not match up well with a governmental need to have youth employed regardless of the job, the interest level, or the contentment of the individual. But the government speaks in an economic language that few of us understand. We asked them to consider co-producing with us and they accepted. We felt in our hearts that we would be able to help them and we knew that they would be able to help us. A relationship based on mutual need and profound hope was made.

Die In Debt remains a working unit of four. Troy and I act as co-artistic directors and Patrick and Minda are our advisors, but we have many honorary (in our minds anyway) members. Ned was the first. He is a man filled with vision and curiosity. He has a knowledge base most Ism compatibles would kill for and an unparalleled generosity of spirit. He is an artist. And he was there very close to the start of something. The spirit of Die In Debt and the spirit of K.Y.T.E.S. met during the actual performance. That combined spirit is what I believe truly unified the two companies.

It was a crazy thing to do. I can still remember the laugh tracks I would hear as I walked up and down staircases. Laugh tracks to my hubris. Who were we to do what we wanted to do? We were who we were and we wanted to do what we wanted to do. What could be more simple, or more humbling? It has to be one of the most essential struggles any artist faces. ENTITLEMENT. Who says I can? Nobody but you, babe.

Troy and I moved quite naturally into intensive producerial roles. His confidence and boyish ability to hear only yes in any response gained us access to undreamt-of landscapes. We applied for funding based on our dreams. We had no tangible performance space and we didn't have a track record. We were rewarded for our audacity and our conviction that we would pull something off. Looking back it's hard to fathom but at the time we knew something and I guess that kind of knowledge has the potential to convince others.

My desire was to stage the piece in a blown-out warehouse. Preferably with one wall open to the devastation and beauty of the city of Toronto. And we found it! It was gorgeous, it was perfect, it was abandoned, it was heaven. It was also slated for the wrecker's ball the same week we were to open. It made it onto our handmade original 200 posters. It was a perfect image but a home it was not to be. We were well into rehearsals, with a cast of anywhere from 35 to 55 depending on the day, and we had no idea where we would perform. I started to imagine it in the alleyway outside my apartment. I wonder what the neighbours would have said.

But Troy, a demon on a bicycle, found a home and things really started to get tense. He found the underside of the Bathurst Street Bridge just days before Metro's finest went in and cleared out the area. It has been a home to the homeless since the turn of the century. It has history and tradition, all of which escaped us when Troy happened upon it. Days later we watched in amazement as newsflashes on local networks showed these people being cleared out. It made no sense. We checked with the homeless association, we wanted to ensure that we weren't stepping on any toes. Then negotiations and a lot of ripped fingernails started with CN Real Estate.

As history tells us, we got the space, the show went on and we contributed something to the city that summer. There was much misinformation in the major press as to what we were all about, but there was also a great deal of interest from people who wouldn't normally consider themselves theatregoers. We learned a lot in a very short time. We learned that conviction will carry you places where other attributes might decide not to go. We had a fabulous summer of proving to ourselves that we could make something mean something. Artistically, communally, politically it was an untoward success. And one that I would like to believe is there for anyone to have. The idealist in me embraces the possibility that absolutely everyone has the right to say and do what it is they want to say and do. The cynic in me misses the feeling that one has when they do just that. As an artist, I am constantly searching for that place of freedom; it doesn't last but it will come again. One just always has to be on the lookout.

(1995)

The Spirit of Shivaree
and the Community Play in Canada;
Or, The Unity in Community

by Edward Little and Richard Paul Knowles

The audience gathered at the old Town Hall in Rockwood, and walked
from there along a tree-lined path by the river to the ruins of the Harris
mill. Along the way, they saw historically costumed figures paddling
canoes, emerging from caves, or haranguing them with grievances. Once
at the mill, they found themselves part of a country fair, with music,
crafts, refreshments, and a lively auction that began with farm imple-
ments but ended with the announcement that the township itself would
be on the block at evening's end. The crowd then moved to an open
space to watch moments in their township's history re-enacted on,
around, under, and above surrounding platforms. Here actors mingled
with, pushed through, or shouted from among the assembled crowd.
The action, using styles that ranged from puppetry to polemic, focused
on 1837, the Mackenzie rebellion, and the story of the so-called
"Rockwood Rebels." The play granted Mackenzie himself status as an
exemplary citizen and thereby connected the cause of the rebellion of
1837 to the proposed "rebellion of 1990": a collective community
response to the pressures of suburbanization and exploitative land
development.[1] For the play's last sequence, the crowd was led deeply into
the mill ruins. Here they mingled closely with the actors at a "townhall"-
style debate about development, conservation, and the future of the
township. The evening ended with a song.

The Spirit of Shivaree, written for and about the community of Eramosa by Dale
Colleen Hamilton, a fifth-generation citizen of the Southern Ontario township, was
performed by the community itself in the summer of 1990 at the site of the historic
Harris Woollen Mill on the banks of the Eramosa River. It was greeted by the regional press as Canada's first community play. That the show's producers had advertised it
more specifically as the first community play in Canada using the Colway Theatre
Trust process, a model developed in Britain in the late 1970s and 80s,[2] made as little
difference to reporters and entertainment editors as did the long history in this country of community-oriented theatre. That history extends from civic and historical
pageantry in the early twentieth century through the workers' theatre movement of
the 1930s to the collaborative and collective creations of "localist" theatre companies
such as Passe Muraille, 25th Street, NDWT, Mulgrave Road, and the Mummers

Troupe, and artists such as James Reaney, Rick Salutin, and David Fennario in the 1970s and 1980s.[3] It is ironic, but not insignificant, that in a theatrical terrain in which a sense of place, local history, and community solidarity are deeply rooted values, the first use of an imported model of this type of theatre, with its accompanying suggestion of authentication through external validation (including the participation in script development workshops of "outside" professionals such as Fennario and Salutin), should be celebrated as a landmark and focus for local pride.

Local pride is one of the things that the community play is designed to foster. This is accomplished through what Julian Hilton calls "rites of intensification" (60)—the celebration, representation, and reification of a community that demonstrates its worth both as the creator/producer of the play and as the object of dramatic representation. Community, however, often defines itself by what it excludes, and the celebration and reification of this process can also lead to an unhealthy kind of xenophobia and an entrenched conservatism. Hilton points to other aspects of community theatre, then, which he calls "rites of passage" (60), which have less to do with affirmation of the community as it is currently constituted or understood, and more with social change, cultural intervention, or community advocacy in the face of a threatening or dominant "other." In Canada this "other" often means a large metropolitan area, as it did in the Eramosa project, where "traditional rural values" were pitted against the stereotypical unscrupulousness of developers and bankers from Toronto. It is along the continuum between an essentially conservative cultural affirmation (the solidification of community identity and values) and cultural intervention (the activist initiation of social change) that the community play locates itself as a site of negotiation in ongoing construction of community.

* * *

The construction of community, or community understood as process rather than as stable entity, is implicated in what social theorists such as Derek Phillips describe as the difference between "territorial" communities, which are defined primarily by geopolitical boundaries, and "relational" communities, which are defined by the nature and quality of inter-relationships among a membership with shared interests (12). Relational communities exist, in varying degrees, as, within, and across territorial ones. The tension between coexisting territorial and relational communities is an important factor in understanding the community play as a site of negotiation between cultural affirmation (rites of intensification) and social intervention (rites of passage). If territorial communities tend to carry with them the received values of shared history inscribed in the definition of place over time, relational communities (while often also sharing histories and values) are more likely to be concerned with issues of common interest such as shared activity, recognition, empowerment, and social change.

Distinctions between territorial and relational notions of community have other implications for the community play as well. Power in our society is often territorially defined (through land ownership, municipal and regional governments, and so on), yet apart from moving out or moving in, membership in territorial communities is non-voluntary. Phillips points out, both membership and values in territorial communities are often "inherited" in the sense that many members will become implicated in the traditions and practices of their communities "before they are able to explicitly recognize and reflect on what they have in common" (14). Yet compared to more voluntary forms of association the implicit hegemony of this unquestioned and unquestionable "inheritance" must also be considered against the fact that territorial communities inevitably include a much more heterogeneous membership than usually the case for communities based on common interests. Relational communities, at least those that are not racially, ethnically, or otherwise prescribed, are more likely to be determined by voluntary participation in the process of community, and its actively and intentionally evolving identity.

Community participation, together with the primacy of process over product, is what best distinguishes the community play from other kinds of theatrical activity that take community as their subject, and it is for this reason that we have decided to begin our discussion with an analysis of the nature of that participation and that process, rather than with the more usual critical account of the script or performance text as product.

In Colway-style community plays, eliciting participation is a principal element in the two-year process of creation. These plays are generally rural in setting and subject, they routinely involve a "core" group of professionals, usually from outside of the community (director, designer, playwright, production manager, etc.), a cast of one to two hundred community members, plus hundreds more in various aspects of organization, administration, research, script development, and production. Colway sees its work as creating theatre not only for, but more importantly with a community. Footage from *Dignity and Grace,*[4] a documentary video about the making of *The Spirit of Shivaree*, reveals considerable concern at a meeting of the professional "core" about "letting go," and the "humbling" process of letting the community "take ownership." The rewards of the process, unlike those of more traditional theatre, are less likely to be aesthetic or artistic than social or cultural, and they are consistently articulated by the participants in the rhetoric of mutual support, solidarity, and renewal of community.

The emphasis on broadly based community involvement in (almost) all aspects of process and performance—Colway uses the term "inclusivity"—distinguishes what we are calling "the community play," as practiced by Colway, James Reaney (in *King Whistle*), or their pageantic predecessors, from the larger body of what we have termed "community oriented" theatre.[5] Most often in community-oriented forms a comparatively small group of theatre artists or workers create a theatrical representation of and for the larger, "host" community, holding, as it were, a mirror up to the community as a rallying point for community concern. In the Mummers Troupe's production of *Gros Mourn*, for example, the company visited a Newfoundland community in crisis over the appropriation of their land for the creation of a National Park. The company engaged in an intensive creation/rehearsal process within the community, and quickly mounted an interventionist production that served to focus and express the protests of the residents of Sally's Cove (see Brookes 78–96). In *Gros Mourn* and similar productions that are predicated on relational notions of community beyond geo-political boundaries, cultural intervention often extends overtly to encompass community empowerment within larger social, political, and legislative structures. The Mummers Troupe in Sally's Cove, Black Rock Theatre in working-class English-speaking Montreal, Theatre Passe Muraille in Clinton, Ontario, Cahoots Theatre Projects in the "multicultural" community of Toronto, or Buddies in Bad Times in the gay and lesbian community of that city, all share an insistence that the hitherto marginalized community represented in the play gain voice and agency within the larger social structure. The theatre, to use Tony Howard's term, functions as a "mouthpiece" (43). In this regard, all community theatre workers, both as "communities" of performers and as representatives of a host community, may be seen as functioning along lines described by Raymond Williams, for whom communities and other forms of association are "the necessary mediating element between individuals and larger Society" (95). In this formulation, theatre companies, which are in, but not entirely of the community, serve as the shifting fissures, or "faultlines," [6] around which change can be negotiated. To a lesser extent, the professional core plays this role in the Colway-style community play.

While community-oriented theatre in general tends to be situated on a shifting border between localist and nationalist concerns, then, the community play's emphasis on celebration and broadly based community involvement makes it the most localist of the community-oriented forms. While it may become regionally or even nationally interventionist,[7] it is primarily concerned with relational notions of community insofar as they exist within the project's territorially defined boundaries. From the perspective of the community play, Williams' "larger Society," at least initially, does not extend beyond the territorially defined community. The community play, as a "form of association," through its relatively vast size, protracted two-year process, and emphasis on empowerment through participation, situates its participants as the mediators in a process of publicly defining the community to be celebrated and, perhaps, changed.[8] The potential insularity of this focus on community is reflected in the words of Jon Oram, the director of the Colway Trust and of *The Spirit of Shivaree*, who says in the *Dignity and Grace* documentary that the community play process "feels a bit like a war, drawing people together. [But] in a war you know who your enemies are. In the community play you know who your friends are."

Initially, the principal elements which the community play uses to draw people together are the "inherited" notions of community-shared territory, shared history, and shared values. Once involved, the "community" of participants, both in their role as mediators, and through participation in the various structures and processes of the community play, present for their "larger society" not only a play which demonstrates behaviour and ideals that are constructed as exemplary, but also an exemplary community structure. As Hamilton herself expresses it in *Dignity and Grace*, and as the "Landscape Architect" puts it in the final scene of the play, "Eramosa Township could be a model" (Hamilton 78).[9]

To this end, in both process and product, the community play adheres to what Derek Phillips describes as the "communitarian ideal" (10). According to Phillips, this concept of community depends on four central characteristics: "a common geographical territory or locale, a common history and shared values, widespread political participation [through collective activity], and a high degree of moral solidarity" (14). The first two characteristics, because of their relationship to "inherited" elements of community, can be considered to be "conceptual" and to be implicated primarily in the form and content of the community play as product. In addition to being "inherited," however, the specific nature of these geographical and historical elements is also subject to a process of selection and negotiation. These conceptual elements play a foundational role as an initial rallying point for community consensus and participation, and they are a particular concern of the small group that is involved early in the process. And, as Colway points out, community support is facilitated by the early involvement of "shakers and movers." These tend to be established and influential community leaders with some history of community representation.

Territory, history, established residency, and representation (in the electoral sense) tend to present an initial image of community in preconceived conceptual terms. The community play process, however, by emphasizing the second two characteristics noted by Phillips—shared activity and moral solidarity—moderates the tendency of territory and story to control the definition of the "shared values" which the play celebrates. These last two characteristics, which can be seen to be primarily processual, are most directly implicated in the community play's creative and communal process.

On the culturally affirmative hand, solidarity, creativity, collective cultural expression, and creative play are constructed and celebrated by Colway as exemplary behaviour in the model community. In addition, the focus on "what best serves the play" (Oram) fosters the two elements which Phillips sees as constitutive of "solidarity": a sense of social interdependence, and a sense of belonging. On the other hand such solidarity (to the extent that it focuses on relational aspects of community) also provides the possibility for reconfiguration within the community across class and other lines. It does so through the encouragement of collective activity in the development of networks, communication, and cultural skills; through the experience of working toward common goals in groupings that may transgress the community's implicit social boundaries; and through the celebration both of personal creativity within a cultural process and pride in shared accomplishments.

In addition, the community play offers its participants various opportunities for contributing to its creative and decision-making process through public meetings, community events, theatre skills workshops, and policies such as "inclusivity" and "democratization." Inclusivity insists that no one who wishes to participate is to be excluded. Democratization is implemented through a central Steering Committee and various subcommittees. The Steering Committee, principally composed of "shakers and movers," is charged with policy-making. It is the core of community representation and it largely controls the conceptual notions of community to be represented. In the interests of community empowerment and autonomy, Colway recommends that no members of the professional core sit on this committee (though in the case of *The Spirit of Shivaree*, in which the playwright was a member of the community, she did serve on the Steering Committee). The numerous subcommittees are each headed by a member of the Steering Committee, and subcommittee members are in turn encouraged to solicit additional support and membership. Subcommittees deal with results-producing functions such as historical research, fundraising, promotion, and the solicitation and coordination of volunteers. A primary goal of the committee structure is to spread the organizational and practical load of the project quickly, while encouraging the broadest possible range of community participation. The number and size of the subcommittees is limited only by the community's willingness to participate. In this regard, a primary strategy of the Colway process is to solicit support from existing community groups, clubs, and organizations which then encourage participation from their memberships. [10]

But if the community play's process lays the foundation for building "the unity in community," as well as for reconfiguring the boundaries within that community, its protracted duration and hierarchical control of conceptual elements also provide ample time for conservative forces—the status quo of community power, privilege, and stability—to organize, exercise traditional leadership skills, and assert hegemony. The possibility of cultural intervention in the community play rests in large part, then, with its processual potential for reconstruction and reconsideration of what community means. But its capacity comfortably to contain that intervention, to hold it in check, rests in large part with the degree to which the community play as theatrical product, through its focus on landscape and history, has tended to define community in terms of the historical continuity deriving from the stabilizing influence of place over time. A community play uses documented and conjectural history to tell and re-tell stories to and about its territorial community, and in the Colway model this territorial focus is seen to be an essential element in community building. On a practical level, focusing on and celebrating "the land" and associated values foregrounds "community spirit" and thus works to elicit participation and helps ensure that the play's representation of the community is non-controversial. On a fundamentally conservative pedagogical level, in telling its story a community play is involved in both remembering and constructing a collective past which, by emphasizing continuity, builds or, in communitarian terms, a "community of memory."

A community of memory engenders solidarity and the continuance of "inherited" values by:

> retelling its story, its constitutive narrative, and in so doing ... offers examples of the men and women who have embodied and exemplified the meaning of the community. (Bellah et al. 153)

In the Rockwood case, the essential and essentially conservative values to be shared—"family and land and heritage"—were depicted as spanning centuries and therefore as being common to exemplary pioneers and contemporary residents alike (83). Through consensus over land stewardship, preservation of farmland, and a willingness to fight for issues of control, the land was reified as a principal mediating element between old and new settler, and among heterogeneous community groups. As the character MacKenzie puts it: "It's nice to know that some things never change" (76).

The Rockwood project was first conceived as a response to issues of land control, and it is not incidental that the script of *The Spirit of Shivaree* is dedicated, not only "to those past and present who call Eramosa home," but also "to the land." Nor is it surprising that many of the most resonant moments in the community plays that have so far been mounted in Canada have had to do with this conjunction of landscape and history, in which landscape somehow (and in both senses of the word) contains history, including future histories. When the news of the MacKenzie rebellion came to the world of *The Spirit of Shivaree* by way of sentinels posted at the tops of the limestone cliffs that border the river and the playing space, it created a stir among the characters, and a chill among members of an audience for whom the historical "feel" of the occasion was immediate and poignant. Even more poignant, and more potentially constraining as the dead hand of the past, was the ghostly presence of ancestral characters—pioneer rebels and their families, including Mackenzie—looming in the windows of the mill ruins, presiding over the proceedings as the voices of history that have, in Phillips's terms, "embodied and exemplified the meaning of the community."

This documentary-style "authentication" and reification of received and reproduced (as opposed to re-created or revisionist) history and its emotional affirmation of the continuity of territorial community over time is reinforced in the play's tendency to ritualize history. *Shivaree* and the other community plays produced in Canada have engaged their audiences as participants in historical pageants, processions, and parades that have preceded and punctuated them. Each of these plays has employed evocative historical icons that again tend to function as conservative, affirmative, and stabilizing forces in the production of value and meaning. These iconic moments are often accompanied by lyrical ballads, marches, anthems, and choruses that reinforce a communal and unifying sense of shared past and present purpose, evoking, at the same time, a familiar resonance of civic boosterism and local pride.

The use of landscape as the unchanging repository of history and value is also inscribed in the historical bodies of actors who, in the case of the Rockwood play, were cast to play their own ancestors. [11] When Richard Lay played his great-great-grandfather, William Lyon Mackenzie, particularly in those scenes set in the present, in which he presided over the interpretation of his past and its meaning for the township's future, the privileging of bloodlines revealed an essentialist notion of identity and a fetishizing of ancestral descent that was essentially conservative, whatever the intentions of the show's creators. At one point in the performance, moreover, Mackenzie clearly elided past and present for the audience as well as for the "ancestrally-cast" actors, when he claimed that "I would never have made it to the border alive without the aid and assistance of country people *such as are gathered here tonight*" (emphasis added). [12] This, combined with the fact that the play-making process is consensual, non-contentious, and therefore generalizing, meant that, again, the interventionist

potential of the process tended to be subsumed in the role of community empowerment (see Little and Sim 58).

The interventionist potential of the historical narrative of *Shivaree*—a story of
armed rebellion—and of the fact that the play's central heroes—the "Rockwood
Rebels" and Mackenzie himself—were advocates of violent revolution, then, was safely contained for the audience by the reassuring icons of continuity embodied in the
use of familiar landscapes, faces and names. And of course neither Mackenzie nor any
other of the play's rebels carried a gun.

* * *

The play's use of landscape, history, and dramatic form were not exclusively conservative, however, and if its interventionist potential was to some extent held in check,
it can nevertheless be seen, even as a theatrical product, to have served in several ways
as a site of negotiation for social change. Even its employment of historical narrative
is less clearly or simply affirmative than may at first appear. The history on which the
play most frequently draws is less the traditional, official, or national history of the
acts of great men, than an explicitly revisionist and localist social history, often popular history, in which Mackenzie, for example, can cite what "the history books don't
tell you" (56). Town and county histories, the records of community groups, local
newspapers, Lion's Clubs and women's auxiliaries—even residents' attics—were
scoured as repositories of local history. *The Spirit of Shivaree*, in fact, staged a debate
at the outset of the action in which versions and ownership of history were contested.
A scene in which a lecture on history by Sir Francis Bond Head, Governor of Upper
Canada, speaking from what in a medieval mystery cycle would be called a *locus*, or
scene-specific symbolic platform above the crowd, was interrupted by a woman who
argued, speaking in French from the *platea*, or public playing area that she shared with
the audience as populace, that "God doesn't only speak English and... history didn't
begin when the white men came." [13] In response to her claim that Bond Head "got the
story wrong," the Governor replies that he is "talking about history, not stories," to
which she replies, "stories are histories and histories are stories," before she is silenced
by an armed guard in an overt exercise of historical power (9). This sequence explicitly demonstrates, not only that "history" as story is ideologically constructed and
coded, but also that to control history is to exercise power. The scene also works to
demystify that power and render it contestable.

The site at which power is made contestable is the community play itself. The
play's carnivalesque eclecticism of genres, styles, and voices demystifies any representational realism and gives the audience a democratic role in re-constructing the
history of its own community, as opposed to a stake in the re-production of a dominant myth of "identity" (and in the suspension of its own disbelief). [14] As celebratory
pageant rubs shoulders with documentary agit-prop, and as declamatory rhetoric
mixes with sentimental melodrama and scenes of sit-com silliness, the audience is
encouraged actively to engage in its own, purposeful, history-making, and to negotiate its past and future history in a marketplace of open debate and exchange.

History, however, is not the only fissure opened for contestation by the community play in general, or *Shivaree* in particular. Community plays tend to attract as participants a preponderance of women, and since traditional histories typically relegate women to oblivion, or at best to supporting roles, playwrights and directors must of necessity, if not by design, resort to one or more of: the examination and excavation of women's roles in history; the creation of roles for women in the plays themselves; or the cross-casting of women in men's roles. Each of these options has its own interventionist potential in a patriarchal culture, and each option was exercised in *Shivaree*. Dale Hamilton was conscious in writing the script of the job of recovering women's lives and histories. As she says in *Dignity and Grace*, "that was a very deliberate act on my part; to remind people that there were women there. And when the men were off meeting or being thrown in jail, [the women] were holding... things together." This process of recovery, in fact, extended to the invention of a non-historical character, "Ensa Cameron," who, like Hamilton herself in 1990, provides an activist voice for change in the represented community of 1837. During the scene depicting the township meeting of the "Rockwood Rebels," the men resolve to "go directly to the Centre Inn Tavern and there within commence to mind our own business" (36). Ensa is the only woman to attend the "political meeting." It is she who objects to the resolution and proposes action, and it is she who hides the fleeing Mackenzie under her skirts when he apocryphally passes through Rockwood en route to Navy Island. "Ensa Cameron," then, plays a powerful women's role in the play, and represents an explicit example of revisionist history.

Equally effective in the revisioning of women's roles in society was the casting of women to play male roles in the play, perhaps most notably the roles of the British soldiers who patrolled the *platea*, intimidated the audience, and arrested the rebels. As actor and production coordinator Janet MacLeod said in the video documentary of the project, "for women to become the vehicles of power like that... was quite a new experience."

The experience of empowerment for the actors, of course, was central to the play as process, but the casting of women as soldiers was part of another potential intervention effected by *The Spirit of Shivaree*. Among its most effective and disruptive devices, in fact, was the play's blurring of the lines between character and actor, and between actor and spectator. This blurring was effected in part by the use of cross-casting, masks, and emblematic costuming, in part by the mixing of contemporary and period costuming and clothing, and in part by the use of the *platea*, the temporally and spatially shifting public arena at the centre of the playing area where "the people," past and present, actors, characters, and spectators, negotiated and contested histories, values, and visions of the future. At one point the action was interrupted by an actor/character who claimed, "I don't want to be in this play anymore. I don't like the part they gave me" (64). Later, in a complex conflation of both historical time and theatrical role, a certain "Bill Mackenzie," in the "ah, fertilizer business," recognizably "played by" the historical character, William Lyon Mackenzie, in turn played by his great-great grandson, says, "I'd like to suggest that *you* hold a public meeting, right here, as soon as the play is over, and that *we* face these issues head on" (emphasis added). When the imagined "crowd" agrees, the character comments to the "real" audience, "me again. You didn't think I'd miss a good uprising, did you?" (66).

Among the most interesting and effective moments in the play, was a series of "contemporary vignettes," as they are called in the script. These are presented as public testimonials spoken from a variety of community perspectives by a seventh-generation man, a farm mother, a subdivision mother, a newcomer, a commuter, and so on, while "the characters are taking off costumes, applying modem makeup, accessories, etc." (60). [15]

This use of the play as a site for public and popular debate was made explicit when the action and the audience moved, physically, to the interior of the mill for the final, "town hall" sequence, which rounded out the framework initiated by the fair, auction, and marketplace of the opening sequences, and returned the play to the people. If one of the virtues of the community play process was, as Jon Oram says in *Dignity and Grace*, that it "resulted in cast members talking about the issues involved," the performance, serving as a kind of carnivalesque marketplace of contesting versions of what the play's closing song celebrates as "home," provoked the same debate within the larger community.

The fair with which *Shivaree* opened is a standard feature of the Colway-style play, but in this case it provided something more, as a framework, than the usual opportunity for broadly-based participation, some fundraising, and a smooth transition into the play proper. Culminating as it did in a theatricalized auction, the opening sequence framed the entire play within the context of community celebration as commercial exchange. Initially, items such as a communally-produced quilt (now in itself an historical artifact) were auctioned off, but capital investment (represented by the developer, "Newman," with his dark glasses and cellular phone) soon replaced "fair" dealing: "Merle and Gordon Cameron," local residents, were outrageously outbid for a much needed pickle jar by Newman, who planned to use it as a decorative umbrella stand. The marketplace had highjacked the fair.

If *The Spirit of Shivaree* presented itself, then, as a carnivalesque and celebratory mingling of people, styles, and genres—as a fair—it did so in full consciousness that carnivalesque play occurs within a public place, *platea*, or "market square" that exists within and is dependent upon lines of economic force that are external to it. In this case these included "fair market value" for pickle jars, antiques, and agricultural land that farmers can no longer afford. In fact the fair is highjacked, as local fairs always are, by a marketplace over which the community has little control. As Peter Stallybrass and Allon White note

> The tangibility of its boundaries implies a local closure and stability, even a unique sense of belonging, which obscure its structural dependence upon a "beyond" through which this "familiar" and "local" feeling is itself produced.... It is a place where limit, centre and boundary are confirmed and yet also put in jeopardy. (28)

Stallybrass and White go on to say that "it is a gravely over-simplifying abstraction...
to conceptualize the fair purely as the site of communal celebration," and they point,
finally, to "the deep conceptual confusion entailed by the fair's 'mixing of work and
pleasure, trade and play,' as a source of anxiety for 'the bourgeois classes,' and implicitly as a potential source of social change" (30).

Among the definitions of "Shivaree" (or "charivari") in the *Oxford English
Dictionary* is "a babel of noise," and *The Spirit of Shivaree* can be seen as such a babel.
As both process and product it can be seen to serve as a carnivalesque marketplace at
which community celebration becomes a bargaining site for the negotiation of values.
These fluid and contesting values in the community play are represented by its rites of
intensification, on the one hand, and its (internally generated and externally imposed)
rites of passage, on the other; by notions of community that are territorially and/or
relationally defined; and by tension between cultural affirmation and continuity based
on conservative notions of history and landscape, and cultural intervention based on
a politics of social change. Perhaps "a babel of noise" is less accurate as a way of
describing the community play, however, than a babel of voices, sharing a territory,
and engaged in the ongoing process of imagining and building there a relational community of common interest.

(1995)

Notes

¹ Statistics Canada figures detailing overall population growth in Eramosa Township
between 1901 and 1986 are reproduced in Little and Sim, (5–6). Organizers of the
community play, using figures from the year-end analysis of population and house-
holds in police villages contained in the Ontario Assessment System "Wellington
County Study," placed the population growth of the village of Rockwood between
1987 and 1988 at an unprecedented 37%.

² The most comprehensive account of the Colway process is Jellicoe. See also Baz
Kershaw's analysis of the community play's political efficacy (168–205).

³ Many of these plays are unpublished, there are few traces at all of many communi-
ty-style plays and pageants, and where there are scripts, they are of course even
more inadequate as representations of process or even of theatrical product than is
usually the case in the theatre. Nevertheless, the reader is referred to Ridout,
Middleton, Wright and Endres, Ryan, Theatre Passe Muraille, 25th Street Theatre,
the Mummers Troupe of Newfoundland, Brookes, Reaney, Fennario, and Winslow.

⁴ The phrase "dignity and grace" is taken from the conclusion of the James Gordon
song that recurs throughout the play:

> We all know
> That this old town has gotta grow
> But can't we do it with
> Some dignity and grace.

5 This larger body includes the Worker's Theatre of Action in the 1930s, the interventionist theatre of the Mummers, Passe Muraille's collectively-created socio-logical documentary theatre, the revisionist historical agit-prop of David Fennario's *Black Rock*, and the increasing body of work in the 1990s by gay, lesbian, feminist, and ethnic theatre companies which relate to specifically defined relational com-munities. Like all community-oriented theatre, these forms originate with a localist impulse—the presentation or representation of community experience to, and for, its constituent members. In overtly seeking to expand their sphere of influence to be regionally, or even nationally interventionist, however, such forms delineate a fur-ther continuum of community-oriented theatre practice—one concerned with issues of local, regional, or even national expression and intervention.

6 We are borrowing the concept of "faultlines" from Sinfield.

7 The Green Paper, for example, a guide to rural land use prepared by a citizen's action group formed in conjunction with the Eramosa community play, has been cited as a model by the provincial Ministry of Municipal Affairs. For a more detailed account of the impact of *Shivaree* on local and regional planning see Little and Sim. It is also worth noting that community plays are not designed for tours or remounts outside of the community that creates them, and the remounting for a second year in the same community of the Fort Qu'Appelle community play, *Ka'ma'mo'pi' cik/The Gathering*, 1992, 1993—the first time a Colway-style play has been remounted—provoked controversy both among community play practioners and within the community.

8 Of the three Colway-style community plays produced in Canada to date: *The Spirit of Shivaree* was conceived by Dale Hamilton as a means of provoking a localized response to increasing pressures of suburbanization (see Little and Sim); Blyth's *Many Hands* (1993) was created to celebrate a theatrical tradition in a community described as experiencing communication problems between a transient "summer theatre crowd" and the resident community; and Fort Qu'Appelle's *Ka'mo'mi'pi'cik* (1992, 1993) was designed to help reconcile differences between white and Native "communities."

9 All subsequent references to the text of *The Spirit of Shivaree* are by page numbers only.

10 In Rockwood, for example, this involved groups such as the Local Architectural Conservation Advisory Committee, The Junior Farmers, two Women's Institutes, church congregations, heritage and environmental groups, the Rockwood School, the Lion's Club, the Grand River Conservation Authority, the Rockwood Recreation Committee, and eventually the township council.

¹¹ In addition to Richard Lay as Mackenzie, members of the Benham, Harris, and Hamilton families played their ancestors in *The Spirit of Shivaree*.

¹² We are quoting from the videotape, *The Spirit of Shivaree*: Eramosa Community Play, June 1990. (Guelph: Hamilton/Fox). The final phrase is not included in the published script.

¹³ For a political analysis of the distinction between *locus* and *platea* see Weimann 73–85 and *passim*.

¹⁴ This winning of the imaginative assent of the audience in the making of history as myths of origin is the typical technique of James Reaney in his *Donnelly* cycle and elsewhere (see Knowles). The term "carnivalesque" and the concept of carnival derive from M.M. Bakhtin and are most fully articulated in *Rabelais and his World*.

¹⁵ These "testimonials" mixed "actual" statements by community members with scripted perspectives prepared by Hamilton.

Works Cited

Anderson, Benedict. *Imagined Communities: Reflections on the Origin and Spread of Nationalism*. Revised ed. London: Verso, 1991.

Bakhtin, M.M. *Rabelais and his World*. Trans. Helene Iswolsky. Bloomington: Indiana UP, 1984.

Bellah, Robert, Richard Madsen, William M. Sullivan, Ann Swidler, and Steven M. Tipton. *Habits of the Heart: Individualism and Commitment in American Life*. Berkeley: U. of California P, 1985.

Brookes, Chris. *A Public Nuisance: A History of the Mummers Troupe*. St. John's: Institute of Social and Economic Research, Memorial University of Newfoundland, 1988.

Dignity and Grace: The Story of the Eramosa Community Play The Spirit of Shivaree. Prod. and dir. by Charlie Fox and Mark Hamilton. Guelph: Hamilton/Fox, 1992.

Eramosa Community Play Archives, U. of Guelph.

Fennario, David. *Joe Beef (A History of Pointe Sainte Charles)*. Vancouver: Talonbooks, 1991.

Hamilton, Dale Colleen. *The Spirit of Shivaree*: A Community Play for Eramosa Township. Toronto: Playwrights Union of Canada, 1990.

Hilton, Julian. "The Other Oxfordshire Theatre: the Nature of Community Art and Action." *Theatre Quarterly* 9.33 (1979): 53–61.

Howard, Tony. "Theatre of Urban Renewal; the Uncomfortable Case of Covent Garden." *Theatre Quarterly* 10.38 (1980): 33–46.

Jellicoe, Ann. *Community Plays: How to Put Them On.* London: Methuen, 1987.

Kershaw, Baz. *The Politics of Performance: Radical Theatre as Cultural Intervention.* London: Routledge, 1992.

Knowles, Richard Paul. "Replaying History: Canadian Historiographic Metadrama." *Dalhousie Review* 67 2.3 (1987): 228–43.

Little, Edward, and R. Alex Sim. *Dramatic Action: How Eramosa Township Faced its Problems.* Guelph: Ontario Rural Learning Association in cooperation with the School of Rural Planning, University of Guelph, 1992.

Middleton, Jesse Edgar. *A Pageant of Nursing in Canada.* Toronto: Canadian Nurses Association, 1934.

Mummers Troupe of Newfoundland. *Buchans: A Mining Town. Canadian Drama/L'Art dramatique canadien* 13.1 (1987): 72–116.

Oram, Jon. "The Marriage of Two Minds." Colway publicity material.

Phillips, Derek L. *Looking Backward: A Critical Appraisal of Communitarian Thought.* Princeton: Princeton UP, 1993.

Ridout, Denzil. *United to Serve.* Toronto: United Church of Canada, 1927.

Reaney, James. *King Whistle. Brick* 8 (1980): 5–48.

Ryan, Toby Gordon. *Stage Left: Canadian Theatre in the Thirties, A Memoir.* Toronto: CTR Publications, 1981.

Sinfield, Alan. *Faultlines: Cultural Materialism and the Politics of Dissident Reading.* Berkeley: U. of California P, 1992.

Stallybrass, Peter and Allon White. *The Politics and Poetics of Transgression.* Ithaca, NY: Cornell UP, 1986.

Theatre Passe Muraille. *The Farm Show.* Toronto: Coach House, 1976.

25th Street Theatre. *Paper Wheat: The Book.* Saskatoon: Western Producer Prairie Books, 1982.

Weimann, Robert. *Shakespeare and the Popular Tradition in the Theater.* Baltimore: Johns Hopkins UP, 1978.

Williams, Raymond. *The Long Revolution.* Harmondsworth: Penguin, 1965.

Winslow, Robert. *The Cavan Blazers.* Ennismore, Ont.: Ordinary Press, 1993.

Wright, Richard and Robin Endres, eds. *Eight Men Speak and Other Plays from the Canadian Workers' Theatre*. Toronto: New Hogtown Press, 1976.

Wabana: A Native Word
Meaning "Place of First Light"

by Denyse Lynde

Some thirty-one years after the closure of the Wabana Mines of Bell Island, Newfoundland, "Place of First Light," "a living interpretation of the island's rich history, packaged in the form of a three hour theatrical tour," opened on June 30, 1997. From the initial research, scripting, physical site preparation and casting to production, *Place of First Light* is an extraordinary success due to its initial conception, large production team, successful blend of tourism, heritage conservation and artistry, and finally, perhaps most importantly, to the seemingly boundless energies of the youthful artistic team.

In a province marked by skyrocketing unemployment, a devastatingly high cost of living and any number of faltering (despite the government's assertions) tourism schemes, *Place of First Light* is a testament to its creators' vision, financial shrewdness and fierce commitment to an "idea." The management team, led by Anna Stassis and Danielle Irvine, was inspired by *The Miners of Wabana* by Gail Weir, a book published in 1989 based on an extensive series of interviews conducted by the author, who is a native of Bell Island. Part of the Breakwater Books series, Canada's Atlantic Folklore and Folklife, *The Miners of Wabana* is a beautifully produced testament to the history of the mines, the labour movement and the tragedies in the "tickle," which as the tour guide in *Place of First Light* explains "refers to the body of water we are crossing"—the tour has begun, of course, on the ferry as it crosses from Portugal Cove to Bell Island.

In each chapter of *The Miners of Wabana*, Weir explores fully an aspect of life on this small, rugged place. In chapter one, "History of Wabana Mines," Weir records the naming of the island, "a rock which resembles a bell," and traces the history of the mines from opening to closing over seventy-one years. In the next chapter, the labour history of the small community, dominated by the colourful David Ignatius Jackman, or "Nish," is traced. In "Tragedies in the Tickle," Weir describes events that occurred during World War II off the coast of this tiny island. These included such routine disasters as ferry collisions as well as more unforeseen intrusions, among them the attacks of German submarines which caused considerable damage until the Canadian navy finally responded.

The Miners of Wabana became the primary source for *Place of First Light*: "A lot of the stories were from interviews that she [Weir] did for the book.... I [Stassis] just thought the stories in here were fantastic" (Coxworthy, "Down Under"). When Stassis and Irvine were joined by actor/writers Robert Chafe and Sean Panting, the project was underway. The writing, while based on Weir's book, quickly took on a life of its own as characters and events were fleshed out. Further research was conducted. Books by Kay Coxworthy, Steve Neary and John Hammond and a tour of the island by Bell Islander Charlie Bown provided further colourful reminisces. As research and writing progressed, considerable time and effort was spent acquiring funds for what would become a project with twenty-five full-time funded positions. Equally time-consuming was the back-breaking work needed to restore the entrance shaft to Mine Number 4. Open to vandalism and the weather since the closing of the mine, this shaft would become the realistically dark and claustrophobic setting of the final scenes of the production when the audience would experience the miner's world first hand. In order to recreate this space, walls had to be cleaned, lighting installed and the mine floor recreated.

The team broke tasks of writing into two areas which would be amalgamated to create the text. Another actor/writer, Selina Asgar, worked on what would become the bulk of the production, the above-ground tour of the Island that moved from Portugal Cove Ferry docks to a bus which toured the entire island. Chafe and Panting concentrated on the extensive underground mining sequence. While the writers were scripting and all were cleaning the mine, the producers were successful in securing funding from Human Resources Canada, the Canada/Newfoundland Agreement on Economic Renewal and the Canada Youth Business Loan Program as well as the support of the Bell Island Heritage Society, the Wabana Town Council and the Bell Island Development Industrial Adjustment Services Committee.

First Light Productions felt that it could create its own unique niche in Newfoundland's developing tourist market:

> In recent years Newfoundland has seen a resurgence in its story telling tradition as several key communities across the island, in cooperation with professional bodies both financial and artistic, have presented their histories through theatre and song. This most often involves the fisheries and life on and off the sea. We differ from what has so far been offered in that our subject matter differs. We want to depict life under the sea: the submarine mines that stretch out for up to three miles under Conception Bay.

In choosing Bell Island for their premier production, First Light Productions wanted to create a "multigenerational" story, "utilizing storytelling methods in combination with more contemporary theatrical styles." The resulting script and production of *Place of First Light* is particularly striking due to the fine writing, strong performances and varied natural settings. In fact the motif of the island "tour" that governs the production effectively places the audience within the world of the drama from the opening moments boarding the ferry through three hours of performance until the light finally floods the old mine shaft and the bus awaits for the final ride to the ferry home.

Place of First Light begins at the ferry dock, Portugal Cove, where the audience is greeted by tour coordinator Julie, played with considerable enthusiasm by writer/actor Selina Asgar. Escorting her "tour" onto the car ferry and shepherding them into the below-deck lounge, Asgar plays the obnoxiously bright and cheerful Julie, determined to get these potentially uncooperative charges through her tour on time and in place. Within seconds of her opening spiel, Julie is interrupted by a late arrival who, although asking to join the group, soon reveals that he knows more about the community than the tour guide. After agreeing with her that whales should be watched for, the mysterious newcomer points out that sharks are found in these waters as well. Seeing that Julie looks a little unwell, he asks if she is seasick. Julie explains why she has her present job and thinks that she has her new charge figured out:

> **Julie**: Me? No of course not, well, not really. Actually I was kinda seasick at training camp.
>
> **Miner**: Training camp?
>
> **Julie**: No big deal really. I was a trainee for Princess Line Cruises, I would have been working there this summer except—*(she puts her hand over her mouth, then exhales deeply)* that they thought I should try to overcome my motion sickness. Which I have really. Part of the reason I took this job, forty minutes on the ferry back and forth, you see, baby steps. *(The miner looks at her and tries not to laugh. Seeing this, the target quickly composes herself as best she can.)* Well enough about me. How about you? *(the miner shrugs his shoulders and smiles).* Now don't be shy, *(coming to a realization)* Oh, I SEE what's going on now, you're part of the tour, right? Dressed up the way you are to add historical ambience!

However, from this point on, nothing is quite the way it should be for our tour guide even though she has her "handbook of historical facts and points of interest." Life, or rather drama, keeps intruding.

In her next attempt to take charge of her tour, Julie begins to tell her tourists— the audience—about the collision of two ferries which is recounted in Weir's book (471). She is interrupted again by a young couple played by Frank Squires and Jackie Hynes, who discuss their wedding plans. While Julie, with considerable interest, the Miner, with bemused affection, the "theatre" audience and the regular ferry crossers eavesdrop, the multilayered approach to storytelling is effortlessly established. The audience is pulled into vignette after vignette as, once disembarked at Bell Island, the audience is shepherded on and off a bus by the tireless, energetic but increasingly harassed tour guide, Julie, as the "formal tour" is interrupted and expanded by various characters from the past. Frequently these two intersecting circles of "tour" and "history" are further expanded by the interest of additional members of the audience, "real" inhabitants of Bell Island who provide another layer to an already complex theatrical context. Thus, in one production, Asgar the performer, no less than Julie the character, was interrupted by a local woman who pointed out to the performer and her audience that she lived "just over there... all her life." Asgar cum Julie graciously accepted the unscripted mini-scene and easily moved the action into the next vignette.

The heart of the text is the history of Bell Island, coloured by comic and tragic re-enactments of figures and moments. The young couple from the ferry reappear at the monument of the Garland disaster, recreating the last moments of that fateful ferry accident which leaves Julie sobbing and unable to continue with her narrative. Sharply contrasting is the next scene at the 1st Coast Defense Battery where the "tour," is disrupted by a soldier from 1942 who is in turn interrupted by a furious farmer who claims the army has shot his favourite cow, Becky. With screams of "cow killers" and "moos" described in the text as *"something like a cow vengeance cry,"* the two characters in pure slapstick tradition go scrambling down the long hill out of sight. Julie, left with her "tour," once again leads them back to the bus and attempts to resume her official spiel. She is, of course, interrupted when once again a stranger joins her group. Like the miner on the ferry, the new arrival, Billy, knows more about the Island than Julie. Julie is relying on her book of facts while Billy "lived" on the Island. All of which becomes a bit of an inside joke for the production as writer/actor but non-Bell Islander Asgar used Bell Islander Weir's "little" book for primary research, while the miner and other recreated figures who love to correct Julie are all played by real Bell Islanders.

The tour continues back on the bus as Julie and Billy describe the murals in town which are funded by various arms of local government and which commemorate the island's rich heritage. At the last mural, one in the process of being restored, the audience is shepherded off the bus, and, yet again, the "tour" is interrupted, this time by a scene played across the road from the mural on a green belt behind a row of houses, one of them supposedly occupied by a miner. Like all the vignettes, history is dramatized in this humorous scene where a miner is not allowed inside his home until he has scrubbed and performed the "second washing." Once Julie thinks she is back in charge, she loses Billy who follows the miner and his wife in hopes of a bit of supper. The actor, Allan Hawco, playing Billy, has headed off to be in place for his next scene although the audience, by this time prepared for anything, are blissfully unaware of this or any of the flurry of activity circling the "tour." As the audience is bussed from location to location where vignette after vignette is dramatized before them, cast and crew of First Light Productions are moving from location to location in the company van, changing costumes and picking up props. Asgar, as Julie, not only shepherds the audience on and off the bus but, throughout the three hour performance, provides interludes of information on local geography and history between the dramatic sketches.

Following Billy's scene with his sister at the monument dedicated to the victims of the German attacks on the iron-ore boats in 1942, the bus takes the audience to the last site, the entrance to underground mine number two. Following a comic turn at the entrance where Wilf, the miner from the opening vignette on the ferry and the miner whose wife won't let him in their house until the "second washing," refuses entrance to a woman whose husband forgot his supper. Of course women are not allowed in the mines and once Wilf leads the audience through the entrance, the audience becomes a group of male visitors.

The first thing that strikes one inside the mine is its utter blackness. First Light Productions crew circles the audience with flashlights pointing to the ground in order to lead them from performance space to performance space. Working almost like an independent section from the tour proper, Wilf leads the audience through this section while Julie remains at the entrance of the mine, ready to assist anyone out of the utter blackness of the mine. Once within the mine, the first vignette opens strikingly; from the blackness within the audience sees two lights approaching which, when closer, are [seen to be] the helmet lights of two miners coming up the mine shaft. As each scene passes, the audience is guided deeper into the shaft, theoretically by Wilf, the retired miner, but practically by the unobtrusive presence of the ground-directed flashlights. Stories that are dramatized outline the back-breaking work, the enormous length of the tunnel under the sea and the reliance on Clydesdales who "knows *[sic]* the mine better than any man down here." The labour history as recorded in Weir's book is dramatized through the efforts of the colourful union activist, Nish Jackman, to sign up new members.

At the deepest point in the shaft, set within what appears to be an alcove, is a table where miners sit for their lunch, play practical jokes and relate ghost stories, dramatically heightened for the audience by the distant, eerie sound of footsteps. The last encounter is between Wilf and a novice miner who, it soon becomes apparent, will not survive the dangerous work, and just as the youngster moves off with "Time to go," Wilf picks up the refrain with "Yeah. I suppose it is. Time to go. Buses are waiting" and suddenly the light floods into the shaft as the crew opens the entrance door. With the sunlight streaming into the mine entrance, the surroundings are instantly transformed, and the shaft is revealed. With the doors open, the audience applauds the cast of First Light Productions and wanders back to the bus for the last trip to the ferry dock. The three hour extravaganza is over.

The cast of *Place of First Light* is a combination of young professionals and Bell Islanders, but there is no apparent discrepancy between the abilities of the two groups. Robert Chafe, Sean Panting and Selina Asgar, all writers/actors, have established strong reputations as versatile performers in and around St. John's. Joined by Frank Squires, Allan Hawco and Jennifer Adams, the St. John's contingent is uniformly strong in various roles. Bell Islanders perform as cast and crew. Particularly memorable are performances by John Doherty who creates Wilf and the Miner and Leah Lewis who plays Dora, the miner's wife. The strength of "Place of First Light," however, lies in the production itself, where all performances are equally supportive and consequently create a taut and cohesive, briskly moving and constantly shifting panorama.

First Light Productions took on a monumental task when it conceived "Place of First Light." Moving an audience of twenty to twenty-five people from the ferry docks at Portugal Cove, across the ferry, over Bell Island, into a mine shaft and back to the ferry docks could have been a logistical nightmare. To compound the situation, twelve actors double to perform over twenty-four characters in a variety of spaces scattered all over the Island, on the ferry and on a bus. The subsequent production is apparently effortless and the result is stunning. Designed as a "living interpretation of the Island's rich history," *Place of First Light* is an exciting and moving theatrical feast. A history lesson may be taught but what remains besides the richness of the stories of Bell Island are the moving dramatizations of the tellers of these stories.

Storytellers and storytelling have long been dominant elements of Newfoundland culture. Recently communities have turned to their history in order to develop a tourism base. Some of these community-based pageants or plays have been more successful than others. The premiere production of First Light Productions Inc., the *Place of First Light* is unique in this period of recent community-based productions. It is most obviously unique, of course, because of the history of this mining community in a province usually associated with fishers and fishing. But the extraordinary quality of this production does not rest in its subject matter but rather in the high quality of writing, the strong and uniform calibre of the acting, and the tight and polished production values. Finally, the vision of producers (Irvine and Stassis) leading to the conception, creation and production of A *Place of First Light* must be applauded. Their efforts, supported by both the professionals and the Bell Islanders, resulted in an excellent production that brought the history of the community to life.

(1997)

Works Cited

Asgar, Selina, Robert Chafe and Sean Panting. *Place of First Light.* Unpublished production script. 1997.

Coxworthy, Kay. *The Cross on the Rib: One Hundred Years of History, Bell Island, Newfoundland.* Bell Island, NF: Kay Coxworthy, 1996.

———. "Down Under." *Evening Telegram* [St. John's] June 27, 1997: 9.

———. *Tales from across the tickle: Bell Island, Newfoundland.* Bell Island, NF: Scott Publications, 1994.

Hammond, John W. *Wabana: A History of Bell Island from 1893–1940.* St. Stephen, NB: Print'N Press, 1982.

Neary, Steve. *The Enemy on our Doorstep: The German Attacks at Bell Island, Newfoundland, 1942.* St. John's, NF: Jesperson, 1994.

"Place of First Light." Grant application and brochure.

Weir, Gail. *The Miners of Wabana.* St. John's, NF: Breakwater, 1989.

The Gaze from the Other Side:
Storytelling for Social Change

by Sherene H. Razack

> Her (story) remains irreducibly foreign to Him. The man can't hear it
> the way she means it. He sees her as victim, as unfortunate object of haz-
> ard, "her mind is confused," he concludes. She views herself as the teller,
> the un-making subject... the moving force of the story. (Trinh, *Woman
> Native Other* 149)

For many of us who would describe ourselves as teaching for social change,
storytelling has been at the heart of our pedagogy. In the context of social change storytelling refers to an opposition to established knowledge, to Foucault's suppressed
knowledge, to the experience of the world that is not admitted into dominant knowledge paradigms. I have found storytelling to be central to strategies for social change
in two apparently different sites: law and education. In law, there is now lively debate
on "outsider jurisprudence," Mari Matsuda's useful phrase for "jurisprudence derived
from considering stories from the bottom" (Matsuda, *Public* 2322). Storytelling is less
new to critical educational theorists and practitioners but the emphasis in critical
pedagogy on voices silenced through traditional education is now being met with calls
to interrogate more closely the construction of subjectivity. That is, the complex ways
in which relations of domination are sustained, lived and resisted call for a more careful examination of how we come to know what we know as well as how we work for
a more just world across our various ways of knowing.

When we depend on storytelling either to reach each other across differences or
to resist patriarchal and racist constructs, we must overcome at least one difficulty: the
difference in position between the teller and the listener, between telling the tale and
hearing it. Storytelling is all about subjectivity: often uncritically "understood as
sentimental, personal and individual horizon as opposed to objective, universal,
societal, limitless horizon; often attributed to women, the other of man, and natives,
the other of the west" (Trinh, *Not You/Like You* 373). When, for instance, the Canadian
Advisory Council on the Status of Women, a quasigovernmental organisation, collects
the stories of immigrant women with a view to their publication, one suspects that it
is the sentimental, personal and the individual that is being sought after. To what uses
will these stories be put? Will someone else take them and theorise from them? Will
they serve to reassure everyone that Canada really is diverse, full of folklore? Who will
control how they are used? Will immigrant women tell a particular kind of story in a
forum they do not control? Such dilemmas are evident wherever storytelling is used.

In this chapter, I propose to situate my introductory comments in the context of storytelling in law, leaving the central part of the paper for a consideration of storytelling and critical pedagogy. I want to suggest, from the perspective of a popular educator who also works in academe doing legal research, that there are land mines strewn across the path wherever storytelling is used, that it should never be used uncritically and that its potential as a tool for social change is remarkable provided we pay attention to the moral vision that underpins how we hear and take up the stories of oppressed groups.

Storytelling in Law

Law relies on a positivist conception of knowledge. That is, there is a straight line between the knower and the known. In law, judges and juries discover the truth from the array of information put before them. There is only one objective truth and it is empirically provable. Reason features prominently and emotion is ruthlessly banished. The rule of law is "the consistent application of prior stated rules," a process theoretically uninformed by politics or ethics (Massaro 2099). Storytelling in law, then, is an intellectual movement that is "a rebellion against abstractions" (2099). Its purpose is to interrogate the space between the knower and the thing known; its function is one of putting the context back into law. Scheppele writes of the conceptual scheme of the observer that stands between him or her and the event. Storytelling is a theoretical attention to narrative, to the nature and consequences of this conceptual scheme. Concretely, it is an interrogation of how courts come to convert information into fact, how judges, juries and lawyers come to "objectively" know the truth: "Those whose stories are believed have the power to create fact" (2079).

Legal rules and conventions suppress the stories of outsider groups. The fiction of objectivity, for example, obscures that key players in the legal system have tended to share a conceptual scheme. Thus judges who do not see the harm of rape or of racist speech are considered to be simply interpreting what is before them. They are not seen to possess norms and values that derive directly from their social location and that are sustained by such practices as considering individuals outside of their social contexts. Stories of members of marginalised groups must therefore "reveal things about the world that we *ought* to know" (Delgado 95). They are "a means of obtaining the knowledge we need to create a just legal structure" (Matsuda, *Public* 2326). Matsuda argues forcefully that "those who have experienced discrimination speak with a special voice to which we should listen" (*Looking* 324). Stories, in the context of law, bring feeling back and they tend to work from experiential understanding (Massaro 2105). How this happens in a courtroom is clear from feminist jurisprudence.

Feminists working in law describe for the court's benefit the nature of women's oppression and then make an argument that policies and practices that perpetuate that oppression ought to be declared illegal. (In Canada, section 15, the equality rights section of the Charter of Rights and Freedoms, is usually invoked in support.) The

Women's Legal Education and Action Fund (LEAF), formed in 1985, is one of the major groups developing and making this argument in Canadian courts (Razack). The challenge has been to bring into the courtroom details about women's daily lives in a forum constructed to negate or silence such realities. For instance, Western law functions on the basis of liberalism where the individual is thought to be an autonomous, rational self, essentially unconnected to other selves and dedicated to pursuing his or her own interests. To present an individual in her community, and further, to describe that community as LEAF has done, as "the disadvantaged, the disempowered, the marginalized" (Razack 74–75) is to pose a fundamental challenge to legal discourse. The individual in her community is less empirically provable, and courts are inordinately fond of empirical proof.

Feminists working in law theorise on the nature of the challenge they pose to law's "truth." Robin West, for instance, sees the process as one of telling women's stories. Thus feminism applied to law consists of flooding "the market with our own stories until we get one simple point across: men's narrative story and phenomenology is not women's story and phenomenology" (West 70). An example of this kind of flooding is the defence mounted by the Federation of Women Teachers of Ontario when they found themselves in court defending their right to exist as a women-only teachers' union. The Federation argued that women were and are an oppressed group and that in this specific context, a mixed sex union would only perpetuate that oppression. The men teachers' federation who supported the challenge to the Federation's right to exist as an all-female institution maintained that women teachers are equal in every way to men teachers; a mixed sex union would serve all teachers best. Whereas the side arguing for a mixed union only felt obliged to point to the collective agreement as proof of equality between men and women, the Federation enlisted the aid of over 20 women, experts in women's history, women's studies, women's unions etc., to flood the court with information about the past and daily lives of women in general and women teachers in particular. For instance, Dale Spender was asked to testify on her research that men dominate in mixed sex groupings. Joy Parr, a Canadian historian, gave evidence that historically Canadian women have had to fight to protect their rights. Management studies testified that "the routines of inequality" blocked women's advancement. Principals, for instance, had to have training in curriculum studies, which one could only get after school, a time when most women shouldered family responsibilities. At times, the tale became highly subjective, as when Sylvia Gold, then president of the Canadian Advisory Council on the Status of Women testified that she felt that the Federation had directly influenced the creation of women leaders. At other times, details about women came into the court-room in full scientific dress. Margrit Eichler, a sociology professor, quantified inequality for the court's benefit and then measured the Federation by 20 indices of inequality. Her conclusion: the Federation advanced women's interests (see Razack 78).

For feminists working in law, storytelling has always been particularly seductive; women's stories have not been told. Until recently, there has been little concern with the difficulties that arise from an uncritical use of stories. There are two features of storytelling in law that bear mentioning. First, how are the stories going to be received? Can the Man hear it the way she means it? This is particularly evident in the courtroom when the story has to do with violence against women, a story that heavily implicates men. A second problem is that one cannot be ambiguous or contradictory when playing this kind of game in a court of law, given the power of law's positivism. The stories are being told to make a particular point and they are being heard in a particular way. It will not be possible to squeeze all the realities of daily life into this framework; some realities are distorted to the point of their being unrecognisable. Canadian Native women in prisons, for instance, are currently wondering if their stories of oppression are "translatable" for the court's benefit.

Indeed, storytelling as a methodology in the context of law can lead very quickly into dichotomies and generalisations that make it difficult to describe the intersections of race, class, gender and disability. Is the search for facts, as Carrie Menkel Meadow, a feminist lawyer, asks, "a feminine search for context and the search for legal principles a masculine search for certainty and abstract rules?" (49). Gender, uncontaminated by race, class, disability or sexual orientation is the prism through which daily life is viewed and differences among women fit awkwardly into the story. When gender is constructed in its pure form, i.e. uncontaminated by race or class or culture, Norma Alarcon has pointed out, the woman thus imagined names herself; her culture, race or class do not name her. Thus, ironically, she remains the old, autonomous, liberal self, only female; another abstraction (357).

Concerns about the "coercive power of stories" (Scheppele 2077) and thus about how they are used and the uses to which they are put have troubled legal scholars working on race critiques of law. Toni Massaro, for instance, has reflected on the consequences of an unproblematic call for stories and context, identifying one important difficulty: in the end, law has to privilege one story over another. A judge has to choose and it is not so much his understanding that is required as certain actions. Furthermore, given the fact that most judges continue to come from dominant groups, they are unlikely to be able to empathise with marginalised groups. In any event, in the area of discrimination, for instance, Massaro points out, empathy is not the ultimate goal. It is not enough to try to find ways to communicate to the judge that discrimination is hurtful. It is equally necessary to convince him or her that an action is morally wrong and requires legal sanction. Massaro suggests that how we hear different stories is therefore dependent on the moral code with which we function (2127). While we experience many unpleasant things, only some are considered both morally reprehensible and "actionable" in law. Justice is all about drawing the boundaries between wrong and right.

Mari Matsuda's work on legal sanctions for racist speech provides a careful reflection on how we might evaluate the stories of victims from the basis of what we as a society consider to be morally wrong. Arguing that a "legal response to racist speech is a statement that victims of racism are valued members of our polity" (*Public* 2322), Matsuda grapples with the complexities of how we decide whose perspectives to take into account in determining the kinds of racist speech that require legal sanction. She notes, for instance, that the typical reaction of oppressed groups to an incident of racist propaganda is alarm and calls for redress, whereas the typical reaction of dominant groups is denial and dismissal of the incident as a harmless prank (2327). Denial of the impact of this form of racism helps to sustain the view that censorship of racist hate messages is a greater harm than the harm of the messages themselves. If we listened to the voices of those harmed by racist propaganda, however, basic principles would emerge that help us to assess the context in which racist speech occurs. Victims of racism make clear that racism must be fought on all levels and that their lives would be improved by an explicit legal condemnation of racist speech.

One immediate criticism of the position that we ought to listen to the voices of the oppressed in determining what is and is not just is, as Matsuda herself observes, the sorting out of who is oppressed and who is not. Anticipating such critics, Matsuda directs us to examine such social indicators as wealth, mobility, comfort, health, and survival which tell us which groups have status. She allows for the fact that oppressed groups participate in each other's oppression but claims that racist speech from a member of a historically subjugated group is not to be judged as harshly as racist speech from a member of a dominant group. The former's racism "is tied to the structural domination of another group" (*Public* 2362). A member of a historically subjugated group forfeits this privilege when she allies herself to the dominant group (2364).

Clearly, deciding which voices to privilege in law is enormously complicated and relies not only on our being able to thread our way through historical domination but also on the clarity of our moral vision. The alternatives, however, are to ignore the voices of marginalised groups or to accept them uncritically. This latter option would leave us with no way of evaluating the difference between Zionism and generic white supremacy, to use Matsuda's example. We would have no guidelines for assessing the context in which stories originate.

Storytelling in Critical Pedagogy

In traditional educational theory, the existing arrangement of society is taken as given and schools "are seen as the means of rationally distributing individuals in what is conceived as a basically just society" (Weiler 5). In contrast, (and like outsider jurisprudence), critical educational theory recognises, as Henry Giroux has put it, that "ideology has to be conceived as both source and effect of social and institutional practices as they operate within a society that is characterised by relations of domination, a society in which men and women are basically unfree in both objective and subjective terms" (Giroux, cited in Weiler 22). Thus a radical or critical pedagogy is one that resists the reproduction of the *status quo* by uncovering relations of domination and opening up spaces for voices suppressed in traditional education. How critical educators do so is once again through the methodology of storytelling. Individuals who develop critical thinking can challenge oppressive practices; the critical educator thus "takes as central the inner histories and experiences of the students themselves," seeking to foster critical reflection of everyday experience (Weiler 22–23).

As in outsider jurisprudence, storytelling for social change in an educational setting is more complicated than the phrase would indicate. In her work on how the
school covertly regulates the production of self-regulating, autonomous individuals,
Valerie Walkerdine stresses that those who are most targeted in the school system, the
poor, the working class and ethnic minorities, also resist and engage differently with
the systems of domination in which they are enmeshed. As Walkerdine put it, "the
constitution of subjectivity is not all of one piece without seams and ruptures" (204).
The voices of the oppressed are not simply left out of the system. Rather, the school
regulates what a child is and children of outsider groups (and all girls) respond in a
number of contradictory ways. The critical educator has to understand how "particular children live those multiple positionings" (204). For example, she writes:

> How might a girl's [socially produced] docility in school produce both
> losses and gains? She might be denied in the status of "active learner"
> and yet at the same time be enabled to maintain another site of power,
> for example by taking the position of mother. Yet she must experience
> pain and anxiety if the contradiction between those positions is not rec-
> ognized and understood as an effect of the pathologising process [i.e.
> where masculinity is the norm]. What, too, if that pathology operates in
> relation to different and contradictory assumptions of the normal? How
> then are the resultant splittings lived? (228–29)

The double strategy which Walkerdine recommends, "one which recognises and
examines the effects of normative models, whilst producing the possibility of other
accounts and other sites of identification" (238), is an important reminder of the multiple and contradictory nature of subjectivity, hence of the complexities of working
with the stories of outsiders to resist domination.

While critical educational theorists like Walkerdine begin here, popular education theorists and practitioners often fail to theorise multiple and contradictory
subjectivities. Paolo Freire's pioneering work on the fostering of critical consciousness
in oppressed groups continues to be applied relatively straightforwardly in North
America, for instance, in ways that stop short of interrogating the category oppressed
for the North American as opposed to the Latin American context in which Freire's
work originated. In Freire's work, as Charles Paine writes, a pedagogy that is radical,
whether in the popular education or in the academic classroom, "must help students
transcend culturally imposed consciousness, allowing them to exit their circular, self-
enclosed, and self-perpetuating 'uncritical immersion in the *status quo*'" (558).
Popular education, grounded in this theoretical approach, writes one practitioner,

> stresses dialogue, group learning, and valuing the participants'
> experience as the foundation for further learning and knowledge. The
> educator is considered a facilitator of a collective educational process,
> someone who is able to question critically different perceptions of real-
> ity and custom, and to contribute to the formulation of *new knowledge*
> that addresses the problems of poor communities and the actions those
> communities want to undertake. (Magendzo 50, emphasis added)

Ironically, popular educators have been slow to critically reflect on their own practices. Ricardo Zuniga, in an article called *La Gestion Amphibie* laments the lack of critical reflection on the part of popular educators and attributes it to an us/them mentality. For instance, the funders (the state) are thought to be the bad guys, thus placing emphasis on the unity and internal solidarity of those who receive funding. It then becomes difficult to critically evaluate the project (other than in carefully constructed reports to the funding agency). Zuniga identifies the tendencies that exacerbate dichotomous thinking and make it difficult to deal with contradiction. The popular educator embodies contradiction, he argues: "he [sic] is responsible for training in a context where only self-training is acknowledged; he does not want to control and he is conscious of the distance between him and his 'clients,' 'collaborators' or 'students.' The problems with appropriate terminology well illustrate the contradictions" (158). The only palliative, Zuniga argues, that is available for this anguish is the reassurance of being on the right side, the alternative to the *status quo.*

If you are on the good side, then you define yourself by reliance on "*le savoir populaire,*" popular knowledge, and not "*le savoir bourgeois;*" a firm rejection of empiricism, positivism and science and a warm embrace of emotions, stories, narratives, nature, spontaneity (Zuniga 162). Stories cannot really be critiqued in this framework; they are unproblematically conceived of as suppressed knowledge. There is an assumption that the living voices (and sometimes the written texts) of the oppressed express a truth that will win out. There is little room for questioning that voice or text as the transmitter of authentic "human" experience (Greene 25). Here the authentic voice rests on a conception of the self as unitary and coherent. Language is seen as simply representing reality rather than constructing it. (Zuniga, however, is only objecting to the oppositional thinking and not to the view of language and voice as straightforwardly representational of reality. Thus, he ends up arguing for more rationality and less emotion.)

Feminists have long warned of the ultimate dangers of dichotomising. With poetic eloquence, Gloria Anzaldua writes:

> But it is not enough to stand on the opposite river bank shouting questions, challenging patriarchal white conventions. A counterstance locks one into a duel of oppressor and oppressed; locked in mortal combat, like the cop and the criminal, both reduced to a common denominator of violence. The counterstance refutes the dominant culture's views and beliefs, and for this, it is proudly defiant. All reaction is limited by, and dependent on, what it is reacting against. Because the counterstance stems from a problem with authority—outer as well as inner—it's a step towards liberation from cultural domination. But it is not a way of life. At some point, on our way to new consciousness, we will have to leave the opposite bank, the split between the two mortal combatants somehow healed... (*Borderlands* 78).

To heal the split, we have to think about our way of life. "The massive uprooting of dualistic thinking" (*Borderlands* 80) which Anzaldua and many other feminists have long called for requires new ways of knowing. Yet, the narratives or stories, of which Zuniga complains, are frequently advanced by feminists as *the* way to challenge patriarchal dichotomies, in spite of the fact that they are primarily described as everything patriarchal knowledge is not. Thus, Bettina Aptheker concludes her book *Tapestries of Life* with this suggestion:

> The point is that more than one thing is true for us at the same time. A masculinist process, however, at least as it has been institutionalized in Western society, accentuates the combative, the oppositional, the either/or dichotomies, the "right" and "wrong." What I have been about throughout this book is showing that the dailiness of women's lives structures a different way of knowing and a different way of thinking. The process that comes from this way of knowing has to be at the centre of a woman's politics, and it has to be at the centre of a woman's scholarship. This is why I have been drawn to the poetry and to the stories: because they are layered, because more than one truth is represented, because there is ambiguity and paradox. When we work together in coalitions, or on the job, or in academic settings, or in the community, we have to allow for this ambiguity and paradox, respect each other, our cultures, our integrity, our dignity. (254)

In critical educational and feminist theory, what are being sought, then, are ways to come to terms with the contradictions of everyday life, contradictions that reveal themselves in the stories of the oppressed and in which are located the seeds for critical consciousness. How does this project take shape in the classroom?

"In the Field"

There is high demand for stories in the classroom—both the traditional academic classroom and the one in which I teach human rights activists at an annual summer college. There, Aptheker's "respect each other" (254), acceptance of tolerance and ambiguity etc., frustrate me however, in the same way that Elizabeth Ellsworth felt frustrated by the fine sounding phrases of critical pedagogy in her influential article "Why doesn't this feel empowering?" Stories intended to serve as an opposition to patriarchal discourse have *not* always felt empowering. This is due, in large part, to two tendencies: our failure to recognise the multiple nature of subjectivity and hence the complex ways we construct meaning, and a failure to develop an ethical vision[1] based on our differences. In the effort to untangle how we are constructed we have sometimes failed to define what it is about the world that we want to change and why.

Ellsworth noted specifically that in mixed-sex, mixed-race courses on racism, students enter with "investments of privilege and struggle already made in favour of some ethical and political positions concerning racism and against other positions" (301). The strategies of empowerment, dialogue and voice do not in fact work as neatly as they are supposed to because there is no unity among the oppressed and because our various histories are not left at the door when we enter a classroom to critically reflect. Her students were unable to "hear" each other. The operative mode was rationality and the stories of various groups had to be justified and explicated using the very tools that held these stories to be inadmissible. (Here the parallel to feminists working in law is obvious. The rules of the legal game structure the tale in such a way that only some parts of it can be told or what is told is unrecognisably transformed by the fancy scientific dress.) Going beyond Aptheker's unproblematic call for a tolerance of ambiguity, Ellsworth suggests that we respect the diversity of voices, of stories as it were, that we recognise that the voices are "valid—but not without response" (305). In other words, the stories must be *critiqued* and she has a number of concrete suggestions for doing so which I would like to address in order to look for a way out of a return to rationality or to an uncritical reliance on stories.

Ellsworth recommends that we work hard at building trust, hence the importance of building in opportunities for social interaction (we do this at the [University of Ottawa] summer college [in human rights] by making the programme a residential programme); that we stress the need to learn about the realities of others without relying on them to inform us; that we name the inequalities *in* the classroom and devise ground rules for communication, (for this we used Uma Narayan's article "Working across differences"); that we consider strategies such as encouraging affinity groups between those who are most likely to share the same forms of oppression; and that we consciously offer such groups the time to coalesce so that individuals can speak from within groups. All of these recommended pedagogical practices come out of her central piece of advice which is that we critically examine what we share and don't share. We work from the basis that we all have only partial knowledge that we come from different subject positions. Most important of all, no one is off the hook since we can all claim to stand as oppressor and oppressed in relation to someone else. These suggestions, which I do practise, do not save me from some of the "ethical dilemmas" that arise frequently at the summer college (although perhaps I could have minimised their impact had I paid closer attention to the ground rules above).

Two incidents from the most recent summer college in human rights illustrate some of the difficulties with a critical use of storytelling. The summer college in human rights, held at the University of Ottawa but sponsored by the non-governmental Human Rights Research and Education Centre, brings together sixty human rights activists who work for social change within an organised group. Thus there are members of groups of women with disabilities, various anti-racist groups, the Assembly of First Nations, lawyers for human rights in South Africa, and so on. Although it frequently happens that individuals from dominant groups work for organisations on behalf of the oppressed, the majority of students can fit, in one way or another, into the "disadvantaged groups." The first incident illustrates the unreasonably high demand for storytelling from those in dominant positions. Here I take some responsibility. The curriculum is designed to encourage storytelling and the pedagogical practices emphasise the need to make a space for different voices and in fact to forge a politics of alliances based on this sharing of daily experiences. One participant in my group, a white disabled woman, frustrated by the silence of a black woman from South Africa when South Africa was being discussed, directly confronted her with a firm "Why don't you tell us your experiences?" Realising the harshness of what was said, another participant, also disabled but male, repeated the request more gently. The trust and sharing of the class, built over 5 days, instantly dissolved. The Black participant, confronted with a request to tell her story, defended her right to silence and then left the room in tears. In the chaos of what then ensued, it became clear that the sentence, so simply expressed by a white woman, innocently inviting a woman of colour to share her experiences of racism, recalled for every person of colour in the room (seven out of twenty and myself) that this was not in fact a safe learning environment. As the instructor and a woman of colour, I tried hard to retain my composure. Later, distressed to the point of tears by the "loss of control" in "my" classroom, and not consoled by the learning value of the event, I wondered how it was that I could have been so powerfully affected in spite of many years' experience of just this type of situation. I recall trying clumsily to explain to a colleague that *we* (people of colour) are always being asked to tell our stories for *your* (white people) edification, which you cannot *hear* because of the benefit you derive from hearing them. Suddenly, the world was still white after all and the pedagogy that insisted that the oppressed can come together to critically reflect and share stories seemed a sham. Other writers of colour have noted, of course, that few people of colour have ever considered learning in a mixed-race environment as safe. For example, Patricia Monture-Angus comments that in her many years as a student and a professor, and often the only Aboriginal person in the room, she has never experienced the classroom as a safe space (67). Yet the pedagogy of storytelling and the presence of a number of subordinate groups, including a number of people of colour, led many of us to throw caution to the winds. What we had failed to consider was how social hierarchies operated among subordinate groups.[2]

Let me leave this story for a while and tell another that occurred in the same context but among all three classes of the summer college. This story illustrates for me the sheer difficulty of understanding across differences and the need for some ethical guidelines for *listening*. The session in question took place in August, 1990. On the day that the Federal Government of Canada, at Quebec's request, decided to send in the army to try to end the standoff between Mohawks and the Quebec provincial police (*Sûreté du Quebec*), the students of the summer college decided to abandon the curriculum and take action. This after all was the basis of the education for social change they had come to get. In the very heated discussions that followed as to the most appropriate actions to be taken, the only two Native participants (not, however, of the Mohawk nation) assumed a leadership role, again in keeping with the principles of the college that struggles for social change must be led by the groups in question. They both endorsed a march on Parliament Hill to protest armed intervention and made a passionate plea (in the form of stories of their lives as Native women) that we all accept this as the only course of action. As in Elizabeth Ellsworth's class, we, the non-Natives in the room, then began to process the story we had heard. Some of us then required the two women to defend their position using the master's tools since we felt that the army was in fact an improvement over the *Sûreté du Québec*, a police force well-known for its racism. In fact, we argued, the Assembly of First Nations who represented Native groups, themselves agreed this was so although they deplored, as we did, armed intervention. The situation soon led to tears (from the Native women), recriminations (from some of the francophone participants who felt that sympathy for the Mohawks came easily for anglophones whose daily lives were not touched by the crisis as were the lives of francophone inhabitants of Quebec), sheer astonishment at the depth of emotion we had observed, and to our general confusion and failure to find a way out of this ethical dilemma. In a different way, the situation was repeated when a native woman from an altogether different reserve (Akwasasne) came to speak against the Warrior societies of the Mohawks, while a Native leader later spoke in their defence. We had to employ the tools of rationality to choose between stories and to determine political action. The brilliant suggestion of Uma Narayan, that we grant epistemic privilege to the oppressed, falls apart when the subject positions are so confused. Unless we want to fall into the trap of demanding that the oppressed speak in a unified voice before we will believe them, we are still left with the difficult task of negotiating our way through our various ways of knowing and towards political action.

Both these incidents led me to reflect on classroom ethics, indeed on ethics in general, in mixed sex and mixed race groupings where there is a commitment to social change. First, I agree with Zuniga and Ellsworth: we do shy away from critical reflection of the practices of those on the "good" side. Ironically, our analytical and pedagogical tools seem to discourage internal critique by calling for respect for different voices with insufficient attention paid to the contexts of both the teller and the listener. Second, the risks taken in the course of critical reflection are never equally shared. This is almost a truism yet we have not been careful to devise a pedagogy that would accommodate it or a political practice that would not sacrifice diversity, again I think because the game of good guy/bad guy discourages it. What would a pedagogy that recognised the inequalities of risk-taking entail? We know more about what it would not entail, for instance Ellsworth's comments that acting as though the classroom is a safe place does not make it safe.

From feminists and practitioners of critical pedagogy alike has come the suggestion that caring is as important as critical pedagogy. For instance, Methchild Hart warned of an overemphasis on cognitive processes (135). We cannot absolutely know what is required in what instances. Is the best we can do to remain open and to care? There are, however, boundaries to our caring which have to be worked out when deciding how far we will commit ourselves to action. Furthermore, these boundaries are hard to discern across cultures and caring sometimes gets in the way. Lynet Uttal, writing of her experience of the differences between Anglo-feminist groups and those of women of colour, notes that in Anglo-feminist groups, the emphasis on providing care and support leads to passive listening of diverse voices. There is seldom any heated discussion or disagreement; those who fail to fit in simply leave the group. She describes Anglo-feminists' "blank looks of supportive listening" and the absence of critical engagement with the ideas proposed (318). Making a related point, Monture-Angus notes that white conference participants who rejected her stories of subordiniation, did so covertly, that is, privately without the knowledge of the non-white participants, thereby avoiding open confrontation (18–19).

Richard Brosio reminds us that our professions notwithstanding, education is not the leading route to social change (75). Perhaps we ought not to have the expectation that a pedagogy can be devised that will help us to transcend the dichotomies and the bind of partial knowledge. Iris Young wisely notes that "too often people in groups working for social change take mutual friendship to be a goal of the group. Such a desire for community often channels energy away from the political goals of the group" (235). I interpret this to mean that we often forget that community has to be struggled for, which I think Ellsworth very forcefully demonstrates by her critical analysis of her course on racism. What might assist us to promote the struggle for community?

If there is no automatic friendship, good will or community, where do we begin? The answer is of course already an axiom among us: we begin with critical thinking and critical pedagogy. But where critical pedagogy has traditionally begun is not far enough below the surface. We have to begin with how we know, giving this more attention than we have traditionally done. Epistemology, perhaps without using the word, has to enter into our pedagogy and our political categories. It is not an auspicious beginning to build on the feminist insight that women appear to know differently to men because the universalising tendency of the category "woman" has been every bit as destructive as the universal category "oppressed" has been in critical pedagogy.

Carolyn Steedman well illustrates the point that how we know what we know is central to our political practice because it helps us to locate the inconsistencies, the cracks we might then use to empower ourselves. Commenting on the fact that all women learn about patriarchy in the family, whether by the father's absence or presence, she remarks:

> What is a distinction though, and one that offers some hope, is the difference between learning of this system from a father's display of its social basis, and learning of it from a relatively unimportant and power-less man (as in the case of her working-class father), who cannot present the case for patriarchy embodied in his own person. (79)

Our different subject positions, borne out in how we know, tell and hear stories, are ignored at our peril. Maria Lugones describes the dilemmas that confront her as a Chicana woman in an intellectual context that is predominantly white, when invited to tell her stories. White/Anglo women, she writes, "can see themselves as simply human or simply women. I can bring you to your senses *con el tono de mi voz*, with the sound of my—to you—alien voice" (49). This at any rate is the assumption behind storytelling. For the woman of colour, however, the situation is altogether more difficult:

> So the central and painful questions for *me* in this encounter become questions of speech? *En que voz* with which voice, *anclada en que lugar*

anchored in which place, *para que y porque* why and to what purpose, do
I trust myself to you... *o acaso juego un juego de* cat and mouse for your
entertainment... *o por el mio?* I ask these questions out loud because
they need to be asked. (49)

If we are sensitive to this difference which Lugones brilliantly demonstrates, and we
heed Ellsworth's practical advice on this score, that is that we problematise what the
limits of our knowing are, based on our different subject positions, I think we end up
realising that storytelling serves various groups differently and that it should never be
employed uncritically in mixed groups.

Trinh Minh-ha's work is a courageous attempt to delineate modes of storytelling,
to explore the complex interplay between the subject positions of the tellers and the
listeners. "There is more than one way to relate the story of specialness," she observes,
and stories can perpetuate domination. For instance, specialness can serve the dominant groups as entertainment, as "that voice of difference likely to bring us *what we
can't have* and to divert us from the monotony of sameness."

> Eager not to disappoint, I try my best to offer my benefactors and
> benefactresses what they most anxiously yearn for: the possibility of a
> difference, yet a difference or otherwise that will not go so far as to ques-
> tion the foundations of their beings and makings. (*Woman* 88)

As a listener, one can be drawn into such a process very easily. I have seen students
literally feeding off the tears of stories from the Third World, basking in the sense of
having visited another country so easily and feeling no compulsion to explore their
own complicity in the oppression of others.

The problems of voice and identity are packed with internal dilemmas not only
for the listeners but also the tellers of the tale. Often women of colour are asked to tell
their stories while others will do the theorising and the writing up. Yet the chance to
speak, to enter your reality on the record, as it were, is as irresistible as it is problematic. What kind of tale will I choose to tell, and in what voice? Trinh Minh-ha asks,
"how do you inscribe difference without bursting into a series of euphoric narcissis-
tic accounts of yourself and your own kind? Without indulging in a marketable
romanticism or in a naive whining about your condition?" (*Woman* 28). There are
penalties for choosing the wrong voice at the wrong time, for telling an inappropriate
tale. Far better, one might conclude, as the black woman from South Africa did, to
keep silent. I found myself exploring, at the summer college, this right to silence and
offer in this regard another of Trinh's observations: "Silence as a will not to say or a
will to unsay and as a language of its own has barely been explored" (*Not You/Like You*
373). As an educator, however, I find the idea of silence extremely unsettling, reminding me of my own compelling interest in encouraging the telling of stories.

In storytelling, then, while asking ourselves what we can know and not know is
important, particularly in terms of listening to others and then deciding how to act in
a particular situation, I think there is a more basic task at hand. This is the task of
calling into question knowledge and being of both the teller and the listener, and

struggling for ways to take this out of the realm of abstraction and into political action. "What we do toward the texts of the oppressed is very much dependent upon where we are," writes Gayatri Spivak (57), echoing a Québécois proverb that "*on pense ou on a les pieds.*" Again I turn to Trinh Minh-ha who has illuminated for me most clearly why neither rationality nor emotional sharing will suffice. Trinh suggests we consider breaking the dichotomy mind/body, reason/emotion, as is done in Asian martial arts for instance, by adding a third category, "instinctual immediacy," by which I think is meant subject position or point of departure. Here, instinct does not stand opposed to reason; it requires us to relate to the world with immediacy, to allow "each part of the body to become infused with consciousness." Instinct requires us to reactivate the "radical calling into question in every undertaking, of everything that one takes for granted" (*Woman* 40). Give up, in other words, the quest for knowledge, that is to definitively know, either through the heart or the mind. Instead, question one's point of departure at every turn so that strategies (such as replacing rationality with emotions) do not become end points in themselves (*Woman* 43).

Trinh Minh-ha is optimistic about her proposal to engage in the ground clearing activity of radically calling into question:

> The questions that arise continue to provoke answers, but none will dominate as long as the ground-clearing activity is at work. Can knowledge circulate without a position of mastery? Can it be conveyed without the exercise of power? No, because there is no end to understanding power relations which are rooted deep in the social nexus—not merely added to society nor easily locatable so that we can just radically do away with them. Yes, however, because in-between grounds always exist, and cracks and interstices are like gaps of fresh air that keep on being suppressed because they tend to render more visible the failures operating in every system. Perhaps mastery need not coincide with power. (*Woman* 41)

The *mestiza* consciousness described by Gloria Anzaldua in her book *Borderlands/La Frontera* requires ground-clearing activity. The future belongs to the *mestizos*, Anzaldua writes, "because the future depends on the breaking down of paradigms, it depends on the straddling of two or more cultures. By creating a new mythos—that is a change in the way we perceive reality, the way we see ourselves, and the ways we behave—*la mestiza* creates a new consciousness" (80). Anzaldua makes concrete the tolerance for ambiguity called for by Bettina Aptheker when she situates it in the radical calling into question of all our subject positions. The first step of the *mestiza* is to take inventory: to ask critically, "Just what did she inherit from her ancestors?" (Anzaldua, *Borderlands* 82)

Pedagogically, then, ground clearing activity is my suggestion for reshaping education for social change. In one way this is not any different from the axiom to continually critically reflect. What it refers to, however, is reflecting critically on how we hear, how we speak, to the choices we make about which voice to use, when, and, most important of all, developing pedagogical practices that enable us to pose these questions and use the various answers to guide those concrete moral choices we are constantly being called upon to make.

Concretely, I envision a more complex mapping of our differences than we have ever tried before. In the case of the summer college, for instance, it will mean that more space is cleared in the curriculum for exploration from our various subject positions. Colonisation from within and without will become a major theme and not just in terms of what colonisation means for Third World peoples but also how it constitutes the colonisers themselves. The project at hand is Spivak's "unlearning privilege" (30) so that "not only does one become able to listen to that other constituency, but one learns to speak in such a way that one will be taken seriously by that other constituency" (42). In the past, it seemed such an enormous task to enter into the classroom some of the realities of various oppressed groups that it did not seem possible to concentrate on how we are "processing" this information differently based on our respective subject positions. In effect, were I to redesign my pedagogical approach in the summer college, I would want to pay more attention to how we know rather than primarily to what we know. It seems simple enough but the complex ways of telling stories act as a reminder that the task is anything but simple.

In law, maintaining a similar vigilance about how we know what we know requires that we pay attention to "the interpretative structures we use to reconstruct events" (Crenshaw 404). As feminists, for instance, we will need to devise alternatives for telling about the lives of women of colour that transcend the narrative about the white woman or the one about the black man. Since the stories of women of colour fit into neither, telling them will require attention to multiplicities, contradictions and relations of power embedded in interpretive structures.

To conclude, I endorse Trinh's passionate plea for a movement away from defining and boxing ourselves into one subject identity:

> You and I are close, we intertwine; you may stand on the other side of the hill once in a while, but you may also be me, while remaining what you are and what I am not. The differences made *between* entities comprehended as absolute presences—hence the notion of *pure origin* and *true* self—are an outgrowth of a dualistic system of thought peculiar to the Occident… (*Woman* 90)

Without absolutes, no true self, no pure origin, it becomes all the more imperative to pay attention to how our multiple identities are constructed and played out at any one time in any one context. The white disabled student might then have not asked for the stories of the black South African; she might have focused on critically examining her own need to hear those stories (to what end?). Similarly, we would not have been paralysed by guilt upon hearing Native women call for a particular form of action which did not meet our rational criteria. We might instead have asked what was affecting our comprehension of events (as indeed they might have asked themselves). In the same way, feminists who go to court might question their choice of narrative strategies *before* they go to court. More secure in our respective commitments to probing beneath the surface of what we know, to how we know, alliances might then be possible between white, heterosexual, able-bodied and middle-class women and women on the margins. In the courtroom as in the classroom, ours "is a responsibility to trace the other in self" (Spivak 47), a task that must become central to our practice.

(1998)

Notes

1   I have used the word ethical to describe a collective reflection on the moral values we each hold. An ethical vision informs our politics in the sense that it is a shared sense of what is right and wrong.

2   This issue is taken up at length by Mary Louise Fellow and Sherene Razack in "The Race to Innocence: Confronting Hierarchical Relations among Women." *Iowa Journal of Gender, Race and Justice*, Vol.1 No. 2, 998–1998. 335–52.

Works Cited

Alarcon, Norma. "The theoretical subject(s) of *This Bridge Called My Back* and Anglo-American feminism." *Making Face, Making Soul. Haciendo Caras*. Ed. Gloria Anzaldua. San Francisco: Aunt Lute Foundation Books, 1990. 356–69.

Anzaldua, Gloria, ed. *Borderlands/La Frontera*. San Francisco: Spinsters/Aunt Lute Foundation Books, 1987.

———. *Making Face, Making Soul. Haciendo Caras*. San Francisco: Aunt Lute Foundation Books, 1990.

Aptheker, Bettina. *Tapestries of Life*. Amherst: U of Massachusetts P, 1989.

Brosario, Richard. "Teaching and Learning for Democratic Empowerment: a Critical Evaluation." *Educational Theory* 40.1 (1990): 68–81.

Crenshaw, Kimberle. "Whose Story is it Anyway?" *Race-ing Justice, Engendering Power. Essays on Anita Hill, Clarence Thomas, and the Construction of Social Reality*. Ed. Toni Morrison. New York: Patheon, 1992. 402–40.

Delgado, Richard. "When a Story is Just a Story: Does Voice Really Matter?" *Virginia Law Review* 76.9 (1990): 95–111.

Ellsworth, Elizabeth. "Why Doesn't this Feel Empowering": Working Through the Repressive Myths of Critical Pedagogy." *Harvard Educational Review* 59.3 (1989): 297–324.

Freire, Paulo. *Pedagogy of the Oppressed* (1970). New York: Continuum, 1984.

Greene, Gayle and Copelia Kahn. "Feminist Scholarship and the Social Construction of Women." *Making a Diference. Feminist Literary Criticism.* London: Routledge, 1985. 1–36.

Hart, Methchild. "Critical Theory and Beyond: Further Perspectives on Emancipatory Education." *Adult Education Quarterly* 40.3 (1990):125–38.

Lugones, Maria. "Hablando Cara a Cara/Speaking Face to Face." *Making Face, Making Soul. Haciendo Caras.* Ed. Gloria Anzaldua. San Francisco: Aunt Lute Foundation Books, 1989. 46–54.

Magendzo, Salomon. "Popular Education in Nongovernmental Organizations: Education for Social Mobilization?" *Harvard Education Review* 60.1 (1990): 49–61.

Massaro, Toni M. "Empathy, Legal Storytelling, and the Rule of Law: New Words, Old Wounds?" *Michigan Law Review* 87 (1989): 2099–127.

Matusda, Mari J. "Looking to the Bottom: Critical Legal Studies and Reparations." *Harvard Civil Rights-Civil Liberties Law Review* 22 (1987): 322–99

———. "Public Response to Racist Speech: Considering the Victim's Story." *Michigan Law Review* 87 (1989): 2320–381.

Menkel Meadow, Carrie. "Portia in a Different Voice: Speculations on a Woman's Lawyering Process." *Berkely Woman's Law Journal* 1 (1985): 39–63.

Minh-Ha, Trinh T. "Not You/Like You: Post-Colonial Women and the Interlocking Questions of Identity and Difference." *Making Face, Making Soul. Haciendo Caras.* Ed. Gloria Anzaldua. San Francisco: Aunt Lute Foundation Books, 1989. 371–75.

———. *Woman, Native, Other.* Bloomington: Indiana UP, 1989.

Monture-Angus, Patricia. *Thunder in My Soul: A Mohawk Woman Speaks.* Halifax: Fernwood, 1995.

Narayan, Uma. "Working Across Differences: *Hypatia* 3.2 (1988): 31–47.

Paine, Charles. "Relativism, Radical Pedagogy and the Ideology of Paralysis." *College English* 50.6 (1989): 557–70.

Razack, Sherene. *Canadian Feminism and the Law: The Women's Legal Education and Action Fund and the Pursuit of Equality.* Toronto: Second Story, 1991.

Scheppele, Kim Lane. "Forward: Telling Stories." *Michigan Law Review* 87 (1989): 2073–098.

Spivak, Gayatri Chakravorty. *The Post-Colonial Critic. Interivews Strategies Dialogues.* Ed. Sarah Harasym. London: Routledge, 1990.

Steedman, Carolyn. *Landscape for a Good Woman.* London: Virago, 1986.

Uttal, Lynet. "Nods That Silence." *Making Face, Making Soul. Haciendo Caras.* Ed. Gloria Anzaldua. San Francisco: Aunt Lute Foundation Books, 1989. 317–20.

Walkerdine, Valerie. "On the Regulation of Speaking and Silence: Subjectivity, Class and Gender in Contemporary Schooling." *Language, Gender and Childhood.* Ed. Carolyn Steedman. London: Routledge & Kegan Paul, 1985. 203–341.

Weiler, Kathleen. *Women, Teching For Change, Gender, Class and Power.* New York: Bergin & Garvey, 1988.

West, Robin. "Jurisprudence and Gender." *University of Chicago Law Review* 55.1 (1988): 1–72.

Young, Iris Marion. *Justice and the Politics of Difference.* Princeton: Princton UP, 1990.

Zuniga, Ricardo. "La Gestion Amphibie." *Review Internationale d'Action Communautaire* 19 (1988): 157–67.

The Working Body/The Working Gaze

by Alan Filewod

> But show something.
> And let him observe
> That this is not magic,
> but Work my friends.
>   Bertolt Brecht, "The Curtains"

The convergence of working-class theatre with labour activism produces a set of theoretical problems that have been in a constant state of reformulation ever since theatre artists aligned their art with class struggle. If political theatre workers can often be heard to complain that they are reinventing the wheel, it is because the act of producing theatre for and in the labouring classes raises recurring questions that find specific solutions only in local practice. As Raymond Williams has noted, "work" has shifted its meaning in the modern age "from the productive effort itself to the predominant social relationship" of that effort in capitalist society (335). Work is therefore a particularly difficult quality to represent on stage, because it can only be made known through the social relationships of working or by its product, the work. On one level, all performances take place in a workspace, because performance itself is the product of work, whether as a job or as a leisure activity—the difference is largely a matter of the organizing social formations which give it meaning. All performances take place on a shop floor; all actors are working people.

This exposes two basic problems. The first concerns the actor, who is both the producer and the re-presenter of work. The question of the working body of the actor reveals a crisis in the industrial place of the acting profession. The outlines of this crisis can be seen in the historical development of performance approaches capable of representing work and at the same time validating the actor as an industrial worker.

The second question is that of the "working gaze," which examines the ways in which working-class spectators watch theatrical performances. Is their reception contingent on class formation? Do particular dramatic techniques reflect this formation more accurately than others?

The issue of the gaze treats two dialectically related problems, from both sides of the stage: the ways in which the worker audience "reads" performance, and the dramatic techniques used by working-class theatres to represent and narrate the world as experienced by that audience.

These two questions, of the actor as worker and the worker as spectator, must be considered in light of each other, because it is in the point of convergence that we find the theoretical position that defines working-class theatre in terms of its role in organized labour. When detached, the two questions dissolve into a vague problem of class inflection. They are in a sense depoliticized. There are numerous historical examples, for instance, of bourgeois theatre that projects itself into working-class audiences. This is, in fact, a commonly played out historical source of the idea of national theatres, following the ideas of Romain Rolland, the late-nineteenth century French writer who argued for a democratized theatre populaire. The basic proposition can be stated bluntly: taking Shakespeare to the masses renews Shakespeare and civilizes the masses. This attitude, with its implication that both actor and text occupy a social space "away" from the popular, has informed entire industries in most western societies, in which professional actors validate themselves as working class by taking their art "to the people."

Clearly, the act of performing to working-class audiences does not authenticate the theatre itself as working class. Nor is the representation of work and working life itself sufficient to define a performance as "working-class culture." It is only when these two conditions meet, when cultural representations emerge out of and play back to specific communities of experience, that it is possible to speak of a theatre of and for workers. This leads to the fundamental proposition that working-class theatre is most usefully defined as a relational practice. As such, it can be analyzed only in terms of the organizing contexts in which relational conditions are stabilized. It is here that the congruency of workers' theatre and organized labour has been historically necessary, because the labour movement has provided the material and ideological environments that enable us to speak of the workers' theatre as an historical movement.

Space/Community

Historically, the project to reconfigure the relationship of theatre and audience in class terms has been approached as a problem of cultural geography that accepts a fundamental mapping of cultural ideology and material space. The place in which theatre happens can originate, confer and confirm social value. This is in part because communities ("audiences") use particular places to stabilize cultural boundaries. Such spaces function as matrices in which communities establish themselves in practice.

Those theatres which have most successfully established themselves as working class are often authenticated by a relationship with such a community-defining/community-defined space. This may be a physical place, as is the case with theatre produced in a workers' club or trades hall, or a symbolic space, usually configured in sponsorship by a working-class organization or community. Often, of course, these two conditions intersect. Political theatre productions that originate in "professional" contexts outside of working-class specificity (as are most theatres) frequently tour to working-class spaces, not because of a romanticized proletarianism of taking art "to" the workers, but because a material identification with a worker-identified space is a necessary step towards class legitimization.

This process has become more complex for contemporary theatres as the industrial reordering of urban centres since World War II has extensively revised class-defined urban geographies. A theatre can no longer claim to be working class simply because, like Joan Littlewood's Stratford East, it plays to the working-class neighbourhood in which it is situated. This is in part because class-defined neighbourhoods are more fragmentary in modern cities, in the sense that working-class neighbourhoods have dispersed with the relocations of industry and have been opened to settlement by other social classes; moreover, contemporary urban divisions are increasingly organized in terms of race as well as of industrial class.

The principle of validation through space, which might be considered a process of particularity, holds in other sectors of cultural activity—in feminist performance, for example, or in popular theatre, in which activist theatres perform in contexts defined by communities in struggle. Commonly, theatre workers in these fields approach the question of space and particularization as a discovery that reveals typifying or naturalized features of the field itself. As the history of class-engaged performance reveals, the contestation of space is a fundamental and recurring issue in oppositional cultural practices.

Working-class theatres have often begun with this principle in mind, beginning their operations by "going to" the working audience. Like the Blue Blouses, like Piscator, the Red Megaphones and the troupes of the Workers Theatre Movement, many of these companies defined an aesthetic based on the coding of the audience-controlled space into the performance. This was the initiative behind the formation of the Mummers Troupe in Newfoundland, 7:84 in Scotland, Melbourne Workers Theatre (with its worksite in the midst of the Jolimont rail yards) in Australia and most of the oppositional theatres of the American left. In practice, however, many such companies find themselves revising these terms. This process is forced by several major pressures. The institutional pressure comes from arts councils that reward artistic success with increased funding and encouragement to stabilize operations with a theatre space. This in turn generates a need to maximize use of the space, and a conceptual redefinition by which the theatre begins to define its performance space as working class and incrementally transfers cultural ownership to the classes that attend, and thus define, theatre spaces. Hence the gentrification by which theatres renegotiate their class alignment in order to survive.

The second, internal pressure is forced by the artists themselves, who seek expanded opportunities to do what they do best: to act in more complex parts, to write bigger plays, to design more elaborate settings, to stage more elaborate spectacles. Because the performance venues that legitimize working-class theatre tend to be funded marginally (if at all), they are less likely to offer these opportunities of scale. By necessity, working-class theatre often privileges a kind of "roughness" that refutes the perceived "polish" of commodified spectacle. This roughness is itself translated as an expression of class authenticity.

…playing back

The fact that a performance takes place in a particular space confers a degree of legitimization, but this itself does not confirm class alignment. Space, in both the geographic and the theatrical meanings of the term, is a materialization of ideology, and as such is the product of contesting forces. One such force is the hegemony of the dominant classes in society, which implicates oppositional forces into its systems of renewal. In these terms, a touring production of *Miss Saigon* playing in the civic centre of a working-class community is not simply evidence of the musical as a "popular" art (as the word is deployed by the mass media) but rather a process of colonization that naturalizes the humanist cultural ideology of the corporate sector.

Political theatre activists have come to an awareness of the economic connections that link performance spaces to this colonizing force. In fact, they have always come to, will always come to such an awareness, because political theatre practice tends to arise out of praxis and consequently can be seen as a constant, recurring process of rediscovery and reapplication of a specific set of basic oppositional techniques. Or, put another way, all resistance movements must discover for themselves what tactics work best; if they invariably rediscover the same tactics, it is because those tactics can only be learned through a process of (re)discovery.

The most important tactic of working-class theatre has been the attempt to take the theatre to the audience, which in its most logical extension has meant taking the performance to the workplace. Playing the shop floor has been an aspiration for numerous companies throughout the century. Although the social conditions that motivate this desire differ greatly, some common reasons can be traced through them.

First, the radical action of renouncing the playhouse in favour of the audience's worksite creates the possibility of reconfiguring the industrial relations of artist and audience by superimposing one workplace on another. This has the effect of acknowledging the audience as a specific political community and asserting the theatre artists as industrial colleagues. When such performances intervene in the workplace during times of routine labour, they can be used by unions to focus analysis or promote morale; when the theatre intervenes during times of labour strife, they can function as both propaganda and expressions of militant solidarity. In both cases, the theatre claims the workplace as its own site of struggle.

For reasons that raise serious questions of gender experience, labour intervention troupes have been attracted historically to heavy industry, to mines, factories and building sites. Increasingly, however, worksite performance is moving away from the factory floor. It is quite likely that in the 1990s, the typical worksite performance takes place not in a male-dominated heavy industry site, but in a mainly female office or service sector site. The proletarian romanticism of the factory performance has evolved into a more utilitarian model that essentially transfers Theatre-In-Education forms into workplaces. Social issues such as domestic violence, racism, sexual assault and equity tend to find more receptive sponsors in public sector and pink-collar unions.

It is worth noting that workplace performance can inadvertently expose deep contradictions between the industrial organization of the theatre companies involved (which are usually small, under funded and financially marginal) and the labour hosts whose struggle they join. As several companies have discovered, intervention in labour disputes can trigger contention within the theatre group when members begin to scrutinize their own working life. This is one of the main reasons why radical collectives have tended to implode in crisis; as the histories of 7:84 and the Mummers Troupe reveal, theatres that are operating in a state of financial emergency cannot easily survive interrogation of their own industrial practices.

The Worker as Spectator

Although it may seem an exaggeration, it can be argued that for most of the nineteenth and twentieth centuries the theatre has been largely a working-class pastime. Nevertheless, it is still associated in popular representations with the social elites that claimed the best seats and perspectives. Above and behind the dress circles and the boxes in which aristocrats flirted and gossiped, we find recurring images of the coarse gods of the gallery who provide the mob background of brutishness that enables the notion of aristocratic sophistication.

These images tell us more about the artists than about the audience. In fact, for most of the past two centuries, the theatre has been largely a working-class entertainment, in that working people have bought most of the tickets. The history of theatre architecture in the first half of the nineteenth century, for example, was a continuous process of building and rebuilding ever bigger houses to seat ever expanding audiences. The gods in their galleries did indeed stomp, leer, raise hell and interrupt, but neither was such behaviour unknown in the more expensive stalls. The received image of the disruptive mob that caricatures working-class audiences in the last century still persists in the image of loutish Bundys noisily disrupting the ballet.

The theatre may have been the main form of working class entertainment for the century preceding Hollywood, but it rarely returned an accurate reflection of working class reality. Far more common was the projected image of working life through the experience of the middle class, whose morality and capitalist ethics regulated social norms.

Consider the enacted representation of the working class male in Tom Robertson's 1867 society melodrama, *Caste*, with its character of Sam, who represents the idealized projection of the working class as the mainstay of the social order. Sam is in all respects a comforting image of the workingman: he is steady, sober, polite, good-humoured, self-educated, skilled and faithful, "not ashamed of my paper hat." But he is also the regulator of class immobility, who makes the astonishing speech that

> People should stick to their own class. Life's a railway journey and
> Mankind's a passenger—first class, second class, third class. Any person
> found riding in a superior class to that for which he has taken his ticket

will be removed from the first station stopped at, according to the by-laws of the company. (Ashley 271)

The contradiction between the viewer and the viewed—the Sam on stage and the Sam in the gallery—may seem obvious in this Victorian example, but the example of modern TV shows how it can be internalized and therefore naturalized. Popular sitcoms depict class not as an economic condition but as a *habitus* of taste and behaviour, as the term is used by Bourdieu. The common American euphemism for working class is "blue collar," which relocates class formation into a lifestyle choice. In TV Land, working-class anger is mutated into a blue-collar libertarian defiance that acknowledges class dissent but enlists it as the most aggressive defender of the status quo—which is repeatedly inscribed as the values of the American heartland.

If the theatre has been largely a working-class venue, why is its image so inextricably bound up in high society elitism? And why do left-leaning artists continually speak of the need to "reach" the working-class audience? How could Piscator have found himself so embittered that he could write, in 1924, that "the proletariat, whatever the reason may be, is too weak to support a theatre of its own" (324)?

The explanation may lie, in part, in the absence of real data about audiences in the modern theatre. Except for a few sociological studies, such as Bourdieu's *Distinction*, there is little empirical information available about the actual constitution of theatre audiences. Most of the available information is anecdotal, non-empirical or informal, lumped together under the umbrella of common sense. This is made even more complicated by the fact that the traditional signifiers of class difference are disappearing in modern daily life, replaced by mass culture signifiers that cross class boundaries. An attempt to define the class origin of a given theatre audience by reading the way they dress, for example, will almost certainly fail. As the Canadian proletarian poet Milton Acorn once said to an acquaintance who expressed surprise that he was wearing a suit to a function, "the working class dresses up."[1] As the ruling classes dress down.

The fact is, most audiences are working people, but most are not situated in and by the theatre as "working class." Twentieth-century theatre has moved from mainly working-class entertainment to a split, contradictory context in which the popular—the accessible, the mass appeal—is an expensive commodity produced by a highly sophisticated and capitalized industry, and the elite—the minority taste, the avant-garde—is undercapitalized, significantly less expensive to produce; materially more accessible but culturally less so. Usage in this sense is in large part class-determined. Funding economics are such that the more popular the theatre, the larger the public subsidy. But proportionately less of the budget is covered by that subsidy, so the tickets are more costly. Expensive tickets are justified by the notion of the pervasive market forces that are summoned to explain most modern corporate price-fixing, and in turn require immense advertising budgets to sustain them.

The experience of modern theatre has exposed a gap between the practice of working-class life and the representation of that life as formed by class experience.

Audiences may be working people, but it doesn't follow that they are labour audiences. In the postmodern world of the pluralized subject and experiential/optional communities, a world that offers new opportunities for identities negotiated through mass culture, the creation of new subclasses, new routes of class advancement, a world marked by the globalization of capital and its subsequent colonizing and redeployment of work forces—in this new world order, the modernist idea of working life as the basic site of identity has been severely destabilized.

Stanley Aronowitz has argued that "the working class is no longer possible as a mythic figure" (150). That the working class exists and occupies a space defined by struggle and resistance is undeniable, although the traditional class signifiers have been displaced. The mythos of the steel town culture has been supplanted by the more brutal class realities of the 1990s, in which, according to recent news reports, there are an estimated 11,000 illegal sweatshops operating in the United States, exploiting immigrant labour in conditions verging on slavery.

Organized labour (which is the voice of the industrialized taxpayer, not the sweatshop slave) claims the power to speak for working people; it thus claims cultural authority over the terms of class formation. For that reason, working-class theatre achieves legitimacy when it intervenes in that formation and defines its audience through the agency of the unions. Working-class theatre constructs its audience through the process of specificity and so participates in the construction of the class that gives it meaning. The returned gaze of that class gives the theatre its purpose in the moment of struggle. The theatre needs that sense of militancy and struggle because it needs a condition to require its intervention. In the stable social order of the Fordist accord, theatre has no place on the shop floor, because its transgressiveness upsets the management/labour balance that is designed to systematize production.

Organized labour functions as a stabilizing field that gives ideological and political coherence to an increasingly diverse subject. For political theatres, labour provides site, audience and problem (or need), the three elements that make theatre possible. But like all formations of identity, the construction of the working class through the process of organized labour is itself negotiated and provisional. Unions have been caught between the hostile forces of new right governments, with their anti-labour agenda, and the pressures from within their expanding constituencies. The struggles for voice by minorities defined by gender and ethnicity, the demand for equity by women and marginalized communities, have begun to collapse the boundaries that have traditionally isolated the public and domestic. Even as organized labour consolidates its place as the articulation of working-class experience, it is under pressure to expand its understanding of work itself. Activist theatre is one of the ways in which the expansion in the workplace expands the notion of the worker and the working class.

(1999)

Notes

[1]   This story is anecdotal—ed.

Works Cited

Aronowitz, Stanley. "Working Class Culture in the Electronic Age." *Cultural Politics in Contemporary America*. Ed. Ian Angus and Sut Jhally. New York: Routledge, 1989. 135–50.

Bourdieu, Pierre. *Distinction: A Social Critique of the Judgement of Taste*. Trans. Richard Nice. Cambridge: Harvard UP, 1984.

Brecht, Bertolt. "The Curtains." Trans. John Willett. *Bertolt Brecht Poems*. Ed. Willett, John and Ralph Manheim. London: Eyre Methuen, 1976: 425.

Piscator, Irwin. *The Political Theatre*. Trans. Hugh Rorrison. New York: Avon, 1978.

Robertson, T.W. Caste. *Nineteenth-Century British Drama*. Ed. Leonard R.N. Ashley. Lanham: UP of America, 1989. 256–314.

Williams, Raymond. *Keywords*. London: Fontana, 1983.

Caravan Farm Theatre: Orchestrated Anarchy and the Creative Process

by Richard Bruce Kirkley

Caravan Farm Theatre, located in the Salmon River Valley northwest of Armstrong, BC, has been delighting audiences with original and unconventional outdoor theatre for thirty years. Since its beginnings in the late sixties as a horse-drawn caravan, the company has long been dedicated to the development of a countercultural theatre and lifestyle in opposition to the technological and consumerist preoccupations of the North American mainstream. With its roots in sixties radicalism, in street theatre and guerrilla theatre and in experiments with collective creation and communal living, Caravan's approach to theatre is fundamentally informed by an ideology of anarchism. Through recent interviews with theatre artists closely associated with Caravan, including actor/playwright Peter Anderson, former artistic director Nick Hutchinson, current co-artistic director Estelle Shook and former publicist Ken Smedley, I inquired into the nature of a creative process underscored by the need to reconcile the tension between individuality and collectivity—a tension central to the practical pursuit of anarchism. The interviews reveal how the anarchistic ideals deeply embedded in Caravan's way of working give rise to an unorthodox, yet effective, creative process that generates performances of great spontaneity and immediacy.

The conception of anarchism that informs Caravan is grounded in a political philosophy that extends back at least to the nineteenth century (Lehning 70–76), which holds that individuals should be free to determine their own courses of action and which therefore rejects all forms of coercive authority exercised by one person or group over others. Anarchism favours a system based on voluntary cooperation and free association of individuals and groups, in which governmental authority is seen as both unnecessary and counterproductive. Yet anarchism also holds that any conflicts that arise between the needs of the individual and society will best be resolved by the parties directly involved, since it is in the interest of all individuals to work collectively to ensure their mutual well-being. Ideally, in a true condition of anarchism, individuals will tend to group together in localized communities, or collectives, cooperating with one another to resolve conflicts and determine common directions through consensual agreement. Hence, one of the forms of social organization with which the anarchist movement has long experimented is communal living, a collective organization dedicated to an egalitarian distribution of property, labour and decision-making. Finally, it is worthwhile to recall that there is a cultural dimension to anarchism, which sees artists as creative individuals who need the freedom to work beyond established rules, forms or conventions in order to release their creative energies and realize their full artistic potential.

This view of the artist informs much of Caravan's approach to theatre. Nick Hutchinson commented that "the idea of anarchism makes people very uncomfortable because it puts them in a situation where there are no safeties. But that's your place as an artist. That's what you do as an artist. If you don't put yourself in that place, you're not going to produce your art." While Nick cautioned that Caravan has never had any explicit intention or objective to establish a theatre company based on anarchism, he added, slyly, that "we were just too good anarchists to do that." Certainly, anarchistic ideals are embodied in the communal organization of the Caravan farm and theatre company, in the consensual decision-making that informs the choice of shows and the design process and in the approach to rehearsals, where the company seeks to liberate their creative energies in pursuit of a deeper interconnectedness, directness and spontaneity in performance.

The communal organization of Caravan has always consisted of two overlapping groups: the farm group—those who look after the farm throughout the year—and the theatre group—those who come to produce the summer or Christmas shows. These two groups are by no means exclusive; considerable crossover has always taken place. For the summer show, the theatre group begins to arrive in late spring or early summer, usually around thirty to forty people, but sometimes swelling to as many as eighty by the time the show is under way. Most of the actors, designers and technicians, together with their families, take up residence on the farm, living in tents or temporary structures. Meals are served in a communal cook-shack, prepared by one or two cooks hired each summer. Washing facilities consist of a single bathhouse—with one bath and one sink. While improvements have been made in recent years—notably a new well and the addition of a few small cabins—living conditions are generally primitive, prompting former Caravan publicist Ken Smedley to characterize the farm as "the Third World of the Canadian cultural community."

Yet many Caravaners willingly overlook the deprivations, since living closer to nature and working in a collective setting generate some significant benefits. One such benefit is the strong sense of community that promotes ease of communication, facilitates cooperation and allows for a greater recognition of everyone's contribution. According to Peter Anderson, "collective living makes the whole process of sharing and exchanging ideas so much easier and more immediate. You don't need to set up a meeting in your busy schedule, by which time your original idea has lost its immediacy." Current co-artistic director Estelle Shook, who grew up on Caravan Farm and witnessed the summer gatherings first-hand for many years, told me that one of the great benefits of living and working collectively is that everyone participates in doing whatever needs to be accomplished:

> The boundaries always change according to the needs of what's happening. People don't get fixed in specific roles.... It's important for everyone to see what everybody else is doing.... That's what unites the company, and makes it easy to live together.

The communal lifestyle forges strong bonds, not only in work, but also in play. One of the great pleasures of life on Caravan Farm is the spontaneous fun that is inevitably unleashed when so many creative people come together in a mutually supportive, natural setting. "You get so many fun things going on," Estelle declared. "This place is an amazing little haven. It weds so many important parts of existence together: the country, the animals, the open space, the music, theatre." The lifestyle encourages a powerful sense of creative reciprocity in which people give each other permission—as Estelle put it—"to become the thing they've always wanted to be." Yet concurrently, the demands of the farm, the production and day-to-day living also teach people to recognize—Estelle again—that "they have a responsibility to something greater than their own little ego, which makes for a better, stronger person"—and a healthier artistic community.

While the communal lifestyle does have drawbacks, overall it generates an environment that allows people to explore their creative potential and push beyond the boundaries or blocks that can develop from the stresses of working within the tighter constraints and specializations of mainstream theatrical practice. This process generally consists of five overlapping stages: play selection, play composition, design, rehearsal, performance. While on the surface this sequence is not dissimilar to traditional production methods, it is in the actual strategies and techniques employed that we see significant divergence.

At Caravan, selecting the play to be produced for the upcoming season usually begins sometime towards the end of the run of the summer show, when the company gathers for a "vision meeting." Peter Anderson describes this session as a time when "everyone throws out their dreams about what they want to do, so that ideas are always generated out of the interests of the collective." The "vision meeting" initiates an open-ended process of brainstorming and discussion that can, in fact, continue for a period of several months, with letters, newsletters and phone calls going back and forth between company members long after they have left the farm and moved on to other work across the country. In the end, the final decision rests with the artistic director; but the choice has always been fully informed by the interests, desires and contributions of the entire company. The result, according to Estelle Shook, is a strong commitment to the project from everyone involved.

Once the project has been determined, the composition of the playscript and the musical score gets underway. While Caravan has produced established classics, most shows have been either an original play or an original adaptation. As the writing takes place, the work is usually informed by the input of the larger collective. The plays often emerge out of political issues of concern to the company and the communities for which they perform. The plays of Peter Anderson's "Farm Trilogy," for example—*Law of the Land*, *The Coyotes* and *Horseplay*—all deal with issues of the natural or agricultural worlds under siege by the forces of industrialization and resource exploitation. Other shows reflect the company's interest in the spiritual importance of humanity's relationship with the natural and animal kingdoms. The Catherine Hahn-inspired collective creation *The Last Wild Horse*, for example, was a large-scale pageant dedicated to the mythology of the horse, both as a powerful symbol and as a central force in building and uniting the communities of the BC interior. Concurrent with the scripting process, meetings with composers—such as Alan Cole, Derek Hawksley or John Millard—take place as the musical ideas for the show develop.

This preparation extends to the design process as well, and it is here that Caravan starts to depart most significantly from conventional theatrical practice, as the company seeks to break down the rigid compartmentalization of theatrical roles and theatrical hierarchy. "In the conventional theatre," Peter Anderson points out, "there's a rigid protocol. Actors are considered rude and out of order if they question or comment on the designer's work." In the Caravan way of working, the actors are included in the design process from the very beginning. Costume, set, mask and prop designers sit down with the actors and discuss the script in detail, soliciting the actors' input on such issues as characterization and costuming or physical movement and setting. This two-way communication continues throughout the rehearsal period, often over meals in the cook-shack or extending directly from the design team's observations of the actors' work in rehearsals.

While conflicts and disputes inevitably arise, their resolution demands the respect and understanding that emerges between actors, designers and technicians as they witness each other's hard work and dedication. The designers associated with Caravan—Catherine Hahn, Molly March and Melody Anderson, to name a few—are deeply committed to this collaborative way of working, as well as to an open-ended process that can sometimes see their creative choices radically altered as rehearsals progress. There is often a strong resistance or caution at Caravan around the urge to set things too quickly or too early—to seek a solution in design when often the most effective, most essential solution can be found in the acting. "If you can find the way," Nick Hutchinson believes, "the less you design, the less you build, the more essential the solution you find." While on one level the design process at Caravan entails a risky, even nerve-racking approach to theatrical production, by removing the creative divide that often separates actors and designers, the company has developed an important, viable alternative to conventional theatre production.

One of the central aims in the development of the Caravan rehearsal process, in Nick Hutchinson's words, has been "to get away from the traditional read-block-detail-run procedure" followed by most theatre productions. While the company may sit down together and read through the play on the first day of work, what happens next is a two- to three-week period of creative exploration. During this initial period, the actors and director—and often the designers and technical crew as well—participate in a series of acting, movement and vocal exercises. While often based on key ideas or images in the play, the exercises are not undertaken with specific objectives in mind in terms of developing material for the play itself, although valuable ideas or insights often occur during the exploration that later may be recalled and worked into the fabric of the performance.

On the surface this exploratory work may seem relatively vague and unproductive, but in fact it serves several important purposes. First, it builds a strong group dynamic, not just between the actors, but—as I have indicated—within the whole company. Second, the exercises and activities liberate the creative energies of the company, enabling and empowering people to bring their creative ideas out into the open. Third, exploratory work allows everyone the time and space to discover each other's interests and instincts as artists. Fourth, it provides an opportunity to work through the material of the play on a deeper level, exploring the images, themes, forces or dynamics that the play embodies. Finally, as Peter Anderson puts it, "it's just fun; it's about having fun as an actor, and as a company."

Over the years, Caravan has experimented even more boldly with this open-ended process. As Peter Anderson explains,

> a direction that Nick and I began moving towards, and that really excited me, was not casting until maybe halfway through the rehearsal process.... I found it very effective in getting all of the actors to think of the play as a whole, and discussing the ideas of the play, and seeing the play from how a director approaches it, rather than with the tunnel vision you apply to your own character—which happens as soon as you're cast.

Essentially, this approach flows from the anarchistic notion of the creative artist as an autonomous, self-determining entity whose creative energies are, in some sense, blocked by restrictive rules and conventions. The exploratory rehearsals and the technique of delaying casting for as long as possible are both strategies for pushing actors away from the comfort of established practice towards a place where they must take creative risks, create out of their own energies and—interestingly—forge mutual and consensual agreement with the whole company to determine both the meaning and the concrete expression of the performance text.

The first phase of Caravan's rehearsal process generates a rich, powerful fermenting of creative juices which proves highly beneficial as the process shifts to the work of patterning and structuring the performance itself. When casting happens, the decisions are informed by an extensive understanding of each actor's strengths, interests and instincts. The task of staging the scenes moves forward relatively rapidly because the actors are now thoroughly familiar, on a deep level, both with the dramatic material and with each other's ways of working. Yet the staging process is not so much about fixing the form and structure of the performance as about finding the creative energies—the *germs*—which animate the actors' ability to engage form and structure in performance. As a director, Nick told me,

> you're always faced with the central contradiction of theatre: you are looking to repeat the unrepeatable. You are looking for the completely "without anticipation." (How many times, as a director, do you find yourself saying to an actor, "you're anticipating"?) What you're looking for is the "flow through." You're looking for the vessel that conducts the water. You're looking to give it form, but as soon as you give the river, or the swirl, form... you have to get out of the way. You have to let the energy itself express the form....

The result of Caravan's creative process, more often than not, is an exuberant, playful, spontaneous energy that suffuses the whole performance. "While you may lose something in terms of a polished performance," Peter Anderson told me, "this is vastly outweighed by the group dynamic." By directly embracing that central contradiction of theatre—"repeating the unrepeatable"—Caravan's creative process empowers the actors' capacities to rediscover and work the energy of the moment in every performance. Responding to a term coined by Ken Smedley, Peter Anderson agreed that

> Ken's term "orchestrated anarchy" describes [the process] very well. It's not pure anarchy; it's very directed and conscious…. When anything becomes set, or becomes enshrined as a structure, then it's time to break that…. As an actor, when you do something that maybe works one night, and gets a laugh, then how do you make that alive the next night? If you copy it—well, it might work—but you're killing something—that thing being the moment. So breaking out of that is anarchic.

At the heart of Caravan's way of working is the search for an approach that frees the acting, the staging, the design, the performance itself, from an overly rigid—and deadly—adherence to technical detail, to imposed form, and allows for a more spontaneous re-creation of form out of the immediate energy of the performance.

There are downsides to the Caravan way of working. The communal lifestyle and primitive living conditions have certainly been known to wear people down. To survive, one needs to have a highly developed and secure sense of identity. One needs to be able to define one's boundaries, and protect one's privacy, while still maintaining a high degree of openness, tolerance and respect for others. The working process is certainly not for all theatre artists. Actors can find themselves in vulnerable places, where they need tremendous support, and sometimes that need can go unnoticed within the larger momentum and excitement of the group. Yet those who find themselves unhinged by the experience tend to be the exceptions. Many artists associated with Caravan return year after year, in large part because Caravan provides an opportunity to work with a process of creative exploration that they are rarely, if ever, able to experience in the mainstream theatres.

Yet the efficacy of the process moves beyond the collective to encompass the audience and even the natural world itself. Producing theatre outdoors requires the risk-taking and unconventionality that spring from Caravan's anarchistic process. For the actor, according to Peter,

> working in the natural landscape puts your own work on a scale where you see yourself within a larger perspective. It's a very liberating effect, realizing you are part of something larger. But most importantly, it's the connection you make with the audience. Because you're outdoors, you're challenged that much more to hold the audience's attention.

The outdoor arena demands the kind of creative spontaneity and liberation the company seeks, since the performance must generate the energy needed to connect with the audience and engage their senses and imaginations. Thus, the entire Caravan process contributes directly to working with performance conditions which, like those of *commedia dell'arte*, demand a sharpness and spontaneity, an ability to "work in the moment."

Yet at Caravan Farm, such moments reach beyond even the immediate circle of the audience to embrace the natural world as well. There is a special magic that can happen in outdoor performance when a spontaneous synchronization of the imaginative and natural world occurs. As Ken Smedley described it, Caravan performances give people

> the experience of going into the natural world, and communing with it in an imaginative, creative fashion, [in a way] that is intensified when you go into that forum and have a creative experience. Every aspect of your essence and your being is heightened to a level that can be transcendent. In the overall synchronicity between what's being created by the performance and, at the same time, what's being created in the natural world, you come to these moments that are absolutely otherworldly, that are transporting, that are fully dimensional moments that you can't experience in any other place, in any other forum.

Witnessing a Caravan performance, audiences can experience moments of unrepeatable beauty and power, when the energies of the actors, the audience and the natural world seem to achieve the kind of harmony that deeply touches the human spirit. Yet for this to happen, the actors must have developed the capacity to engage such moments—for they don't come about purely coincidentally. The magic happens because the actors, and the company as a whole, have created a way of working that responds spontaneously to the immediacy of each performance moment.

(2000)

Works Cited

Anderson, Peter. Personal interview. 28 April 1999.

Hutchinson, Nick. Personal interview. 30 April 1999.

Lehning, Arthur. "Anarchism." *Dictionary of the History of Ideas: Studies of Selected Pivotal Ideas*. Vol 1. Ed. Philip P. Wiener. 4 vols. New York: Scribner's, 1973. 70–76.

Shook, Estelle. Personal interview. 30 April 1999.

Smedley, Ken. Personal interview. 22 April 1999.

Theatre Inside-Out:
An Educational Monograph:
Alternative Theatre in Prisons

by Richard Payne (edited by Steven Bush)

"A theatre without opinion is not a theatre."
(George Luscombe qtd. in Friedlander 52)

April, 1981. From inside a Canadian federal prison, inmates stage political participatory theatre (for an "outside" public audience) earning national as well as regional recognition. This is the story of taking Alternative Theatre inside and giving it to the prisoners. And learning from what they do with it.

Theatre of Survival: An Enemy of the People

The day comes when I walk into Matsqui Institution, a high–medium-security federal prison in Abbotsford along the Fraser valley more than an hour east of Vancouver. Institutional Theatre Production Society, established some years before with Leon Pownall and the Langara College Theatre Department, has evolved into an in-house apprenticing program that teaches the inmates basic theatre skills. They are permitted to give public performances to visiting audiences one month of weekends a year. I.T.P. Society has once again earned supportive reviews in the local press, this time for Ibsen's *An Enemy of the People*. And I see exactly what I have been looking for: that irresistible energy when actors take the space with deep-in-the-bone authentic purpose; raw, vibrant, truthful, and necessary. I make contact in the after-show gathering with inmate company director Ron Sauvé, who has steered the show with his steely integrity as the persecuted Dr. Stockmann. And so it is, within a few more months, I get a call from Ron; they are looking for a director for their next show. Interested? Of course I am.

Coming Inside

The deal is this: University of Victoria pays my salary, but the inmates audition me first. All I can think is: just be straight with them. I know theatre, they know prison, so I suggest a fair trade: they keep me out of trouble, and I use only skills which can become theirs, to use in future shows. A good faith bargain is struck. The choice of play has not yet been made. I propose the obvious: an ensemble satirical farce, based on a clearly absurdist view of society, but one that is played full-out, in the round, with audience interaction; to cut to the chase: a new production of my political clown play, *Alfred Jarry's Circus Ludicrous Presents "Boss Ubu."*

Theatre of Absurdity: Adapting Alfred Jarry's Ubu Roi

I first adapted *Ubu Roi* on a more traditional campus, Carleton University, in collaboration with the raucous playwright and satirist Brian Shein, who declared that, if I wanted a Clown Circus, Jarry must be his own Ringmaster. The prime Père Ubu (Bozoesque MegaMacbeth) of the day was Idi Amin Dada, and allusions were obvious and easy to render. The more we clowned it, the more savage several moments became; and yet the show remained bright and hysterically funny. This "living political cartoon" powered an ensemble of nearly 30 young adults who had no training.

Now, as I come to imagine the reworked script moving even further from gross bombast to savage satire, the Prison Theatre seems a most perfect forum. We don't need a mere Amin or Khomeini (or Reagan or Mulroney) holding the headlines hostage—we also have the near insanity of the Canadian penal system, right in our collective face. The prisoners love the anarchistic ancestry that *Ubu* celebrates, the fact that Jarry's original lampoon in just two evenings of performance in Paris in 1896 ushered in the Avant-Garde and Modern Theatre. *Ubu* was an unexpected assault on Western and Classical sacred cows: history, heroism, and self-styled civilization. It was indeed radical back then; it could be again, if delivered with a grin. The politics of this venture appeals to them immensely, no problem; it is the risk of undertaking "clown" performance that has them concerned.

Getting Started

Actors are always vulnerable at some level, students even more so. Add to that the prison environment, where every move you make is critical to your survival; at all times, you are scrutinized, judged, and assigned meaning within a closed (and sometimes dangerous) community. This is not mere childhood fear-and-loathing over tacky birthday party entertainers or a shabby circus: more than the outside houses, their fear is humiliation in front of the preview crowd, made up of the other 90% of the prisoners at Matsqui, who are outside both the academic program and the inmate theatre.

One early session, I have the actors on the floor, barking merrily like seals or some such. The coffee urn in the corner also serves other inmates who work next door in the crafts workshop. A guy swaggers in to score a cup, stops, and takes in the scene. Ron, my ever-watchful Assistant Director, simply says: "Hey, it's cool." The guy shrugs okay, gets the coffee, leaves. One rehearsal, I rush in, unload my pockets onto the side of the stage—keys, tissue, notepad, wallet—and jump into the session. Ron walks up to me, hands me back my stuff, says: "Hey man, this is a prison. It's full of thieves."

Early sessions go well. We are having fun and we are starting to work like a team. I don't know what relationships, histories, or tensions exist among any of the participants, over in the rest of their day, but they seem to be able to leave their baggage at the door when they come in here to work, to play. This may be a lifeline for some, the only "good time" available, something they can have some control over. And they have worked hard to make me comfortable.

The guards are another matter altogether. Some let me know right off that I am not welcome, "giving the animals a free education they don't deserve." When I check in at the main guardhouse, I am greeted with: "Oh, coming in to rehabilitate the prisoners today?" No one believes in rehabilitation, maybe not even me. I remind myself they have a lousy job.

As the clowning work progresses, I bring in, once a week, Dennis's ten-year-old daughter, Kelly, who is fiercely loyal to her dad. She looks the guard square in the eye—no way anyone is going to put her off; I wish I were as confident as she manages to be. It is splendid having a child in the room; everyone loves her visits. Dennis and Kelly are assigned clown turns together in the play. Later, when Dennis gets a 72-hour UTA (Unescorted Temporary Absence), he and Kelly go clowning together in a local park.

We start to tackle the script. Only on its feet, with several goes, does anything start to come together. But when it does, there is sheer zippola in the room. They are getting off on the crazy humour. I beg, borrow, or rent (not steal) an arsenal of props and production supports from outside, to allow our circus the level of mock-spectacle called for.

I have to sit with the Assistant Warden and go through everything; the bear costume, okay; the squirt gun, no, size and shape too close to real. Apparently, two inmates have tried to exit in drama club costumes and makeup during one visitor's evening last year; I make a mental note: makeup workshop, not a good idea. But clown wigs, oversize shoes, no problem.

Little do I know that some evenings, as they line up for count in the ranges, before retiring, some of our troupe snap on their clown noses. They make as if not wearing them, as they call out their I.D. number, and strangely, the guards pretend likewise. (What is it about that red nose…?)

Going the Distance

Task: Research of commedia dell'arte ensemble situation-building and stock clown-character types.

Strategy: Watch their descendants on evening television. Dennis, who plays the naive and soon-to-be deposed President Fred of Ubetcha, finds his doppelganger in the Governor on *Benson*. Gary, as Ma Ubu, goes for Miss Piggy on *The Muppet Show*.

Now we have something of a dependable common language, as we build characters and turns.

Task: memorizing, getting off book, line runs.

Strategy: none required. They have plenty of time and opportunity, stuck in here, when I am outside. (Would that we could this do to all actors.)

Task: attending rehearsals, continuity.

Strategy: depends on the circumstances. Gary, playing a central lead role, is suddenly in solitary (for only a week, thank the theatre gods!). Something went down in the rest of his day, though not at his instigation; he did what he had to. We rehearse around him as best we can. End of that day, heading for the main gate out. Wayne Knights (the UVic co-ordinator) and I are walking along a paved pathway, across from the Solitary wing—a two-storey brick affair with arrowslit-sized windows.

(A voice rings out: "Hey Richard!!" We stop)

Richard: *(calls back, in a shout)* Gary?!

Gary: Yeah!! Second Floor, one from the end!!

Richard: *(stares now at a specific black slit in the stone edifice)* How ya doing?!

Gary: What did we do in rehearsal today?!

Richard: Started Act Two. Ron will get some notes to you!!

Gary: Okay!!

Richard: *(turns to Wayne)* The funny thing is, this all feels quite normal to me, now. Another typical Matsqui workday.

Wayne: Oh yeah.

Sexual Politics

Task: casting two dozen men in a mixed-gender story.

The company has been asked to bring in descriptions or sketches of the clowns they are hoping to create. Now they are choosing costume pieces from racks of borrowed theatre inventory. Al (muscular, now halfway crossing the identity line) has brought in a joker from a deck of cards, a pretty safe choice. I point to an option on the rack. What about this French maid's outfit? Al gives a short gasp, widens eyes, double-takes, checks out how serious I am. Within ten minutes he is a splendid creature with fluff hat and feather duster and gorgeous red shoes. After holding back for weeks, Al now comes totally alive, having fun and taking chances.

Charlie, on the other hand, is a fully female presence; she is not sure how she is going to fit in, but is serious and potentially courageous as an actor. I give her the role of Mavis, the First Lady, a Sarah Bernhardt spoof in austere whiteface. Very tragic, and ever so self-consciously elegant. She is completely female in some crazily very right way. She inspires the cast, and will catch the praise of the critics. And so it is we integrate the transsexual prisoners into the company. The sexual-sector tensions amongst this year's drama troupe members (of which, remember, I am blissfully unaware) evaporate.

Rediscovering the Family

Now I am surrounded by a crazy mix of people—nearly two dozen zanies of every stripe—who have to function as a tight ensemble. I tell them about seeing *Short Eyes* in New York, and about the fully professional ex-inmate company who called themselves "The Family."

And then the question comes: what kind of family are we?

Onstage, in George Luscombe's self-defining play, *Hey Rube!*, the theatre-worker's life is portrayed in the guise of a small circus troupe on the road, having to survive. With *Short Eyes*, The Family are empowered to present, essentially themselves, an alternate family unit with collective skeletons in the closet. Now, at Matsqui, I need a family structure that feeds these guys 24 hours a day, as actors on the boards and as prisoners behind bars. And so we take on a play within the play that the audience will never know. I declare ourselves to be a commedia dell'arte troupe of the Middle Ages. A pack of families that work and live together, train on the job, and watch their collective backs.

If this is who we are as a troupe, who must we then be as individuals? Using the roles they are already assigned onstage, we extrapolate backwards, to understand where we each fit into the travelling circus family. I make a proposal: "The troupe's founder, a famous clown, has two sons, who now run the company as senior partners. Don here, who plays the old fuddy-duddy character, is the elder son. But now he's long in the tooth, and doesn't have the stamina anymore for the big lead roles. Besides, he tends to wander off or forget his lines."

Everyone laughs, because Don, who is quite a bit older than the rest, and has been around for what seems like forever, has indeed been messing up a load of nearly-identical cue lines. He grins, nods in agreement.

"So, Ron, the younger brother, is the main performer now, the one we build our shows around. As head actor, he also trains the apprentices." Ron not only plays Ubu, but assistant directs, produces, and propels the whole venture.

And so on. Everyone gets a personal history and a place on the theatre collective's family tree, one that equally suits their roles as actors and as personalities. There are no longer any troupe members who are outside our inner sanctum; vets and newcomers, straight and other, all enjoy the right to belong. This new level of mutual support empowers us in the crunch period.

The final three weeks are a blur. Somewhere in there I realize I have really put my foot in it, because I am now directing from the stage, in costume. Someone had got his parole earlier than expected. After looking over the company abilities and role distribution, Ron and I agreed that I would take over the part—that of Alfred Jarry, the insane ringmaster of the whole hallucinatory circus. As I said, we each of us got a "family role" that fit.

Hi-Jinks Behind the Scenes

The final weekend before the play opens. I drive out the nearly two hours, to run the last Full Dress Rehearsal. Everyone in the company is geared up to the max. Yet after three months of work, I walk into the reception blockhouse, only to be told: "Gee, we can't find your pass. Guess we can't let you in today." They do allow me to send a written message back to Ron, to run the session in my absence. And I turn and drive home.

Circus Day! Sideshow

The project enjoys unusual variations on last-minute snafus common to all theatre ventures. Missing prop, a really nice suede vest—(mine!)—someone has got in and pinched it. Dennis: "Don't worry about looking for it, it will be converted into bed-slippers by the end of the day."

Then the Musician is missing, or rather, detained. Boyd, who plays Boss Ubu's one-man clown band (for sound effects) from the side of the stage—"The Boss Pops"—is off to a court hearing; no way of knowing when he'll be returned. We drape a sign over his drum set—"BOSS POPS Gone to Court"—which at least gets us another chuckle. Boyd crawls in by the end of Act One—to a round of applause from the house, and the cast. The show really does go on.

I too undergo an adaptation, in a most memorable performance accident. As Jarry, I open the play by bursting out of the Grand Entrance, atop a bicycle, in the follow-spot; with a triumphant "Ha-ha!" I hurtle directly downstage across the raised circus ring. On this night, my rear wheel misses the ramp, and I careen sideways onto the cement floor in a tangled heap, all in front of the audience, variously delighted and horrified. At least, I took none of the house out with me.

In the deafening silence that haunts all theatre-workers, all I can think is, ONE, there is a glass liquor flask in my belt, for a later bit of scene business, mere inches above my groin; is it (am I) still intact? And TWO, Keep Going! I apparently do, monologue uninterrupted, clambering back up onto the stage with one leg rammed right through the spokes of the crippled front wheel. The inmates, both in the lighting booth and backstage, are simply killing themselves laughing at my onstage predicament. But from this night on, because I manage to keep going, I am given a subtle new level of respect. My nickname is now "Wipe-out."

Circus Day! The Main Tent

Night after glorious night, we have real theatre, and, crazily enough, real circus.[1] The audience laughs easily and often, encouraging the cast forward. The clowns are open, and so the show grows and grows. What the prisoners say they value most is the chance, not only to make the public laugh, but to go out and mix with them. As a Janitor Clown comes down a row, and stops to dust off someone's head, or pick a piece of mime-lint off a three-piece suit, barriers dissolve. We are pleased to see we have more seniors and children in attendance than ever before. Any scenes that might discomfit the guards certainly delight the audience. In one typical clown turn, the palace guards try to tie up a prisoner with a long yellow rope. They become a desperate jumbled clump; the victim crawls out between their legs, to lope for freedom. The clump, now tied only to itself, grumbles and, in unison, hops and drags itself offstage.

The View from the Stands

The recognition of the troupe's achievement is concretized by both audience interaction, which is bubbling, and by the universally enthusiastic reviews out in the public media. In *The Vancouver Sun*, Wayne Edmonstone gives up half the Entertainment Section front page. "The irony—in fact, the honest comic absurdity—of staging an Anarchistic play inside a prison can by no means be lost on its captive cast and they quite simply play the living hell out of it, to their own delight and inevitably, in the face of such raw energy and enthusiasm, to that of their audience as well" (Edmonstone).

But the coup of "scooping" the Vancouver theatre scene that month is overtaken when we get a glowing review from John Lazarus on CBC-Radio's "Arts National": "With Ron Sauvé as Ubu, voraciously greedy for power and then abusing it with fierce joy, we are constantly forgetting, and then being reminded, of where we are…. *Boss Ubu* is a gleefully defiant bellow from within the prison walls" (Lazarus).

The View from the Ring

After the intermission, the play resumes with general troupe clowning all over the house. Up in the ring, John and Mike, who have taught themselves to juggle for this play (driving everyone around them nuts up on the range), proceed to juggle tennis balls to one another right across the ring, over or near my head as I preside over the various turns and direct traffic. Every night they do different things, draw me into their world of activity, challenge me, even taunt me. They are doing perfect ring clown work without being shown. That unit of improv, for me, is my chance to just play. For a few moments, I really do belong.

The other, and far more extraordinary experience, comes after the show goes down, when we mix with the public for about twenty minutes before the clear-out. I will never forget the hesitant enthusiasm with which audience members, many of them college age, approach to enter into discussion—some undecipherable blend of fear, fascination, admiration, puzzlement, what? In these moments of awkward caution, I remember one actor's spin on prison theatre: "We're not animals, goddammit. And once we make real contact with them (the audience), they know it, but they don't know how to put that together with the place we have to live, or how we got here." For a brief moment, I have experienced what the guys face, here and later back on the outside, for much of their lives. A final border that cannot be crossed.

The hardest thing, in all this work, is to recognize that I too, to the troupe members, will always be, can only be, an outsider, no matter how well we connect or work together. I will never truly know, or be part of, their real world. The theatre we share, as co-workers, is a fine moment, but it is only a controlled hallucination. And I am being pulled back outside the fence.

This is their theatre, and it is time for me to go. And it is time for two of them to leave, as well; without telling us, they had arranged to delay their release date, so they could finish the run of the play.

(2000)

Acknowledgement

Steven Bush wishes to thank Debbie Green (Head of Reference & Research Services) and Don Sklepowich (Media Specialist/Audio Alchemist, Media Commons) at Robarts Library, University of Toronto, for their generous assistance in tracking down hard-to-find citation details.

Appendix: Letter from Patrick Keating [2]

Hello

My Name is Patrick Keating. I'm sure that means nothing to anyone reading this. Anyways… I met Richard in 1980. He introduced me to theatre. He was teaching a theatre course at an off-site campus of the University of Victoria. I thought I was taking a course that would help me with writing. He brought in an adaptation of *Ubu*

Roi... Alfred Jarry's *Circus Ludicrous presents Boss Ubu* that he wanted to produce. I had no idea what was in store. One day Richard came into the classroom decked in full clown regalia and started doing his clown turns and I remember thinking there is no way this clown is going make me crack a smile. Trust was, and I imagine still is, a scarce commodity in a Federal Penitentiary. But he persisted and eventually got that smile and a couple more. How could you not be taken with a man who was willing to come into a high security penitentiary and try to teach murderers, drug traffickers and bank robbers the Laban theory of flick and dab in preparation for a clown show. He even came through the front gate in full clown and let the Guards search him. They did their job, shook their heads, and said "Might as well come in, the place is full of fucking clowns." The production went up and it was a huge success. I put off my release date just so that I could stay and finish the course and the show.

He also arranged to bring in a production of *Happy Days* that a local company Tamahnous Theatre were doing in Vancouver. That was the first live play I saw. I called that company when I was released and my education in theatre continued. As in most things to do with life it isn't always exactly a straight line. But thirty years later I'm still working in theatre. I think Richard would be proud of that... I know I am. Every day I'm glad of the opportunities and the possibilities. And every day I'm glad that someone like Richard Payne took the time to share his gifts with a bunch of men locked behind walls and razor wire. Richard knew and taught me that theatre can make a difference.

Richard, I know you'll be fine because wherever you are I'm sure "...the place is full of fucking clowns."

(2010)

Notes

1 *The Vancouver Sun* Entertainment Calendar for Wednesday, April 1, 1981 announced that *Boss Ubu* opened Thursday, April 2 and played "Thursday, Saturday and Sunday throughout April at Matsqui Medium Security Institution, Abbotsford" (Entertainment). The notice advised that "to facilitate gate clearance early booking is advised"—ed.

2 This letter was written expressly for the public tribute to Richard Payne on July 5th, 2010.

Works Cited

Edmonstone, Wayne. "…Relief from inmates." *The Vancouver Sun*, 6 April 1981. D1.

Entertainment Calendar. *The Vancouver Sun*, 1 April 1981. D3.

Friedlander, Mira. "Survivor: George Luscombe at Toronto Workshop Productions." *Canadian Theatre Review* 38 (1983): 44–52.

Lazarus, John. "Arts National." CBC-Radio. 16 April 1981.

Whose Community? Whose Art? The Politics of Reformulating Community Art

by Honor Ford-Smith

Memory-boxes: a letter, a rose, a photograph juxtaposed and framed by a wooden box provoke a meditation on the uprooted and transnational lives of Spanish-speaking women. A large mural called *Greetings to Taniperla* frames a handball court in Scarborough, Ontario. The mural is both a replica of and a response to the original, created in Ricardo Magon in Chiapas, Mexico, and later destroyed by the Mexican army. Artists, students and Catholic priests from Mexico and Canada contribute images to the piece.... Giant puppets dance like fantasies on the grass in a community play which synthesizes a traditional Chinese story with a commentary on the environment. In Regent Park, Toronto, a group of black youth talks about what creating a play might mean for the image of their community.... In advertising space on a Buffalo city bus, photo montages by Canadian artists Carol Conde and Karl Beveridge's "Theatre of Operations" juxtapose human health needs with the alienation and performative aspects of commodified medical care (Conde and Beveridge, "Theatre"). Drawing on theatre methods developed by Augusto Boal, the pair collaborate with union members and later rework images in discussion with workshop participants drawing on an artistic vocabulary influenced by the anti-nazi artist John Hartfied, the theories of German playwright Bertolt Brecht, Soviet and Chinese revolutionary art.... In Montreal, Teesri Duniya Theatre extends the notion of performance beyond the limits of the stage. Collaborating with Montreal Arts Interculturels (MAI), together they mount a professional production of Jason Sherman's *Reading Hebron*, a play about the 1994 massacre of Muslims at prayer in the Hebron. Alongside the play Teesri Duniya held community outreach meetings and exhibited community-produced drawings at the MAI to dramatize community responses to the issue (Little).

All these descriptions demonstrate that the practice of community art encompasses a lively range of peoples, activities, spaces and forms. Community art is becoming a discourse in its own right, gaining increased recognition within the categories of some public and private sector funders and cultural institutions and developing a particular language for its practice. It is bringing together folks from different social spaces in a mixture of symbolic activities and it is generating its own educational programs both within and outside of traditional training in the arts at colleges and universities. These developments have been a long time coming but nevertheless they raise a number of questions. First, there is the question of timing and context. What does community cultural expression mean in the current context of the enormous expansion of global capitalism—an expansion which is commodifying almost everything, transforming both the potential of cultural production, as well as the way we think of communities, nations and the state? Second, since the arts and their cultural values do not exist independently from authorizing social institutions, (though their relationship to those institutions is never transparent), in whose interests does funded community art operate? Third, since the power and possibility of any practice is contingent on the responses it generates, and the way it is taken up, what critical practices will serve the development of community art? Is everyone an artist? If the legacy of high art is the notion of its autonomy from the babble and contamination of the tin pan values of the marketplace, and its critical evaluation in terms of this autonomy, how then do we evaluate art which claims to dissolve the division between artist and community, society and life, to open a space for the claims of the under-represented and the marginal?

In this very short discussion, I want to argue that the incorporation of community art into the categories of public and private funders and other institutions necessarily means that it becomes a space for struggle between a number of competing social, political and cultural interests. While I endorse its support by public and private institutions, its incorporation into these agencies as a cultural category has important consequences for notions of both "community," "artists" and "art". I propose that the process of incorporation and development needs to be led by the artists and the community members who struggle to make the means of all forms of artistic production accessible equitably to all and who are prepared to scrutinize the practices of Canadian cultural institutions. It needs to be led by those who advocate for varied and plural art forms and artistic identities through which the arts can speak to multiple audiences. Without this, community art is in danger of becoming a process which can be used both as a brightly packaged form of welfare and as a means for the manufacture of the myths which justify traditional narratives of Canadianness and the Canadian status quo. I also argue for an increasingly hybrid definition of community and community arts—one which allows for diversity of practice, rigorous critique of practice and which challenges the essentially conservative dichotomy between professional and amateur, between product and process by including more inter-sectoral dialogue between diversely positioned artists and communities. These strategies I hope will allow community art to preserve its function as a meaningful critical social intervention and will work against its domestication.

Throughout the article I use a critical frame that avoids discussions of the autonomy and formal qualities of particular art projects. Instead I examine community art in terms of its social context, the identities of those involved in doing it, the mode of production in which it is positioned, the practices and relations to which these give rise, the narratives and images it circulates and the uses to which the work is put. I write from the perspective of a teacher/artist who teaches in a community arts program and who brings to Canada twenty years of experience in community and professional theatre in the Caribbean and elsewhere. I therefore see community art through my location as a hyphenated teacher-artist and a hyphenated Canadian, that is, a Jamaican-Canadian who like many others, inhabits more than one culture on this planet.

Most of the examples on which my argument is based are inspired by work which took place at the time of the Community Art Biennial in 2000. They are thus woefully Toronto-centric, but I hope that I will be provocative enough to stimulate some talk back from the west, east and north which are under-represented in the discussion. I begin with a summary of the struggles which have led up to reformulation of granting policies in some cultural agencies in the last decade and then move on to an analysis of what is at stake in the legitimizing of "community art."

Cultural Struggle and Cultural Crisis

One reason for the recent reformulation of categories like community arts in arts organizations and funding agencies in liberal democracies like Canada, Australia and Britain, is that artists and other cultural producers have fought for it. Their fight has both challenged narratives of what it means to be Canadian and what counts as having cultural value. Two examples of these protests are those of the Lubicon Cree in 1988 and those of the African Canadian community in Toronto in 1989 and 1993. The Cree, supported by other aboriginal groups across the country, mounted a widely publicized protest organized against the exhibition "The Spirit Sings," mounted by the Glenbow Museum in Calgary. They pointed to the hypocrisy of Shell having funded an exhibition purporting "to show the richness of the early contact culture" at the same time as they were bulldozing gravesites and interfering with hunting and trapping. The protest also critiqued the colonial discourses that controlled the representation of Native peoples in cultural institutions. The protest was broadened to include repatriation, the display of sacred objects, and the representation of Native peoples in museums and galleries (Inuit Art Foundation). Again in Toronto, Arts Organizations supported by communities successfully prevented the closing of the Harbourfront Centre, one of the city's most popular public cultural sites. These and many others events make it clear that cultural production is not seen as cordoned off from social and economic struggles, but rather that many see a link between how they are represented in cultural practices and how they are ruled.

The work of artists, writers and performers from many different social and geographic locations have challenged the boundaries between different categories of art (high/low, professional/amateur, collaborative/individual) and between producers and consumers of culture. Many cultural workers as well as unrecognized ordinary folks have argued that access to the means of cultural expression is a basic human need, one that conditions our ways of understanding the economic, social and political processes around us, and shapes our identities and our human relations. Long before the internet, many anonymous and unnamed folks as well as intellectuals such as Walter Benjamin, Augusto Boal and Rex Nettleford argued that the right to participate in meaning making through the languages of art goes beyond the consumption of the artistic products as privately owned commodities produced in controlled institutionalized spaces. The "artist" is not simply a skilled person whose existence is dedicated to individual freedom of expression but someone who also speaks from within and about a collective or community and who is often deeply involved in creating that community's narratives of struggle, desire and possibility.

Art can be produced out of equitable collaborative relationships and in many ways can be about the terms and results of that collaboration. While artistic products should themselves be accessible, the means and languages of artistic production also need to be democratized in different ways. Scholars like Stuart Hall and Pierre Bourdieu have argued, in different contexts, that "art" is not a fixed category but rather one which is a constantly changing forum for the re-negotiation of cultural values and relationships. As Jameson and Miyoshi put it, "Whoever says the production of culture says the production of everyday life—without that your economic system can scarcely continue to expand and implant itself" (67).

Sharon Fernandez, formerly the Cultural Equity Coordinator at the Canada Council for the Arts, proposes that what we have witnessed is a social movement for cultural equity which emphasizes "*the importance of myriad practices of artists located within different community contexts*" and that this transforms the meaning and potential of art and culture. She contends that artists across the country are working in such myriad and multifaceted ways that the linearity of the concept high art/low art simply cannot apply. In regions where contexts are more grassroots and state or market-driven cultural infrastructure less immediate and ever present, artists have closer ties to the local social issues around them. In other settings artists operate more and more transnationally developing communities which they can nurture across national borders through the internet. Politically, provinces such as Saskatchewan or Newfoundland are very socially conscious and their art practices reflect this. Also artists are racially and culturally diverse and have very different approaches to cultural production. Throughout the 80s artists like Richard Fung, Lillian Allen, Dionne Brand, Afua Cooper, Clifton Joseph, Leonore Keeshing Tobias, Monique Mojica, Marlene NourbeSe Philip, Paul Wong, Sylvia Hamilton, Jin me Yoon, Midi Onedera, Djanet Sears, and Zab Mabongou were among those responsive to community social, cultural and political concerns.

In the seventies and eighties, artists connected to popular social movements formed new cultural institutions which responded to the needs of under-represented groups like women, workers, gays, lesbians and bisexuals and others. Some of the strongest protests which Canada saw in the eighties and nineties were waged by communities of colour and First Nations groups around their exclusion from cultural institutions and around what counts as art. The debates raised at events like the *Writing Through Race Conference* of the Writer's Union of Canada in 1994, made it quite clear that many Canadian citizens and residents did not see themselves represented in national cultural narratives (Tator, Henry, and Mattis 86). Scholars of colour like Sherene Razack asserted that popular narratives of Canadianness expressed in Canadian art and literature depicted the country as empty land peopled by enterprising rugged white male settlers who tamed the wilderness and reaped material and social rewards at the expense of first nations and people of colour. These colonial narratives make class, gender and race differences invisible or position aboriginal bodies and bodies of colour in subordinate, marginal ways while glorifying the values of pioneering self-made men who overcome the icy hardships of the north. Razack argues that it is important to be critical about the ways in which stories of the nation position Canadians in relation to each other since these affect how we think of our own power and identity in the everyday. Her argument forces us to ask: to what extent are residents and citizens prepared to consent to relations of ruling within a nation whose images of itself exclude, or make a hierarchy of, different racial, regional and ethnic histories and experiences and maintain the uneasy hegemony of a select group? For a country which depends on immigration for demographic stability, this has very serious implications for governance.

The transnational movement of peoples across borders results in the movement and mixing of multiple modes of representation from outside and inside the Western tradition. Additionally, the deep regional, class, and ethnic differences within Canada itself also result in a multiplicity of art practices and identifications. All these elements combine to revise ideas about what is valued as art, music, performance and literature. They have led to what Cornel West called in the 1990s, the new cultural politics of difference; that is, a cultural politic which compels cultural critics and artists to re-conceptualize their vocations and "to reveal as an integral component of their production, the very operations of power in their immediate work contexts (academy, museum, gallery, mass media)" (West 120). Power works in complex ways through cultural institutions to produce what can and can't be said and heard, to define categories and authorize genres, and it is important to be fully aware of the multiple levels on which this takes place.

In the 1980s and 1990s, the challenges that authorizing cultural institutions faced in Canada provoked a variety of reforms at both policy and programming levels. The Ontario Arts Council, for example, addressed challenges through establishing particular programs. The category "community art" which had previously referred to art in the regions, was expanded to include work with special interest groups, ethno-racial, linguistic and geographic groups—a shift which meant that the work went beyond funding to arts development in provincial regions. An Aboriginal Arts section was established in 1985 to serve status and non-status First Nations and Métis community organizations and schools. In 1991, the Canada Council established the First Advisory Committee on Racial Equality to look into creating greater cultural equity among diverse communities and to deal with the question of access to council programs. The work of the committee resulted in the establishment of a new policy around racial and cultural equity, greater inclusion of under-represented groups on staff and board and attention to ways of making the council's program more accessible. An equity office was created to monitor and work for the implementation of cultural equity policies.

These reforms came as a result of protest, resistance and struggle (see for example Philip; Nurse; Fung). The outcomes stressed that the practice of art that serves these different communities is highly diverse and that policies need to take account of historic inequities such as systemic racism. The gains in the 1990s are to be celebrated. Having said so it needs to be recognized that access to the means of cultural production is only a first step toward full systemic transformation of cultural institutions. Once greater access is achieved, and assuming that this gain is not turned back, more complex contradictions begin to emerge. For changes to have full effect, questions of distribution and consumption also have to be addressed and assessed. Informed critical engagement with the work produced, as well as changes in the content of education about the arts and culture in schools, colleges and universities, all need to be addressed. The process of production, distribution, reception and critique are all part of a complete ecology of cultural production.

Three elements were stressed in writings about community art by agencies and practitioners: production across and with under-represented social groups—that is increased access to the artistic modes of production, collaboration among communities and artists, and storytelling as the preferred method of representation and performance. Often these stories were testimonials based on personal experience. A publication written in 1998 by Angela Lee for the Ontario Arts Council, then reviewing and changing its approach to community art, asserts that community arts are as much about process as product, that they involve a co-creative collaboration between artist and community, and that they are increasingly seen as an effective way to address social and cultural concerns and as a way to make the arts accessible, supported and appreciated by larger segments of society, to integrate non-western artistic activities and art forms into expanding concepts of what the arts are. Lee's discussion implicitly demonstrates the ways in which the idea of community art owes much to participatory and popular education practices which were formerly associated with social movements in Latin America and in particular with Freirean educational theories and strategies which emerged from literacy campaigns and stressed community education based on the life world around subordinated learners (Freire). This gave rise to the work of Boal in Theatre of the Oppressed, aspects of the work of Patricia Ariza (Colombia), Sistren Theatre Collective (Jamaica), Rosa Luisa Marquez (Puerto Rico) and Theatre Yuyachkani (Peru) among many others (Ford-Smith, Taylor and Constantino).

The concept of community art currently in use connotes something beyond a gathering of people who come together to make art in a particular social or geographic location, with or without formal training in the arts. Implicit in the origins of the term is the idea that art production in community contexts is linked to social movements that give voice to the systemically excluded from access to cultural resources, skills, knowledges and institutions. Julie Salverson, for example, quotes a working definition put together by Ontario artists and cultural workers in July 1992, which describes popular theatre as a "theatre for, with and by specific communities—who have not been given access to resources in our society—our interaction with these communities implies a participatory process that may include—development and collection of stories from individuals affected by an issue—[and] accountability to the participating individuals and their communities" (Salverson 120). This definition points to the fact that the origin of the term community art involved the idea of a social and political intervention in the interests of social justice for the marginalized. Salverson goes on to critique the ways in which this definition sometimes homogenizes communities, thus erasing vast differences between those who make up any given group. She points out that the practice of popular/community theatre can subtly discourage popular theatre artists from reflecting on their own artistic and pedagogical needs and disciplines and their own cultural biases and discourages reflection on the way these (suppressed) needs enter their practice in contexts where there are enormous differences, particularly around difficult or traumatic experiences. This insight suggests that disciplines and institutional systems through which artists or facilitators get scripted into community art practice need careful examining.

Hegemony, Institutional Power and the Idea of Community

The institutionalizing of any discourse as a result of struggles confers a gain in power. But such gains are not absolute. They come full of contradictions. The terrain on which gains and reforms are won is ever-shifting. There are many issues at stake in the institutionalizing of a practice which has roots in struggles for social change. The work of Italian social theorist Antonio Gramsci helps us analyse the meaning of changes in cultural discourse when he proposed long ago that it is at the level of culture that consent for governance is negotiated. Gramsci viewed culture as a force field of relations shaped by conflicted tensions and interests. Cultural hegemony, he argued, is secured not via the obliteration of subordinate cultures, but via their articulation to dominant culture and ideology. Giroux and Simon summarize the concept of hegemony when they write:

> For Gramsci, the exercise of control by the ruling classes is less characterized by the excessive use of officially sanctioned force than it is through what he calls "the struggle for hegemonic leadership"—the struggle to win the consent of subordinate groups to the existing social order.... In Gramsci's view such a pedagogical process must work and rework the cultural and ideological terrain of subordinate groups in order to legitimate the interests and authority of the ruling bloc. (Giroux and Simon 8)

In other words, dominant groups who incorporate the demands of their subordinates have to decide what they will change about themselves or give up in order to keep power and control. Similarly, subordinates have to decide what they will give up in exchange for having some of their demands met. This is the process which is currently taking place in Canadian cultural institutions in the context of the shrinking of the nation state under the expansion of capital. It is the outcome of the process of hegemony which will determine who ultimately benefits from the reforms of arts council policy and programming in the late eighties and early nineties.

There is much to be gained from speaking within an institutionalized discourse, as cultural theorist Gayatri Spivak has pointed out (Spivak). The acquisition of a place from which to speak and be heard and a particular language through which to interpret practices are not things to be scoffed at. But Gramsci helps us see that there is nothing essentially or finally democratic, subversive or even equitable about such an acquisition. We have only to think of the way in which medical discourses on gynaecology, race or mental health have been used, to see that any discourse can be appropriated, misrepresented or used in contradictory ways by diversely positioned groups—even as its regulatory procedures give rise to particular ways of seeing and naming the world, even as lives are simultaneously enhanced or denigrated. Nevertheless, the acquisition of a language for seeing and naming the world confers a gain in power. It is pedagogical and so produces subjects. It makes more visible the space for reflection, action and negotiation. In the case of community art, greater support from cultural institutions allows more people to participate in the work. It affects educational programs and offers opportunities for deepening critical approaches.

In the Canadian context, the crucial question is who will provide the leadership of multiple historically marginalized communities as they work to gain from increased public representations of their realities. This is what at present hangs in the balance and is part of the current terms of the struggle. Politicians and professional managers of national, provincial, and urban cultural infrastructures are certainly conscious of what is at stake in the reworking of national narratives of Canadian citizenship. But it is equally important for artists, cultural producers and consumers to be able to name, independently, the ways in which the process of hegemony is proceeding under the new programs and policies. One way of doing this is to examine the social positioning of those leading the reworking of national narratives and narratives of community, the relationships generated by the process, the context for the work, the modes of production in which the work is located, the spaces and places where it is generated and the ways in which those narratives and images are taken up and used socially.

Cultural Hierarchies, and the Defence of Community Art as Political Intervention

One project which graphically illustrates some of the questions which have to be negotiated by cultural organizations, community artists and others took place in Toronto in the summer of 2000. Minsook Lee, a cultural animator, was employed by the Laidlaw Foundation to develop a project for Take Part!, an initiative in cultural democracy begun by the foundation. Minsook Lee designed a program which built on a previous collaboration between the Toronto Environmental Alliance and CUPE Local 416, which includes sanitation workers. The project brought together four visual artists with union members and environmentalists and facilitated dialogue about the environment. The work developed in the context of a political debate about what Toronto should do with its garbage. As workers, activists, and teacher-artists worked together discussing environmental issues, the project resulted in the painting of collectively designed murals on the side of publicly owned garbage trucks. The planned paintings were submitted to the city for approval and the murals were painted on the garbage trucks. The project was launched at the same time that the controversy over moving the city's garbage to the Adams Mine, an abandoned iron mine in Kirkland Lake, Northern Ontario was growing. One drawing—that of a truck leaving Toronto full of garbage, with men with pig-like faces in suits counting money—was interpreted by the media as a graphic critique of the project proposing the dumping of garbage in Kirkland Lake. The city government became alarmed and one city councilor, Bill Saundercook, then head of a City works committee, interpreted the mural as accusing city politicians of corruption and ordered the critical mural painted over, something project members learned after the fact (Barndt, Lee, and Pacific).

The media reported the incident and the groups involved held a press conference. On a CBC discussion of the matter one art critic pronounced on the work of the artists, declaring the murals inferior art objects. The groups held a press conference censuring the city's action and determined to repaint the mural elsewhere. They were to receive further support from the Laidlaw Foundation for this, but when the repainting of the mural coincided with the municipal election, an election in which Saundercook was running, Laidlaw made further funding conditional on an appropriate "communications strategy" and suggested a post-election repainting. No such public relations strategy materialized and so the foundation did not renew the contract of the officer, Robin Pacific, who researched, initiated and developed its venture into community arts. Her assistant, a student intern, was also suspended. The mural has not yet been re-painted and the group has not taken any more funding from Laidlaw.

Throughout the fall, the mainstream media in the city gave widespread coverage to the question of whether the Adams Mine should serve as site for Toronto's garbage, but little attention was paid to the censoring actions of the politicians or the response of the private funding organization by any arts or civil organizations. So far no group of artists, politicians or citizens has come forward to investigate the matter and comment on the garbage truck fiasco publicly in spite of the fact that the silencing of the work took place in public space. Metro garbage trucks are after all, not owned by the works committee or the councillors who chair it, they are owned by the residents of Toronto.

I am quite sure that if something like this had occurred in Havana or Caracas, it would not be long before we would have heard loud protestations about the censorship of artists in Third World dictatorships from many North American media houses. In due course, we might even have had a major Hollywood film about the heroism of those involved and the terrible effects of repression on the artist's lives. Canada is a liberal democracy which never misses an opportunity to perform what it sees as its superiority to countries like Cuba on the world stage by claiming to support the practice of basic human rights worldwide and by claiming to support freedom of expression. Yet in its own yard the disciplining of cultural workers commenting on political issues in publicly owned space has gone without full public discussion or censure from arts groups, unions or city politicians of any persuasion.

There are many questions to be asked about community arts on the basis of this story. The first question is why has there been so little investigation and discussion of the matter from the perspective of cultural workers? Apart from the obvious question of censorship and political manipulation around the question of the environment, there are questions to be raised about the role of arts managers and funders in such a controversy. Why have arts agencies, and in particular Laidlaw itself, failed to publicly defend the right of the community arts projects which they fund to produce politically critical material? The images generated by the garbage trucks were taken up as a strong political critique. The work of artists as different as Brecht, Boal, Lacy, Neruda, Darwish, Wodiczko, Soyinka and countless others across time and place, demonstrate that political critique has always been one of the longstanding purposes of art. If the right of communities and artists to make political statements is not defended by artists or those who support them, then what we have is a situation in which so-called "community" art becomes a way of massaging and managing social consent by offering welfare to the most marginalized, in a bright new decorative package with all the attendant hype of public relations.

Several community artists I interviewed for this article described previous experiences of censorship, though not always by the state and not always by blatant destruction. Deborah Barndt recounts an incident in which the gallery of the Etobicoke Civic Centre removed a photo of a demonstration from a series of photos she was displaying and refused to put it back. Carol Conde and Karl Beveridge describe violently hostile reactions to their exhibition at the AGO in the seventies because it critiqued the politics of the art world as elitist.

Another question worth asking is: would such blatant acts of silencing be possible where an unpopular critique was undertaken by a prominent popular singer, actor or ballet dancer? That is, would it be possible if the artists in question were positioned in a more heavily capitalized and commodified area of the arts or in one of the high arts? Is community art something that lends itself to manipulation because it is somehow "low" art, less and positioned on the borders of the cultural marketplace?

My answer to this would be yes and no. Silencing and disrespect for cultural workers is not limited to community arts, though community artists probably experience it more often. Censorship can be imposed or it can result from selective oversight wherever cultural work threatens to have social uses that threaten powerful groups. So-called "high" art has often been censored in covert and overt ways. But ironically it has been able to mount a defense through claims of artistic autonomy and by recourse to the liberal freedoms—the right to freedom of expression. The theatre of Athol Fugard in South Africa was able to survive and circulate stories about the everyday abuses of apartheid in the 1970s precisely because of its use of elitist artistic forms and transnational appeals beyond the local communities to which it referred. A membership club and initial recourse to arguments about artistic excellence and universal appeal all were used to keep it alive, even though it was simultaneously openly critiquing both those things by producing highly political theatre of testimony (Kruger 154–55.) This kind of rhetoric was never used to defend the garbage project perhaps because the project challenged the concept of the autonomous art by taking art into public space, by drawing on the stories of union members and by juxtaposing art and garbage. What language then can art which is political and participatory invoke in its defense?

Many artists opt to work outside of the cultural marketplace because of disillusionment with the self-referential limitations of the art world. They see their work in collaboration with non-artists as a way of redefining the kinds of discussion which produce the arts and the role of the artist. The arts, for many of these producers, are a way of intervening in power relations through representational practices. For many, community art gives artists and practitioners who do not feel connected to the mainstream arts a place to express their ideas about the world and their desires for what might make it better. Folks who feel excluded by the racialized and class marked institutions and tastes of middle class art lovers find in spaces outside of this field of culture a chance to perform the stories they live by for each other. Collaborative art making that connects formally trained artists with folks who don't consider themselves artists at all creates a hybrid space from which ever-changing stories emerge to shape the human relationships. The commodified, highly individualistic, metropolitan based obsession with formal behaviours, disciplines and genres, and inter-textuality associated with arts institutions are elements which provoke other artists to create spaces which position art as related to social life in the everyday. It is the ambience of formality and the rigidly regulatory procedures that accompany these that lead many artists and audiences to the view that cultural institutions producing high art are elitist and exclusionary.

But the idea that "community" is somehow a pure space, which is more inherently democratic and utopian and which exists in a space uncontaminated by the ideologies of the marketplace, does not necessarily follow. The painting out and silencing of the garbage truck project graphically demonstrates that there is no pure space anywhere and that cultural production is always both a covert and overt site of struggle. The idea that the work of the artist comes from and is connected to pure or transcendent space is an old one which has haunted the work of artists since the romantics and before. It depends on the opposing notion of contamination, because pure space can only be so if contamination exists elsewhere. The binaries pure/impure, authentic/inauthentic, rarely apportion value equally. They are accompanied by the apportioning of greater power to one side of the binary—in this case to that of the richer arts institutions which are defined by discourses of universal transcendence and not by intervention in contemporary social or political issues. This line of reasoning taken to its conclusion implies that community art depends on its opposite—art produced in autonomous and self-referential spaces and/or art produced in the market place. So much for social change!

Artists who make art with subordinate, impoverished, marginal or racialized communities feel the effects of this binary line of thought in the way that they are seen and treated by so-called professionals and by cultural institutions. Their work is often openly patronized as second class artistic practice by the professional arts community. Like the artists who worked on the garbage truck project, they find themselves treated as unskilled, producers of "serious" and perhaps "worthy" but somehow "bad" or "crudely didactic" art within the hierarchies of formal artistic institutions. Their work is justified as social work or adult education—rather than as a serious mode of cultural representation that renders complex thinking and carefully developed skills. These attitudes have material consequences. If one examines the budgetary figures on grants to the arts, it is vividly clear that, even though allocations to community arts and racialized groups have increased, allocations made to institutions like the Ballet or the Opera, for example, are far greater than any to aboriginal arts programs, works by artists of colour or community productions. The practice of community art, up to 1996 when the internet took off, has traditionally relied on a mode of production that was semi-autonomous from the market and undercapitalized. It was a mode of production comparable in some ways to the informal sector or to peasant production. When it moves beyond this marginal position through the uses made of it, it tends to be censored or to be redefined within another disciplinary category.

On the other hand, social, political and labour organizations concerned with social equity or fighting for better conditions have a history in which the arts are seen either as functionalist tools for education or as a frill on the serious work of making social change on more fundamental "hard core" issues—such as jobs, housing or health. In spite of the sterling work of some artists and union workers around this matter, artists still have trouble being taken seriously as workers within the hierarchies of the labour movement. For some, artistic work is connected to the need for pleasure—a luxury to be dealt with after basic needs are met. For others the arts are contaminated by centuries of patronage by the rich and powerful and are not comprehensible by the average philistine. The idea that the artist is a worker is a difficult one to grasp, especially where the artist is not producing for exchange on the market. Artists collaborating with communities find themselves between a rock and hard place—between at least two competing discourses, one on arts and one on the politics and marketing of labour.

Two observations emerge from this: first, it is not so much the process of making cultural representations which incurs feelings of alienation from the mainstream among many artists working with under-represented and impoverished groups, but rather the way in which the workings of power through cultural institutions legitimize regulatory practices that limit how art communicates, to whom and how it can be used by audiences; second, cultural institutions—especially public ones—require constant scrutiny and continued criticism from communities affected by their policies if they are to serve taxpayers and all communities equitably. But such scrutiny must also be accompanied by scrutiny of the cultures of the market and the aesthetics of commodification or else the picture will become one sided. Analyses of community must be accompanied by a relational analysis of the public sphere and the corporate sphere.

In Ontario, broadly speaking, increased interest in community based projects from organizations like the Trillium Foundation has come alongside cuts in funding to individual artists at the Ontario Arts Council. Under the conservative provincial government, in the context of free market expansion, this has been accompanied by decreased support for social programs and increased privatization. Richard Fung argues that in this context, the term "community" can be invoked as an attempt to extend and re-legitimize the neo-conservative agenda and the power of politicians and policy makers. Commenting on recent developments in cultural institutions, Fung contends that many bureaucrats who claim to speak on behalf of "grassroots communities" experience a considerable gain in their power as a result of speaking for communities of which they are not members. Populism can work to legitimize neo-conservative power while marginalizing critics from non-dominant groups who have led the struggle for access to cultural institutions over the last decade. Fung argues that dominant groups can re-work and maintain their power in the guise of including others while in reality limiting the potential of the critical voice from within those communities and the transforming of power relations. This analysis makes visible the process of hegemony at work. One important conclusion to be drawn is that critical artists and audiences need to be involved in leading the process of change if it is to benefit those it claims to serve. Secondly, a more complex understanding of the concept of community as one which spans difference is also key.

Community is usually understood in two ways: first, as a geographically located group and second, as a group which defines itself as a community on the basis of having a particular shared interest or bond of association. Communities, but especially naturalized communities (i.e. communities which you don't get to pick membership in, those which you inherit or are born with—those of sex, nationality, race, age, physical ability), carry with them stories about their bodies or histories which define who they are and how they are seen by others. Through these representations, we make sense of our relationships with each other, decide who's in, who's out, who's important and who's not. Most of us make use of these stories about who we are to determine what we can become, when and how we might enter the scenarios thrown up by life. We invest in them and use them to define or limit our possibilities.

Stories and images of community, unlike our biologies, are not naturally constituted. They are made and unmade over time in cultural production and are often replete with stereotypical myths. The Jamaican community, for instance, has had to fight the Canadian press over consistent representations of Black Jamaican men as criminals. It is not that there are no Jamaican criminals, but that the majority of Black Jamaicans who are not criminals are rarely represented if at all. Over time, portrayals of Black Jamaicans as "bad immigrants" has gained currency and it serves to define its opposite "good Canadians." Definitions of identity usually depend on the denigration of another opposing group. Group identity is made by differentiating one group from other, relationally. Problems arise where groups apportion value to each side of the comparison, giving one side more importance than the other. Material and social rewards are invested in this process accordingly.

When the term "community" is invoked in discussions about community art, it usually refers to groups which are different from the dominant (white and middle class) norm. The moral authority of these groups derives from notions of essential authenticity. The "grassroots," "the working class," "the south-Asian community," and so on, all signal homogenous entities which are just as often contested from within. Material and social resources and rewards are invested in these definitions according-ly, when the trouble is that no community is entirely homogenous or entirely fixed. Any given community is full of internal differences which must be muzzled to pre-serve apparent unity. The ideal of unity can and does serve a strategic function in struggles for change, but often, it also contributes to the dominance of certain groups within those groups.

When we think of any given "community" we tend to define group identity according to dominant images in circulation and not to the groups which challenge these stereotypes from within the community. For example, popular images of the "black community" are unlikely to bring to mind black lesbian mothers. Poet and activist Audre Lorde spent much of her life challenging ideas of black and feminist community homogeneity and the ways in which it worked to penalize and exclude those who differed from the dominant heterosexual, able-bodied male norm. Acknowledging and working with the notion of diversity between communities and affirming the right of critical voices to speak from within communities may be one way to deal with those who seek to manipulate particular marginalized groups in their own interests. A notion of hybrid communities may work against the trend to fix par-ticular groups in ahistorical ways.

Obstinate Memory, an exhibition of memory boxes made by Latin American women, produced for Community Arts Biennial in 2001, illustrates the power of com-plicating the concept of community. Women from the Centre for Spanish Speaking Peoples in Toronto worked with visual artist Amelia Jimenez to make, assemble and juxtapose objects in small boxes. These objects were images of memories drawn from their past, their lives in their many countries of origin and their present lives here in Canada. They were auto-ethnographic symbols which gained symbolic meaning from the way the objects were displayed against each other. The ruptures and discontinu-ities of the women's lives were expressed in objects like stones from Lake Ontario, fragments of letters from relatives in South America, keepsakes from childhood. All these were expressed in work which demonstrated the shifting boundaries between individual/group, world/nation, and dramatized investments in more than one nation, north and south, third and first worlds. The ambivalence of the objects them-selves offered ways for spectators to actively respond to the arrangements of objects through projecting their own narratives onto the objects, even as the process offered the women a place for mourning and remaking of self in the context of the group. The boxes served as a momentary framing for snapshots of the process of identity as a work in progress, not an ongoing or fixed position. The process was collaborative in that each individual discussed her work in the group and with Jimenez, but each woman created her own box.

Obstinate Memory challenged ideas of nationality and community as fixed con-cepts and offered a way of crossing the borders of difference in the imagination of the women and the audiences they addressed. The women recreated their transnational worlds in the maps they made of their lives. They were simultaneously positioned in many sites, speaking not as one but as many voices located in many locations—South and North American, women of different classes, ages and locations in the Canadian immigration hierarchy. The work troubled ideas about cultural purity and community as fixed entities. *Obstinate Memory* defies classifications of community arts as celebratory, oppositional or transformative (Pacific). It is an example of art which offers participants a chance to act as "the mediators in a process of publicly defining the community to be celebrated and perhaps, changed" (Little and Knowles 111).

I have argued that while the category of community art has developed in response to struggles for greater cultural equity, its incipient institutionalization raises a number of new challenges. There are many more struggles ahead if an equitable cultural landscape is to be brought into being. Setting up a separate category of community arts within arts funding is one way of addressing the matter of cultural accessibility, but it does not necessarily address the problem created by the binary community/mainstream. It does not necessarily challenge the authority and traditional legitimacy of these institutions as signifiers of normative cultural power and "western civilization."

In the long run if community artists are to effectively advocate for themselves as cultural workers and defend their right to be as critical as they wish, they will have to come up with two things: allies and a language for defending their work. Such a language will have to confound the old binaries of high/popular art, professional/community artist and so on. One way to do this is to generate critical languages appropriate for assessing art as a mode of cultural intervention and not as a naturally constituted practice based on autonomous, self-referential languages. This does not mean that the work produced should emphasize the literal, the naturalistic and sloganeering. Art which crosses boundaries and makes social and political intervention needs simultaneously to generate support across different groups of artists and community in order to survive and defend itself even as it retains the right to a complex language of signs.

Critical artists and informed community members have an important role to play in the leadership of this process and need to continue to work for the development of the discourse, if it is not to be taken over by those who claim to speak for groups they do not represent. I have argued that if the critical edge of community art is to remain, a more complex understanding of community is needed, one which acknowledges differences within, rather than one which stresses inner homogeneity. I have suggested that the practice of community art itself needs to build on varied approaches, supported by critical work which theorizes problems arising from current practices. While the establishment of the category of community art is a significant step, the binary which undergirds the relations between community artists and traditional artistic disciplines needs to be undermined by critical engagement with the power relations which inhere in those institutions and by developing opportunities for more cross sectoral collaboration and dialogue. The divide between community artist/professional artist and between artist/worker and the binaries which underlie them may not be one which serves either group well in the long run. Artists of all kinds need forms of organization which defend them as workers and which at the same time allow points of divergence and points of contact in their work. As community art becomes incorporated into the categories of public and private funders, communities of all kinds need to work to defend its socially critical nature, so that it does not become a means for greater social control of the most marginalized or a second class practice inferior to professionalized practices.

Communities and artists working with them may need to take a lesson from the trickster hero. They may need to shape shift and strategically retain the lesson of the slippery sign while allowing for multiple interpretations of it. They may need to cut and mix the language of critical education for social action with the rhetoric of artistic autonomy in ways which do not set up an inflexible dichotomy between professional and community, high art and popular art. The use of a hybrid critical language for community art may be important for community art discourse, if it is to survive manipulation and command support.

At the start of the new millennium, the market is more pervasive than ever. Production and consumption regulate our lives in unprecedented ways, creating identities, proposing what to do and how to act. While the marketplace is oppressively present, it is impossible to retreat to a pure space its relations have not transformed. Social theorists Michel de Certeau and Dick Hebdige suggest that consumption isn't just making idiots of us (hard to believe if you watch TV for five hours) but that there is creativity and resistance written into the way we respond, cut, mix and make a bricolage from the paraphenalia of stuff around us. Ways of reusing symbols help to constitute new positions from which to think about and demand new possibilities. Indeed, commodified popular cultural forms such as reggae and rap have provided a space for insurgent Black diasporic identity formation, springing up as post industrial cottage industries within the multinational reaches of the cultural industries. There may be many lessons here for the artists seeking to work in hybrid ways in the present period of expansion and regulatory developments in the field of subsidized community arts.

(2001)

Works Cited

Barndt, Deborah. Personal communication, 2000.

Barndt, Deborah, Minsook Lee and Robin Pacific. Personal communication, 2000.

Benjamin, Walter. "The Work of Art in the Age of Mechanical Reproduction." *Media and Cultural Studies: Keyworks.* Ed. Gigi Meeakshi Durham and Douglas Kellner. Oxford: Blackwell, 2006. 18–48.

Boal, Augusto. *Theatre of the Oppressed.* Trans. C.A. and M.L. McBride. New York: Urizen, 1979.

Conde, Carol and Karl Beveridge. Personal communication, 2000.

———. "Theatre of Operations." Accessed 30 November 2010. http://www.cepa-gallery.org/exhibitions/condebev/index.html.

de Certeau, Michel. From *The Practice of Everyday Life. Cultural Theatre and Popular Culture.* Ed. John Storey. Athens, Georgia: U of Georgia P, 1998. 483–94.

Fanon, Frantz. *Black Skin, White Masks.* New York: Grove, 1967.

———. *The Wretched of the Earth.* New York: Grove, 1963.

Fernandez, Melanie. "Community Arts and the Ontario Arts Council". Unpublished paper, 1998.

Fernandez, Sharon. Personal communication, 2001.

Ford-Smith, Honor. "Sistren." *Cultures in Contention.* Ed. Douglas Kahn and Diane Neumier. New York: Signs, 1985. 84–91.

Freire, Paulo. *Pedagogy of the Oppressed.* Trans. M. Bergman Ramos. New York: Continuum, 1994.

Fung, Richard. Personal communication, 2000.

———. "Working Through Appropriation." *Fuse* 16.5–6 (1993): 16–24.

Giroux, Henry and Roger Simon. *Popular Culture, Schooling and Everyday Life.* Granby, Mass: Bergin & Garvey, 1989.

Gramsci, Antonio. *Selections from the Prison Notebooks.* Trans. Q. Hoare and Geoffrey Nowell Smith. New York: International Publishers, 1971.

Hall, Stuart, ed. *Representation: Cultural Representations and Signifying Practices.* London: The Open University/Sage, 1997.

Hebdige, Dick. *Subculture: The Meaning of Style.* London: Routledge, 1979.

Inuit Art Foundation. "Sharing Power." Accessed 30 November 1993. http://www.inuitart.org/foundation/art-resources/sharing-power.html.

Jameson, Fredric and Miyoshi, Masao. *The Cultures of Globalization.* Durham, NC: Duke UP, 2003.

Kruger, Loren. *The Drama of South Africa: Plays, Pageants and Publics Since 1910.* New York: Routledge, 1999.

Lee, Angela. *Community Arts Workbook…another Vital Link.* Toronto: Ontario Arts Council, 1998.

Little, Edward. "The Reading Hebron Community Project." *alt.theatre: cultural diversity and the stage* 1.4 (2000): 6–7.

Little, Edward and Ric Knowles. "The Unity in Community." *The Theatre of Form and the Production of Meaning: Contemporary Canadian Dramaturgies.* By Ric Knowles. Toronto: ECW, 1999. 107–20.

Martin, Lee Ann. "First Nations Activism through the Arts." *Questions of Community: Artists, Audiences, Coalitions.* Ed. Daina Augaitis, Lorne Falk, Sylvie Gilbert and Mary Ann Moser. Banff: Banff Centre Press, 1995. 77–90.

Nurse, Donna Bailey. *What's a Black Critic to Do? Interviews, Profiles and Reviews of Black Writers.* Toronto: Insomniac, 2003.

Pacific, Robin. *Initiatives in Cultural Democracy: A Report to the Laidlaw Foundation.* Unpublished paper. Toronto,1999.

Philip, M. NourbeSe. *Frontiers: Selected Essays and Writings on Racism and Culture.* Stratford, ON: Mercury, 1992.

———. "Who's Listening? Artists, Audiences and Language." *Questions of Community: Artists, Audiences, Coalitions.* Ed. Daina Augaitis, Lorne Falk, and Sylvie Gilbert. Banff: Banff Centre Press, 1995. 129–49.

Razack, Sherene. "Making Canada White: Law and the Policing of Bodies of Colour in the 1990s." *Canadian Journal of Law and Society* 14.1 (1999): 173–84.

Said, Edward. *Culture and Imperialism.* New York: Random House, 1994.

Salverson, Julie. "Change on Whose Terms? Testimony and an Erotics of Injury." *Theater* 31.3 (2001): 119–25.

Spivak, Gayatri Chakravorty. *The Post-colonial Critic: Interviews, Strategies and Dialogues.* New York: Routledge, 1990.

Tator, Carol, Frances Henry and Winston Mattis. *Challenging Racism in the Arts in Canada: Case Studies in Controversy and Conflict.* Toronto: U of Toronto P, 1998.

Taylor, Diana and Roselyn Constantino. *Holy Terrors: Latin American women perform.* Durham: Duke UP, 2003.

West, Cornel. *The Cornel West Reader.* New York: Basic Civitas Books, 1999.

Pedagogies, Politics and Practices in Working with Youth

by Edward Little and Rachael Van Fossen

In 1997, following consultation with federal, provincial, territorial and municipal cultural departments, various arts councils and almost 200 Canadian artists and arts professionals, the Canadian Conference of the Arts (CCA) released its "Arts in Transition" report. Amongst other findings, the report concluded that education, training and funding of artists in Canada tend to continue emphasizing a "modernist model" that places primary value on the artist as solitary creator—an approach oriented overwhelmingly to the development of artistic skills. While the report acknowledged that this model "has produced and continues to produce many exceptional artists and works of art," the CCA also voiced the concern that "many younger artists find the model confining, unable to accommodate their desire to work more closely with communities and to incorporate social and ecological issues into their art" (6).

Over the past three years, our experience with students entering the new undergraduate specialization in Drama for Human Development (DFHD) at Concordia University supports this finding of the "Arts in Transition" report. Applications for admission have risen sharply since the program's launch in 1998, and, during the interview process, students speak consistently of their desire to train in, develop and practice theatre arts that engage directly with social, political, environmental and therapeutic concerns. The DFHD specialization is one of five program options leading to a Bachelor of Fine Arts degree in Theatre, and all students, regardless of area of specialization, are required to complete a core group of classes in Design, Production, Performance and Drama for Human Development.

The DFHD program focuses on localized, participatory and culturally democratic approaches to theatre arts. Introductory courses, designed with classes of first-year students from all specializations in mind, examine various perspectives on the role and function of the artist in community and on the relationship between the audience and the performance event in various models of alternative theatre practices. Upper-level offerings include Drama Therapy, Popular Theatre and Theatre with Young People.

Another upper-level course, Theatre with Diverse Populations, is aimed at preparing students for individualized "special projects," which may involve internships, community projects or other placements.

Theoretical Approach

The program promotes a vision of theatre artists as cultural workers: artists trained in representation who are socially informed and knowledgeable about various approaches to social, interpersonal and intercultural communication. Whereas popular theatre practices are often seen as somehow apart from, or excluded from, more "mainstream" approaches, DFHD, as part of a theatre department offering co-requisite courses in performance, design and production, insists that these be recognized as symbiotic, complementary elements in a vigorous, inclusive vision of theatre. DFHD emphasizes approaches that are to varying degrees "participatory" and/or "inclusive." Participatory approaches make the fundamental distinction that artists are working *with* participants, as opposed to a potentially patronizing attitude that we are designing activities *for*, or producing work *about*, specific communities or populations. This approach aims to connect artists and communities, with an emphasis on "getting to know" the particular population through methods of direct interaction.

Among the "inclusive" approaches studied are forms which are simultaneously interdisciplinary, intergenerational and intercultural in conceptualization and practice. Representation both *of* and by diverse social and cultural constituents of a project's "host" community is key. Such communities may be defined geographically or by common bond, ethnicity or interest, and students can explore how these notions of community—combined with the nature of participation and inclusivity—determine form.

In interdisciplinary practices, this might be reflected in the use of giant puppets, masks, local stories and legends, original and traditional music and song and the celebration of specific community skills and talents.

Theory in Practice

The application of these theories with specific regard to children and youth plays out in a number of ways in the DFHD program. Following basic education and training in group skills, theatre animation and ethical concerns involving localism, cultural appropriation, witnessing and testimony, students undertake a preparatory course known as Theatre with Diverse Populations:

> *Theatre with Diverse Populations*
> Design and preparation of appropriate drama or theatre activities with specific populations. Working as a team, students will learn to employ community development principles in planning and implementing a theatre program with a targeted population or community group. Topics include specialized learning and teaching strategies, animation skills, needs assessment, and program evaluation. This course will prepare students to carry out independent projects in upper-level courses.[1]

This course concentrates on the kinds of theoretical paradigms and practical skills prerequisite to designing and undertaking "special projects" involving university/

community partnerships and alliances with specific populations. Since 1998 we have completed a number of these projects which directly involve youth.

In Partnership with Black Theatre Workshop

Thami and Isabel involved a tour of Montreal-area elementary schools carried out in partnership with Black Theatre Workshop (BTW) in February 2000. The show, created to celebrate Black History month, featured original songs, choreography and interactive storytelling techniques used to link selected excerpts from BTW's mainstage production of Athol Fugard's play *My Children! My Africa!*. Conceived and directed by Ted Little, all of the linking material was created collaboratively by students enrolled in DFHD courses. Their challenge was to conduct relevant research into both form and content, then create fifty minutes of theatre introducing the idea of apartheid to culturally diverse groups of elementary-aged children in an entertaining, accessible and interactive show. An important aspect of the project was to allow the students to have considerable input into the form of the piece itself—its tone, feel and use of language—as well as its goal to educate and foster mentorship and communication between students in their late teens/early twenties and younger children.

A number of students involved in the *Thami and Isabel* project continue to work on ongoing youth projects at BTW today. Last summer BTW piloted a three-week summer theatre project for teens called the Young Performers Initiative. Participants received preliminary training in various theatre skills, including improvisation, scene study, stage combat, drumming, playwriting and directing. In the final week, the seventeen teenagers each chose one of these areas in which to "specialize." The group then went on to produce a short interdisciplinary theatre piece containing all original material. BTW plans to expand the program in summer 2001, and several DFHD students who first became involved with BTW through *Thami and Isabel* are playing key roles in the summer project's development.

In Partnership with Weston School

Students have also become directly involved in working with youth through in-class work in the Diverse Populations course, under the leadership of Rachael Van Fossen. In winter 2000 (the first year the course was offered in the new program), DFHD students developed a short program with a Grade 7 class from the nearby Weston School. This school functions outside of the public school system, with intentionally low student/teacher ratios and a disproportionately high number of pupils who, for a host of reasons, have had difficulty succeeding in the regular system. Concordia students in the Diverse Populations course, in consultation with the Grade 7 teacher, began by putting together a list of objectives for their program. Included in these were goals they wished to achieve for the sake of their own learning (primarily about applying theory through practical experience), as well as the work on theatre skills and, perhaps more importantly, the improved self-esteem and social skills that they wished to achieve in working with the twelve-year-olds.

Because the DFHD program advocates meaningful and significant contact with project participants whenever possible, and given the time constraints of a three-credit, one-semester course, the twelve students in the Diverse Populations course were divided into teams. Each team worked with the same group of four or five Grade 7 students, focusing largely on improvisation skills and content development for a final presentation to be performed for the whole class. This smaller "team within a team" approach allowed for considerable flexibility within groups; as a result, the Concordia students were able to adapt more readily to the particular needs of individual participants. In each team, content was determined by the seventh-graders themselves and ranged from a suspense horror-mystery piece to a somewhat more sociopolitical piece from the self-named Woman Warrior Tribe (all the Grade 7 girls in one group), which incorporated song and tightly choreographed dance as a celebration of the power of womanhood.

Current Partnership with Teesri Duniya Theatre

This year, Rachael and "Diverse Pops" will work closely with a large-scale undertaking led by Ted and Rahul Varma of Teesri Duniya Theatre. "The South Asian Youth Project: Culture, Participation, and Community Development" is being seeded with $10,000 in start-up funding from Centre d'Études et de recherche sur l'Asie du sud (CERAS); it will be conducted in partnership with Teesri Duniya, the South Asian Women's Community Centre (SAWCC), the Hindi Quebec Association, the Drama for Human Development Program and CERAS.

Now underway, the entire project will take twelve months to complete and will involve cultural research, experiential job-shadowing, formation of an intergenerational theatre troupe (with training in theatre skills and performance creation), travelling "edu-prop" theatre presentations to community organizations and groups and a final showcase performance/presentation in a venue to be determined. The project is predicated on the belief that active participation in socially and culturally relevant art will inform and educate youth about their ancestral heritage. This participation will also provide them with skills and opportunities to develop deeper, richer, more meaningful engagements with their contemporary Canadian cultural experience within the context of their South Asian roots. In this way, the project members hope to highlight the potential of theatre to produce more active and informed citizens who recognize their important role in evolving, diversifying and influencing the path of multiculturalism for the benefit of all Canadians. All aspects of the project, including preliminary educational and cultural sensitivity workshops, discussion forums, photographic displays, creative writing workshops and theatrical and paratheatrical events, will be conducted under the auspices of a Steering Team comprised of youth representatives working with members from the stakeholder organizations.

The project aims to form and consolidate links between Canadian South Asian youth across historic religious and/or cultural differences, and to provide a basis from which to continually renew these links. Accordingly, one of the first priorities of the project is to establish a Youth Action Team consisting of South Asian youth living in Montreal and drawing on as many diverse South Asian backgrounds as possible (India, Pakistan, Bangladesh, Sri Lanka, Nepal, etc.). The members of this core group will be selected based on their level of interest and their potential to train as youth leaders and peer educators who will use theatre to address issues of concern to the South Asian community in Canada. Over the initial stages of the project, the Diverse Populations class will work closely with the Youth Action Team to prepare for assuming more effective leadership roles in the Steering Team and in all other aspects of the project.

To ready the DFHD students for some of the specific challenges that they are likely to face in this project, and as part of their initial research into the population, the Diverse Populations course organizers will host in-class guest speakers and workshop leaders from a range of relevant fields and community affiliations. To date, for example, the class has arranged sessions with Dr. Varda Mann-Feder, a specialist in adolescent development and applied human sciences, and Dr. Hiteshini Jugessur, a community worker experienced with diverse South Asian populations in Montreal. Training in the use of specific techniques from Rachael's artistic practice involving methods of working with social, cultural and generational diversity in community-based projects will also figure prominently at this stage.

These preliminary aspects of training the DFHD students, assembling the Youth Action Team and establishing a relationship between the two groups will take place in January 2001. Following this, over a period of eight weeks in February and March, the Youth Action Team will work closely with the DFHD students and adult members of the Teesri Duniya's Edu-prop Troupe to design outreach activities aimed at involving significantly more youth as the project develops. The work begun by the Diverse Populations class over this period will thus be taken up by the Youth Action Team, in partnership with the Edu-prop Troupe, and will continue to the end of the project.

Conceptually, the Diverse Populations class will be acting as both mentors (in a sense providing preliminary training in animation skills, theatre games and activities to an outreach team of South Asian youth) and animators (animating the group to begin to identify content, activities and innovative theatrical forms that will "speak to" youth in the larger project). Departing from a "roles, rules and risks" model for youth and community development practices (Heath and Smyth 10), a primary goal of the work with Concordia students will be to provide the Steering Team with a set of recommendations about how to design and implement the project in a way that excites youth, speaks to youth about issues of concern to them and allows youth to express their own perspective(s) on these issues.

Challenges

Many of the issues that the project expects to deal with are both complex and controversial. For the youth themselves, we expect that issues surrounding culturally defined notions of sexuality, sexual behaviour and marriage will be significant. Parental concerns about premarital sex and cross-cultural and interfaith relationships and marriages, combined with a persistent taboo surrounding sex education and family discussions of sexuality, are an everyday reality in the lives of many South Asian young people. On the other hand, a common concern voiced by members of stakeholder organizations is the biased nature of certain religious and cultural resources which largely dominate the "South Asian" experience available to these youth in Canada. Some project stakeholders not only cite the limited nature of these resources in terms of immediate social relevance but also voice a concern that impressions left by these resources may even hinder South Asian youth from assisting their parents' generation to make the transition to Canadian society, or from becoming fully participatory members of a multicultural society.

Other issues, such as those of more immediate concern to organizations like SAWCC, include literacy, discriminatory immigration policies, trafficking of refugees into Canada using false documentation and historically taboo subjects such as domestic violence, sexual abuse and the empowerment of women. A particularly complex set of issues involves the possibility of negative role-modeling occurring in the homes of many of the most marginalized. According to Dr. Jugessur, many new immigrant families and almost all refugee families in Quebec face institutional and systemic problems stemming from resources that are either inadequate, inaccessible or ill-conceived in their delivery. For refugee families in particular, lack of employment and restricted access to education, health and social services while making the transition to Canadian society often lead to depression on the part of parents. For all displaced families, the sense of loss and isolation results in a chronic sense of helplessness, a failure to seek further education and/or language and occupational training, ongoing dependency on social assistance and self-perpetuating marginalization from more established members of the South Asian community in Canada.

Of course, the kinds of issues and problems identified as facing Canadian South Asians are by no means restricted to this population. They are, in various configurations and degrees, evident in mainstream, minority, immigrant and socially marginalized populations alike. Furthermore, for any population, the very act of naming complicity in such problems runs a very high risk of contributing to stereotypes and furthering isolation and division. To effectively use theatre arts to open up lines of communication around such issues in non-threatening, non-confrontational ways is but one of the challenges facing the South Asian Youth Project. Informing, sensitizing and assisting young peer educators and other participants to take both responsibility and leadership regarding such issues and problems will require considerable diplomacy, expertise and support from members of stakeholder organizations.

Maintaining constructive communications across any differences of opinion which may arise between variously mandated stakeholders is a further challenge facing the project. To this end, it is essential that the Youth Action Team, the DFHD class and its instructor all consult and report to Teesri Duniya and the Steering Team on a regular basis. Early on, as part of their course work, the DFHD students may themselves design and propose a mechanism for this consultation process.

Question of Follow-up

As with most projects of this type, the question of what happens after the culminating performance has taken place is important to consider.

In the case of the South Asian Youth Project, the involvement of the Diverse Populations class will have ended long before the project reaches completion; ongoing training in theatre skills and performance creation will be taken up by Teesri Duniya. Similarly, the primary goals of the mentoring process with members of the stakeholder organizations involve: (a) promoting education, activism and volunteer work; (b) encouraging youth to take responsibility for problems within their communities (especially when they themselves may not be directly affected); and (c) developing new lines of communication that create greater opportunities for youth to become involved with volunteer organizations in long-term ways that are meaningful and supportive for all parties.

This points to a significant advantage to working in partnership with organizations outside the university where follow-up activity can be taken up by these host group(s). Some DFHD students have themselves initiated follow-up activities with partner organizations, wishing presumably to build on positive in-class experiences and on the sense of satisfaction they felt based on feedback from participants. There is a certain irony worth noting here—despite the fact that the DFHD program stresses the importance of a long and meaningful process when working with non-professional community people, the limitations of three-credit, one-semester courses are such that a lengthy process is difficult to accomplish. Some of our best students wish to engage with the people and the work itself in a deeper way, and, as emerging artist-entrepreneurs, they have set up continuing follow-up activities themselves.

With Weston School, Rachael and her students are working to implement a Theatre with Young People course that would allow DFHD students to work with Weston students on an ongoing basis beginning in fall 2001. In the meantime, two upper-level students, Anisa Cameron from DFHD and Sarah Blumel from Design, have undertaken an interdisciplinary "special project," also at Weston, designed to support and build stronger links among Grade 7, 8 and 9 girls, who are outnumbered approximately four-to-one by the boys.

The logistical difficulties of initiating and maintaining links with off-campus schools and community groups can be daunting. There are also risks associated with taking on difficult or sensitive material with people whose lives are directly affected by the issues, risks to which popular theatre workers consistently attest. In a university setting, these risks are further compounded, in part because the DFHD students are essentially doing hands-on work as artist-animators with relatively little practical experience (although, to be fair, some DFHD students do have significant experience before they apply for admission to the program).

It is heartening to take note of the number of emerging and established Canadian theatre artists who are choosing to focus on community-based work. The DFHD program is designed to fill a need—a need that until recently had not been addressed in a systematic way—for undergraduate post-secondary theatre studies in both old and new participatory forms that incorporate psychological, political and social issues and challenges.

Ultimately it is through art that these issues and challenges will be addressed most effectively. In the case of the South Asian Youth Project in particular, and of the DFHD program in general, we trust that the aesthetic languages of the stage have the potential to hold and represent a multiplicity of perspectives, whether these come from different generations, different cultural or religious backgrounds or simply differences of opinion.

(2001)

Notes

[1] This course description incorporates proposed revisions to the current Concordia Undergraduate Calendar. The revisions were approved by the Theatre Department in fall 2000.

Works Cited

Canadian Conference of the Arts (CCA). "The Arts in Transition Project. Report and Discussion Paper." Ottawa: CCA, 1997. *Concordia University Undergraduate Calendar 2000–2001*. Montreal: Concordia University, 2000.

Heath, Shirley Brice and Laura Smyth. *ArtShow: Youth and Community Development Resource Guide*. Washington, DC: Partners for Livable Communities, 1999.

Little, Edward. "Avoiding the Missionary Position: Diversity and The Other in a New Undergraduate Theatre Programme." *alt.theatre: cultural diversity and the stage* 1.4 (2000): 8–10.

————. "Cultural Democracy and the Enderby and District Community Play." *Canadian Theatre Review* 101 (2000): 56–59.

————. "Cultural Diversity/Cultural Democracy." *alt.theatre: cultural diversity and the stage* 1.3 (1999): 10–11.

The MarshFire Guild System:
Mobilizing Community Resources

by David Fancy

The 75 members of Marshfire People's Theatre Company in Sackville, New Brunswick, presented a seven-night run of *The Great Big Mosquito Show* in August 2000. The project involved people from varied backgrounds—from actors and dancers to painters and musicians, to educators, therapists, meditation teachers, reiki practitioners and convicts.

We especially targeted for involvement youth at risk of becoming dependant on government social services. A space in a local foundry was converted into a temporary theatre, and people from local cultural constituencies, including anglophones, francophones and aboriginals, gathered to stage stories from a particularly turbulent time in the region's history.

Creating the generous space

MarshFire's principle objective is to stimulate community health by creating a "generous space" for local populations. Both physical and emotional, creative and ideological, this "generous space" was envisioned as being a place of collaborative creative exchange between individuals of differing socio-economic and cultural backgrounds, of all ages, abilities and interests.

To create the "generous space" we engaged in partnerships with a variety of cultural and educational organisations in order to offer mentorships and youth training programs. This permitted us to eventually provide free open workshops in music, puppet-making and performance to members of the general public.

Being an entrepreneur

MarshFire also engaged local business and financial establishments to request funds for the project. Now, although the end result of the project was intended to be something beautiful, lyrical, prophetic, critical, fun and participatory, it wasn't long before I realized that 85% of the labour would be entrepreneurial grunt work. Not without its charms and benefits (such as having to describe your event over and over, all the while gradually getting a clearer picture of it yourself), this kind of promotional work occasionally risks pulling you off course.

The key was to describe the project in language that those whom we were addressing could relate to, but avoid getting caught up in the assumptions implicit in that particular discourse. Obviously, each funder had a specific desire they wanted fulfilled in giving us money. For example, we received funding from foundations whose objectives are community-oriented philanthropy, from provincial millennium funding bodies whose objectives were heritage celebration and from businesses who wanted to be part of something that was marketable and had a "buzz" to it.

The most eventful and fruitful discourse clash inside the company came when arts and market objectives met head-on, especially the problematic langauge of the staff of the marketing company who gave us a huge amount of promotional support. Terms such as "value creation," "target audience" and "brand recognition" can have an awkward resonance at best, but they began to sound somewhere between the hostile and the hilarious when used to plan the promotion of a community-based cultural event. Still, the marketers' contribution to the project was a determining factor of success.

An early and determining partnership was that with a local training organization which solicits Human Resources Development Canada funding for bilingual community integration programming in southeastern New Brunswick. Together, we applied for a Youth Services grant and were able to hire 14 people between 16 and 30 years of age to participate as the core group of the project.

Creating the guilds

Twelve months before the production, names were given to different groupings of professionals whose help would be necessary to create the event. We knew early on, for example, that we would need a lawyer to process our applications for not-for-profit incorporation and charitable status. And so The Fast Talkers' Guild was established "for all those dealing with the law and regulations." We formalized the system in the early stages by making a simple brochure which articulated MarshFire's objectives and introduced the concept of guilds. We then approached a local barrister and solicitor, explained that membership in the Fast Talkers' Guild would mean participation in a multifaceted arts-based community project and result in the recognition and fun associated with the (anticipated!) success of the event. The lawyer agreed, helped us with our legal needs, and the company became legally registered.

More guilds were established and positions filled: the Big Bills Guild for those involved with money (insurers, accountants and eventual bank sponsors); the Spellcasters' Guild for those involved in communications; The DigiWalkers' Guild for those involved with computers, and so on. Light doses of wit in the guild namings prompted intrigue in community, and our organizational legitimacy and currency as conversation piece was established.

Guilds served as a buffer

By creating the guilds, we managed to avoid the branding of our site, programme and advertising with corporate logos. We were able to use our own design environment and simply list sponsors when there was space. We tried to maintain the principle that we were inviting sponsors into an already clearly articulated space, both in terms of aesthetics and ideology, and so were largely able to get them to leave their corporate identities at the door.

In addition to having frequent tours of the work site for guild members and members of the public, we listed the guild groupings in the programme rather than simply displaying logos. We wanted to show the professionals and businesses involved that they had an integral role to play in the creation of the production and, by extension, the health of the community.

Inclusion a cornerstone

A quick look at the programme for the production demonstrates how the guild system brought together a broad spectrum of funders and gift-in-kind givers to the event, including wealthy benefactors, Correctional Services Canada, and the local high school music department. As the guild system gathered speed, the business community rallied around the event and spoke about the project's eventual success with a certain amount of proprietary pride. Guild members frequently spoke out about the new perspective on the arts and on community development that they had gained through working on the production. In one interesting scenario, the designers from the ad agency expressed relief at their creative control over the advertising in what they called our "lo-fi" environment. We frequently spoke of the "generous space," and the concept itself became increasingly multivalent, as guild members articulated their own take on the term to each other, to us, and to our public.

Also very important was the exposure of our so-called "marginalized" participants to "successful" professionals. A number of the youth became distinctly more positive about their own futures when they came in contact with the "successful" professionals. Similarly, the change of perception towards youth in the community is still playing itself out, but the core youth participants have all gained an increased sense of citizenship and freedom in a town they have, in some cases, been living in for nearly 30 years.

The Ethical Risks of the Guild System

We encountered, or at least flirted with, the major ethical difficulties of taking money from corporate and government sources. At the risk of denying the corporatist environment in which the whole event was situated, we democratized our articulation of the guild system by suggesting that everyone in the community had an equal if different contribution to make, be they a banker as a member of the Big Bills Guild, or a grade 5 band member with the Floorshow Guild for volunteer performers.

If there was any corrective in the process for perhaps promoting the suspect notion of "the good corporate citizen," it lay in the redistribution of resources towards our clearly articulated "generous space." In this light, the collection of over $200,000 in cash and gifts in kind over six months for a project without precedent in the region becomes more an act of alchemy or even Robin Hoodism than of whitewashing dirty dollars.

The final redeeming factor of taking money from a variety of potentially suspect sources was that we were able to offer ticket prices of $5 and $3, the total sales of which amounted to approximately 2.5% of our overall budget. This way, we were able to extend the fruits of our collective adventure as a gift to the local communities that had participated.

Three Major Strengths

A system modeled after the infrastructure that supported medieval Passion and Miracle plays had several strengths: inclusion of the giving participant in the project's "generous space;" the possibility of tracing the cause and effect of assistance by the sponsor; and the creation of a buffer zone between the sponsor and the organization.

In light of the above, then, we feel this model for community involvement is highly transferable, and is likely to work in most similar situations.

(2001)

Strategic Narratives:
The Embodiment of Minority
Discourses in Biographical Performance

by Nisha Sajnani

This brief introduction of the participants in the project is entirely reductive, but it does serve the purpose of acquainting the reader with the participants involved as well as provide certain qualifiers necessary to the overall project.

Amy Thomas is an American citizen, currently immersed in the process of immigration, who has been living in Canada with her husband since 1998.

Mahshad Aryafar and Pardis Zaregar immigrated to Canada from Iran in 1996 and 1997, respectively.

Danusia Lapinski, whose parents emigrated from Poland, was born in Canada in 1956.

Nisha Lynn Sajnani is my full name. My parents emigrated from Malaysia in 1973, after their parents had escaped persecution as Indian Hindus living in the newly formed Muslim State of Pakistan during the partition of 1947. I was born in Canada. I am a second-generation South Asian Canadian woman, who is invested in reading and writing the texts assigned to me by my country, my family, and my extra-familial communities. My engaging in this project was fuelled by a utopian vision of transnational communities and a desire to uncover the dynamics that limit, circumscribe, and mute the potential totality of what we articulate, express, and live as visible and invisible minorities within our imagined and political communities.

I invited four close friends to collaborate on a collective biographical performance project in late December of 2002, which resulted in a performance piece entitled *The Body Politic: Common Conversations on Gender and the Nation.* It was originally performed as part of the R/Evolution II Humanities conference, held at Concordia University in Montreal in March of 2003, and was staged again, in late August of the same year, for the University of the Streets: Controversies in Feminism café series in Montreal. This paper documents the process undertaken as we prepared to re/present our personal and collective memories of immigration, integration, and assimilation into Canada's multicultural mosaic. Biographical performance provides an art form and a platform for individuals marked as visible and invisible minorities. When it crosses and blurs the borders between separate minority discourses, it has the potential strategically to unsettle dominant interpretations of Canadian identity.

One thing we all had in common was our hyphenated identities. Lubna Chaudhry, a woman of Pakistani heritage who immigrated to the US with her parents, explains: "Cultural hybrids, those who straddle more than one culture, are the inhabitants of the 'third space,' engaged in the creation of yet another culture, a new story to explain the world and our participation in it, a new value system with the images and symbols that connect us to each other and to the planet" (82). As Chaudry suggests, the concept of the "third space," originated by Homo Bhabha, is useful to the understanding of the hybrid experience. This space represents the in-between zone, in which individuals who were born between cultures or raised in a multicultural environment can articulate their lived experience in order to create the meaning of their multiple and contingent identities. This becomes especially necessary in an environment in which nation building has been the project of a white, able-bodied, heterosexual, male majority, who have historically maintained control over the political, cultural and economic tools of production and reproduction. From the outset of this project, our attention was drawn to the voices missing from the narration of the nation's identity—the voices of women, and specifically of those marked as Others in their land (Aujla).

Setting the (Multicultural) Stage

Thirty years have passed since Canada's multicultural policy was first articulated and presented in the Canadian Parliament as a model for the integration of immigrant ethnic communities and as a hallmark of Canadian identity. It emerged under the charismatic leadership of then Canadian Prime Minister Pierre Elliot Trudeau. The proposed mechanism and underlying assumption was that greater self-esteem about one's own culture would lead to a greater tolerance of that of Others. This perspective is echoed in various readings of multiculturalism that support the policy as an innovation in equality, respect, and tolerance for individual differences (Rummens).

This discursive revolution permitted the formation of a social subjectivity based on colour and on Otherness. Himmani Bannerji, a South Asian feminist and educator provides a useful lens from which to critique Canada's management of diversity. She suggests that Trudeau's open-door immigration policy was motivated, in part, by the expectation of capitalist industrial growth and the aspiration of creating a liberal democratic nationhood. The former British colonies, in particular, provided cheap labour, both skilled and un-skilled, as well as the democratic basis for converging Otherness. Bannerji concludes that "color, the cognate of race, refracted into indirect notions of multi-culture and ethnicity, was much on the mind of the Canadian state" (30). Colour was translated into the language of visibility, thus giving birth to a new spectrum, or rainbow, of citizenship. The new Canadian subject was interpellated as visible minority, stressing both being non-white (and therefore visible in a way that whites are not) and being politically a minor player. Ironically, this preoccupation with colour also obscures the degree to which invisible minorities, those who are white in colour but do not come from British or Western European heritage, experience exclusion in Canada.

Bannerji's voice is not alone. Neil Bissoondath sees the policy of multiculturalism as being responsible for ethnic ghettoization and the failure to achieve unity amidst diversity (Bissoondath). Homi Bhabha's use of the term "musée imaginaire" (*Location* 247) is also useful in describing the attitude of a pluralistic democratic society towards the benefits of displaying cultural diversity and also demonstrates how diversity is contained and collapses into state impotence. By locating the identities of its diasporic communities within a fixed grid, the dominant host society can maintain its hegemony. Bhabha also sheds light on the conflict within the diasporic subject. He speaks of the "disjunctive, borderline temporalities of partial minority cultures" ("Cultures" 56), as a consequence of not sharing the same history with the liberal, dominant group. Canadian multiculturalism, as it is, currently celebrated, reinforces this space of temporality, through the endorsement of the term visible minority, which is at once an acknowledgment and a containment of the presence of something perceived as foreign within the body of the greater whole. As a result, invisible and visible minorities occupy an ambiguous position within the nation's space.

The Canadian Multiculturalism Act demarcates the parameters of our social subjectivity and of our terrain as political agents. It demands that we contend both with the nation as imagined community and with the nation as a concrete political entity. The policy functions as an expectation and, at the same time, an injunction and inscribes and prescribes a suggested narrative for the space to which the minority is limited. This policy interpellates both visible and invisible minorities in negative, albeit unequal, ways and has resulted in the persistence of a colour hierarchy, so that those called minorities are excluded from the process of contributing fully to the formation of (trans)national identities and communities. It is from this context that our biographical performance project derives its efficacy.

(Re)Defining HERstories

We came together as a group of five women from different cultural communities. Through an acknowledgment of this divide, we formed an alliance and prepared to transgress the borders of our myriad identities. Our performance emerged from a series of conversations in which we attempted to recognize our differences as well as our common challenges. Over ten weeks, we embarked on a creative journey of unpacking racial stereotypes, exploding gender definitions, and defining personal politics, frequently while sitting over dinner and a glass of fine wine.

The emergence of personal narratives, the stories we have been told and the stories we tell ourselves and each other as we construct our identities, entered into our conversation naturally, as we oscillated among desires to communicate with, convince, and contradict one another. Dan McAdams, a narrative therapist, suggests that "human beings are storytellers by nature and storytelling appears to be a fundamental way of expressing ourselves and our world to others. Stories provide a natural package for organizing information, helping us to shape the meaning of daily events, and communicate what we experience to others" (qtd. in Rubin 13).

This process of storytelling required a willingness to listen as well as to speak. Sometimes you had to reach a certain volume to be heard, so great was the enthusiasm and fervour at our dinner table. It was a tender balance, and I can attest to many frustrating moments where the conversation would seem to void itself of meaning after a certain hour and leave each of us contemplating our commitments to the overall project.

As we theorized, positioned, and imposed our selves in relation to each other, we became aware of the willingness necessary to attend to the many questions that arose as we transgressed the familiar and ended up, often, on uncomfortable terrain.

We decided to withdraw from the group process for a week and work on our own monologues—based on the stories we had shared with each other—with the intent of weaving them together into a coherent script. I drew much of the inspiration for my text from the stories we had shared over the previous weeks. The time we had spent as a group had created a generous space in which my experiences growing up as a second-generation South Asian, Canadian woman could exist alongside the diversity of experiences shared by my collaborators. Over the next few weeks we met and witnessed the development of each other's texts and experimented with methods of bringing each story to the stage. This process was met with a variety of responses from the group. Those with more experience with theatre were much more directive in their staging decisions, and those who desired direction in embodying their scripts were able to receive feedback on aesthetic structure. The process opened up several possibilities for collective storytelling and for reflecting on the new questions that emerged as we experimented with how each of us fit into the Other's story.

Sheila Rubin, a drama therapist, sheds light on the personal efficacy of our collective endeavour. She suggests that an awareness of our personal narratives can help us develop a sense of identity, reclaim a fuller sense of self and gain perspective and a deeper sense of meaning. "Without a stable community or a storyteller to keep track of our personal and collective narrative, people today have become keepers of their own stories"(13). Deena Metzger says that gathering information about ourselves, recalling memories, and putting together a life story are activities that change us. It is in the act of storytelling that we remember and re-member those parts of our selves that have been alienated (Metzger).

Ebron and Tsing's articulation of minority discourses is useful in demonstrating the political efficacy of our collective endeavour. They suggest that the scholarly attention given to the processes of marginalization, while useful in distinguishing the relationship between margin and the centre, has also limited the space in which dialogue can occur across and between marginalized positions. Their call is to "women writing culture to move beyond understandings of culture that have kept women confined inside cultural communities" (390). The phrase "the personal is political," usually associated with feminist discourses, could be, by this logic, equally true for minority discourses, in that resistance to further marginalization is wrought through the creation, with other minority groups, of an oppositional body politic.

(Re)Configuring the Multicultural Aesthetic

I began to envision this project as one of community building that could extend beyond the platitudes about interracial hegemony into mutual respect. Our conversations revealed several dilemmas about how to go about the project of speaking our personal histories, without being immediately relegated to a fixed cultural point of reference. We wanted to produce critically reflective and complex images of ourselves, without playing right back into an us/them binary in which we reinforced notions that our cultures were somehow to blame for the challenges we faced.

We tackled this dilemma in several different ways. In order to avoid having our performance read as a collection of separate, authentic cultural narratives, we needed to imagine more creative weavings among our so-called communities. We began to devise an aesthetic that could support the personal explorations of each of us, without feeding into the very cultural taxonomy we sought to disrupt. We decided to present our monologues in the form of an anthology, interspersed with sound bytes of the conversations recorded over our ten weeks together. In this way, I believe, we demonstrated the ways in which our embodied narratives emerged from a dynamic merging of perspectives across multiple margins. The potential to dismantle essentialist notions of culture became tangible through this approach to staging our situational and hybrid identities.

I find support for this approach in my reading of Sheila James, playwright and director, who says that a political act of resistance must consist of the production of images which contain descriptions of lived experience while referring back to the historical and present relations of exploitation (James). This is especially essential in a political climate in which a liberal, empiricist method of thinking in terms of essential categories is seen as pervasive. Una Chaudhuri also warns against the practice of interculturalism as a form of taxonomic theatre, as it can easily slip into a form of neocolonial universalism, in which separate cultures are seen as harmoniously co-existing—almost homogeneous—but are denied equality on the basis of their inherent differences. She provides a context from which to see art as a reflexive act that has direct sociocultural implications and challenges practitioners to redefine cultural identities, especially in the absence or erosion of the nation state or an immediately accessible national identity. Chaudhuri presents performances as cultural negotiation, rather than merely cultural expression, and as the site where the experiences and meanings that constitute culture can be actively explored and redefined in a continuous process (Chaudhuri). Bhabha's concept of "interstitial agency" is also useful here in speaking about the ways in which the performance of personal narrative is able to refute the binary representation of social antagonism. He suggests that the project of re/presentation among minorities cannot have longevity or authority as its goal but rather must reclaim and name minority's re/visions of their own community histories. In this way, we not only allow for a re-signification of the past and a reinterpretation of the future but also create a space for working through present fissures in the naively assumed transparency of the national narrative (Bhabha, *Location* 334).

(Re)Presenting Community

We first performed our collective biographies as part of the R/Evolution II Humanities Conference at Concordia University in Montreal. The performance was attended by approximately forty guests, who were mainly academics engaged in similar projects around culture and identity. Our second and third performances were open to the public at large and were attended by people interested in questions of identity, multiculturalism, and biographical performance. We held an open discussion forum after the latter two performances, as a way of inviting those who had witnessed our stories to share their own reflections, observations, and experiences. Witnesses to these performances most immediately identified with the struggles, challenges, and images presented in our monologues, which resonated with their own experiences in some form.

Definitions of Canadian identity were amplified in the testimonials of audience members, as they began to analyze the boundaries and responsibilities associated with citizenship. One audience member's questions on voting as a sign of community engagement incited an energetic conversation on the experience of alienation from the processes of self-determination in a liberal democracy. Other conversations that evolved from this performance focused on the healthy formation of identity relative to our ancestral relationship to the physical land upon which we live.

The process and performance of naming and reclaiming our experiences created a space for us, as participants, to embody our willingness to attend to the dynamic, shifting nature of our co-existence. To borrow a lesson from drama therapist David Read Johnson, "[T]he act of creating something from nothing, shaping personal material into aesthetic form, transforming suffering into beauty or art is very empowering" (qtd. in Rubin 19). By this act, we take charge of personal material and issues, rather than being controlled by them. Our collective collaboration in attending to the stories we had chosen to tell brought about a deeper awareness of self and self in society. The act of engaging in a public presentation of self opened our experiences to being witnessed and legitimized. From what I witnessed during the post-performance discussions, it was also a redressive experience for the audience, who spoke of having gained access to their own stories of identity and agency and to questions of belonging, authority, community and citizenship.

Conclusions

Biographical performance provides a way of "looking back to move forward," to borrow an approach from a well-known black feminist, bell hooks (*Teaching*). It is memory work, not for nostalgia's sake, but rather as a strategy for change and for a more meaningful communication between individuals and communities. Our biographical narratives seemed to shift into sociobiographical narratives where we were telling the story of one community, our community, and by this act, inviting others to conceive of themselves in relation to one another in the telling of their stories. Throughout our process, we created the conditions for a performative consciousness—a consciousness that pays attention to the Other's truth, a consciousness that rejects combative debate in favour of the development of the aural capacity, the ability to listen and really hear the Other, as if words and actions were privileged performances. A performative consciousness demands openness, vulnerability, cultivating self-knowledge and assuming responsibility for our own thinking.

Canada has increasingly been forced to deal with the diversity of its national population. The changing racial and ethnic composition within its borders has led to controversy about what it means to be Canadian, as well as concern over the possible weakening of the nation's boundaries. I find that biographical performance can embody a counter-hegemonic politic when it insists upon multiple representations of desire. The process involved in such a project involves a persistent willingness to tolerate the ambiguity associated with how we ingest and interpret the world around us while negotiating our inscribed and prescribed identities. The performance of these negotiations presents a challenge to Canadian cultural relations because it temporarily dethrones the essentialist view of the cultural Other. It leads to uncertainty and therefore creates the conditions for an intellectual practice based on receptivity.

The process implicit in staging (socio)biographical narratives provides the framework necessary for the exploration, definition, and (re)presentation of historical, political, social and cultural influences, as they relate to our positions and spaces of agency within our familial, inter-ethnic and national communities. Here, performance is not just a reflection of preconceived ideas about intercultural co-existence but a dynamic entity that informs what can be reproduced in human action and reaction to societal, political and economic ideology.

Our (socio)biographical performance provided a means of democratic cultural expression that stimulated dialogue, amongst ourselves and with our spectators, on the themes reflected in the performance. In a liberal democracy the cultivation of a public voice is a necessary and urgent project. This form of performance praxis offers individuals and communities the space to realize themselves as cultural producers, able to (re)author and frame their individual and collective histories, as well as produce critically reflective images of themselves.

Through the staging of our own stories, we sought to contribute our voices to the narration of the nation and to attend to the politics of identity and experience. The lucid, temporal and urgent nature of live performance is what rendered it an ideal vehicle through which to mirror and embody this ambiguous third space and render visible our personal and collective experiences of growing up hybrid in Canada. Performance remains an exercise in moving fluidly between frames of action and awareness, where living is experienced as a creative and spontaneous act. I believe that performance that stems from collaboration, as exemplified by this project, is the deliberate extension of this principle into the collective life of our communities. In a world where the often-anxious experience of displacement is all but foreign, a revolutionary space is created through (socio)biographical performance that invites new configurations of bodies in community.

(2004)

Works Cited

Aujla, Angela. "Other in their Land: Second Generation South-Asian Canadian Women, Racism, and the Persistence of Colonial Discourse." *Canadian Women's Studies Journal/Les Cahiers des femmes* 202 (2001):41–47.

Bannerji, Himmani. *The Dark Side of the Nation: Essays on Multiculturalism, Nationalism, and Gender.* Toronto: Canadian Scholar's Press, 2000.

Bhabha, Homi K. "Cultures In-Between." *Questions of Cultural Identity.* Ed. Stuart Hall and Paul du Gay. London: Sage, 1996. 53–60.

———. *The Location of Culture.* London; New York: Routledge, 1994

Bissoondath, Neil. *Selling Illusions: The Cult of Multiculturalism in Canada.* Toronto: Penguin, 2004.

Chaudhuri, Una. "Beyond a 'Taxonomic Theatre': Interculturalism after Postcolonialism and Globalization." *Theatre Journal* 32:1 (2002) 33–47.

Chaudry, Lubna. "Fragments of a hybrid's discourse." In *Emerging voices: South Asian American Women Redefine Family, and Community.* Ed. Sangeeta Gupta. New Delhi: Sage, 1999. 79–91.

Ebron, Paulla and Anna Lowenhaupt Tsing. "In Dialogue: Reading Across Minority Discourses." *Women Writing Culture.* Ed. Ruth Behar and Deborah A. Gordon. Berkeley: U of California P, 1995. 390–411.

hooks, bell. *Remembered Rapture: The Writer at Work.* New York: Henry Holt, 1999.

———. *Teaching to Transgress: Education as the Practice of Freedom.* New York: Routledge, 1994.

James, Sheila. "South Asian Women: Creating Theatre of Resilience and Resistance". *Canadian Theatre Review* 94 (1998):45–54.

Metzger, Deena. *Writing for Your Life: A Guide and Companion to the Inner Worlds.* San Francisco: Harper, 1992.

Rubin, Sheila. "The Role of Storyteller in Self-Revelatory Performance." Masters Thesis. California Institute of Integral Studies, 1996.

Rummens, Joanna Anneke. "Redefining the Canadian Ethos: Towards a Trans-Cultural Citizenship Charter." *Canadian Issues, Thèmes Canadiens.* Montreal: Association for Canadian Studies (February, 2002): 15–18.

Imagination and Art in Community Arts

by Julie Salverson

I want to start with poetry. "It is difficult to get the news from poems, yet men die miserably every day for lack of what is found there" (cited in Rich, ix). Words from a poet, William Carlos Williams. I fell in love with art as a child. I grew up and wanted others to know this language, this difficult place of desire and danger, this invitation to imagine. This language for the inexpressible. In my early twenties I was working in theatres across Canada and started to feel a split between my late-blooming political awareness and my love for art. I became involved in the peace and solidarity movements, and I would go from a rehearsal in a mainstage theatre to a community organizing meeting and think, "Wouldn't art be a useful way to help this process of learning to live together in neighbourhoods?" I started imagining how this could look. I wanted to make theatre in community centres, to—as I put it then—"get the untold stories told." I was very lucky in 1981 to get a Canada Council Explorations Grant to develop a play for an audience of people who were mentally disabled. I found out, by accident, that developing a play *with* this audience was much more satisfying—was electrifying even—than merely developing one *for* them. The accident was this: I was doing a series of weekly workshops with a group of about fifteen adults, most of whom lived in group homes. I did improvisation exercises with them. It was dreadful—experimenting and failing. Then one evening while we were all sitting in a circle, a man arrived late. He was in his early forties; David was his name. He always wore a cowboy hat and carried a lasso. He'd gotten lost on the subway and wanted to talk about it. I let him. Then, for some reason, I turned to the rest of the group and said, "Has anyone else ever gotten lost?" Everybody had, and the energy in that room exploded. So I said, "Well… why don't you get into three groups, and one make a song, one a scene, and one a dance about what it's like to get lost."

That accident changed my life. It revealed the electricity that happens when people speak and are heard, and it also illustrated that what we offer as writers or dancers or musicians or painters is simply another language for that speech. A language that shapes loss and love and hope into a form. And those images that take that language beyond the everyday—that raise it to something that can make us all tremble, just a little—those are poetry. This is true whether the images are musical, visual, or theatrical. Our job as artists is to seek out, find, and name them. Of course, it isn't quite that simple. Who, and why, and when, and where also must be addressed, as well as historical, cultural, and ethical frameworks. I'll get to some of that in a moment.

The project in 1981 grew into the almost-ten-year-run of a company in Toronto called Second Look Community Arts Resource. It's hard to imagine now, but in the early 80s you had to really persuade most arts organizations to give you a grant that involved communities; most thought that kind of work was social work or education. The Toronto Arts Council was a notable exception; also, interestingly enough, were the churches, which had seen how art and politics are not so separate in other cultures. I think, by the way, that now the balance has tipped the other way: you have to make the argument not for community but for art. We are still polarized. However, in 1981 Second Look worked collectively, god help us, and we made it to community centres [in Toronto] such as Regent Park, Central Neighbourhood House, and Scadding Court. And we developed plays with sole-support moms and with young people. Plays about AIDS, about dealing with welfare and the street, about racism: many issues. And what happened was that I got very tired of the kind of theatre we were making: the issues took over the art. So, around 1990, I left. I worked full-time with Theatre of the Oppressed, moving around Canada and a bit in the US, working with Headlines Theatre in Vancouver. And again, I got tired of the theatre we were making and I left. I went to England, but even a rejuvenating stint with Welfare State International and the celebratory adventures of their very politically astute community arts didn't help. I had learned a lot over fifteen years—from popular education, from Paulo Friere, from liberation theology, from development education—but still I was tiring of the need to argue for art. I thought this thing about art was my problem, was about my personal taste. I had been busy trying to make the revolution, but I had gotten lonely for the theatre. I thought that art had to take a back seat to community development, to social change. I thought art was (as Honor Ford-Smith has, ironically, many times described to me theatre for development in Jamaica) to "sugar the pill of the more serious business of education." But over the next ten years—spent mostly writing and teaching writing, sometimes in community projects, sometimes in schools—I redis-covered poetry and theatre. I realized that what I'd thought was my personal taste (wondering, "Is the form beautiful, political, powerful, edgy?") was actually a matter of ethics. I came to this in part from going back to school myself, doing graduate work, and learning about how people struggle through the difficulty of building memorials, creating public memory, translating testimony: things I realized I was doing in participatory theatre. Most of my work has been with survivors of violence. What could the connections be between the form of the theatre we make and the degree of respect and complexity afforded to the stories we tell? I'm going to turn very briefly to some of the projects I've done in the last ten years, and—in postcard fash-ion—highlight the main things I've come to care about.

First, something I call *the lie of the literal*. Art is a language for imagining differ-ent futures, experiencing the past and the present from other angles, and learning to live. I did a play and video with refugees in Toronto in the late 1980s called *Are The Birds In Canada the Same*. The participants were from a number of countries: all artists, all displaced, all survivors of violence. Most participants found it a very valuable experience—but one man did not. He played himself in the play we devel-oped—a play I wrote based on the discussions and improvisations carried out—and he found himself plagued by nightmares and, essentially, re-traumatized by the experience. We don't like to talk about this kind of thing, about the mistakes. What happened during this project prompted me to ask a number of questions. When I learned more about trauma and how it operates—the importance of working through trauma, not recycling it melancholically—I realized that the structure of our process had not allowed this man a chance to work through but only to repeat. This is slippery stuff and there are no formulas, but this experience led me to coin the phrase "the lie of the literal." Here is a short paragraph from an essay I've written about this:

> I am proposing an alternate approach to popular theatre practices (particularly in respect to how such practices engage and represent personal narratives) that speaks a story not as a fixed, knowable finite thing but as an open one that changes and carries with it the possibility of reformings and retellings. "Risky stories," stories of emergency and violation, need to be constructed in such a way that the subtleties of damage, hope, and the "not nameable" can be performed. I am not suggesting a theatre which privileges the aesthetic over the material, the "look" of a theatre piece or story over the urgency of its conveyed meaning. I am suggesting that if the overly symbolic is the evasive, the overly literal is the lie. ("Performing Emergency" 184)

Theatre is not real life. When we reproduce the real life story—in the name of authenticity, of material evidence, of telling the story "correctly"—we often reduce it. People who work with trauma survivors will tell you that the importance of telling a story and having it witnessed is crucial to living with loss. But also critical is having a form outside oneself to "step into" that allows someone who has experienced trauma to "see it" outside of herself. So, when I work with people who are vulnerable, or survivors, I work with the imagination, the invention, the image to step into, not the "real story."

My second point is related to the first, this idea of a too literal telling of a story that reduces its complexity—and, in a way, its dignity—and can run the risk of focusing more on pain than on agency. This time, though, I'm talking about what I call an aesthetic of injury in arts projects with survivors of violence. In another essay I wrote,

> Some years ago I was invited to see a short play at a community college. Student actors and their director had developed a dramatic performance drawn from stories by Bosnian children who had lived through war and extreme violence. The piece opened with the actors lying on the floor doing breathing exercises and inviting the audience to call out thoughts evoked by the idea of land mines. Phrases such as "incomprehensible," "stop it," and "dead, dead" were grimly and vigorously taken up by groups of young performers and turned into tableaus of disaster, which segued into first-person narratives declaring stories of loss and dismemberment tempered with heroics. My disenchantment with this play is not at the expense of the student actors, who no doubt approached the project with sensitivity and the preliminary skills their level of training would allow. What disturbed me was a sense that the students were not present in the performance, were not noticing themselves in the picture, and, consequently, that we as audience members were neither asked nor

able to implicate ourselves. Audience and actors together were looking *out* at some exoticized and deliberately tragic *other*. Even more discomforting than the voyeurism, I felt a participant in what was the almost erotic quality of the manner in which the actors performed pain. Several audience members expressed being extremely moved by the whole thing. But what, I wondered, was our obligation as witnesses to this story, to this unacknowledged pleasure? Yes the audience was moved, but by and towards what? ("Change" 122)

Playwright Daniel David Moses, in both his creative and critical writings, challenges the limits of tragic mimesis (or tragic forms of representing stories). As Moses puts it,

One of the words that always comes up in Native gatherings, and particularly among Native artists, is that it is part of our jobs as Native artists to help people heal [...] To me it sounds as if this [white] guilt is the opposite thing: it seems that you don't want to heal, you want to keep the wound. In romanticism you're dancing around a wound. You have these great desires, these great idealistic possibilities, and then they're cut down and things end in death and it's very sad and beautiful. I've seen the attraction of it [...] but it strikes me as really sick. (qtd. in Appleford 22)

Moses is talking about contemporary mainstream theatre, but his comments apply to what I consider an aesthetic of injury within theatre for social change in English Canada. I suggest that a preoccupation with the experience of loss and a privileging of trauma as a mode of knowledge—both in popular theatre practice and in witnessing and trauma literature—provides an essential yet limiting framework which fixes testimony within a discourse of loss and the tragic, and often presumes testifying to be a monologue not a dialogue. I am beginning to suspect that theatre can offer something here to trauma theory. After all, the interpretation of the act of survival is an act of representation. Which notions of mimesis, of translation, of performance, inform how we live and represent surviving? Can such representations be more than the burden of loss as an absent presence?

The last postcard illustrates a point about the relationship between politics and art. In England in 1958, drama critic Kenneth Tynan accused Romanian absurdist playwright Eugene Ionesco of separating art from the world, and of leading audiences up a "blind alley" (qtd. in Ionesco 89) with an "escape from realism" that led nowhere except to art as a world of its own, answerable to none but its own laws. Ionesco responded by saying that ideological art is inferior to the doctrine it claims to demonstrate, and that if anything needs demystifying it is our ideologies. He says Tynan is making a false distinction between realism and non-realism and is talking in fact about "only one plane of reality, the 'social plane,' which seems to me to be the most external, in other words, the most superficial" (91). The absence of ideology, Ionesco says, "does not mean the absence of ideas: on the contrary, it fertilizes them" (93).

Ionesco is suggesting, I think, that bad art is bad politics. And that distinctions in style—realism is "real life and serious," the absurd or comedic is "frivolous"—are false dichotomies. I want to suggest the same about the ways in which we classify art, in particular "community arts." Right now I am writing the libretto (with composer Juliet Palmer) for an opera about the atom bomb. This project involves research on every level: the professional arts world; the people of Deline, North West Territories (where uranium was mined); the activists in Port Hope, Ontario (where it was refined); researchers in New Mexico (where the Manhattan Project tested the bomb); Hiroshima and Nagasaki. This project is about art, and politics, and history, and communities. It is related to a poetry workshop I do with Ruth Howard at Davenport Perth Community Centre and to the oral histories my students at Queen's University perform with World War II Veterans. It's a strange thing we do in the western world, separating art from life and forcing it into categories. Not everybody does it this way.

I am going to wind up with some of the things I love about collaborative arts projects, and some of the things I hate. I love how excited an old man, Henry, gets when he writes a poem and then listens to the potent silence when he reads it aloud to a group of strangers at a workshop: the hush that falls over the group, the murmurs. He thinks, "I did that, I made them feel that." I love when people who have been fighting about how to keep their children safe in their neighbourhood sew together over a community-centre table and find out they all love the colour red. And when a group of people who all love the colour red sew together over a community-centre table and find out they can join a coalition trying to keep their children safe. And they join, and they bring their strong red banner. I love that.

I hate when I am at a political conference and it is going on all day, and at the break one of the organizers asks me, "Can you do some theatre for an icebreaker, so we can all relax a bit." Theatre as an ice breaker. I hate that. Or when I get a call from a community centre asking me to put some kind of play together about International Women's Day, and then they give me a list of issues that the play needs to "address." I hate that. And when International Women's Day is two weeks away and the person on the phone tells me to "just make sure they have fun"—I hate that even more.

Am I against fun? Am I against issues? Hardly. So what's the problem? The problem is that throwing an exercise or a play together on the fly is an insult to everyone, but most of all an insult to the terrible beauty and staggering potential that art offers should we be willing to meet her on her terms. The problem is that the world is a confusing and scary place, and we need every ounce of imagination we can muster together with the skills to put that imagination into form. This is as true for Henry writing his poem as it is for Margaret Atwood writing her next book.

I always remember some painter telling me in elementary school, "If you want to paint, learn to hold a brush. And then learn to look." The problem is that "art" has become a dirty word. I understand why: we all know about elitism and the arts as a marketplace. But we have gotten so tangled in trying *not* to be elitist, we have thrown out the proverbial baby with the bathwater. The child lives. Her name is art. I want her to come back.

In my twenties, when I started Second Look Community Arts Resource in the early 1980s, I said theatre was a tool. I hate that too. The dictionary calls art "a human creative skill or its application." This is what I think my job is: to work with people who haven't chosen to make their lives about art, but want art in their lives. To introduce skills, a language, another way to speak. Another way to look. That's why I called the company Second Look. By the way, we called ourselves "facilitators" in Second Look, and I hate that too. We wanted to pretend we all knew the same things, which is ridiculous. We all knew the same, more or less, about life, but Henry didn't know how to speak his poem to the back of an auditorium until someone showed him how to open his throat. If you are an artist and someone in a group hires you to show them how to use a paintbrush, then for god's sake show them. If you don't, you are the one making art this big mystery, this special, elitist thing. Hiding our skills as artists is paternalistic and really a way to make ourselves special.

We also did a great deal of collective creation in Second Look, and I want to say a word about that. Collective creation is a misnomer. Creating collaboratively is about people sharing and shaping the details of their dreams, their accidents, their longings. This brings debate and friction and excitement and, perhaps, discovery. And it's only good—rewarding, challenging, questioning—when it's hard work, even if that hard work only lasts thirty minutes. You don't get substance by hauling words and images out of people crudely and quickly, and you don't get it by telling artists to follow your ideas about what issue is currently relevant. Trust them, trust the artists and the people, let them dig deeply and play with their world, and they will surprise you and themselves. That's their job.

Writer Jeanette Winterson says,

> [A]rt has deep and difficult eyes [...] art is a foreign city, and we deceive ourselves when we think it is familiar. No one is surprised that a foreign city follows its own customs and speaks its own language. Only a boor would ignore both and blame his defaulting on the place. Every day this happens to the artist and to art. (4)

Learn to hold a brush. Let someone teach you. Teach someone. Learn to look differently. Art is a language. Respect it. However little or much you engage in it, do it fully. And give painters and sculptors and musicians and writers and designers and actors and all these people who devote their lives to a craft the respect you would give an athlete, or a physician, or a teacher, or a builder: any serious worker who has spent time and energy and heart doing this thing in the world. Learn its language, just a little. It will give back to you tenfold.

(2004)

Works Cited

Appleford, Robert. "The Desire To Crunch Bone: Daniel David Moses and the 'True Real Indian.'" *Canadian Theatre Review* 77 (1993): 21–26.

Ionesco, Eugene. "The London Controversy." *Notes & Counter Notes: Writings on the Theatre.* Grove Press, 1964. 87–108.

Rich, Adrienne. *What is Found There: Notebooks on Poetry and Politics.* New York London: W.W. Norton and Company, 1993.

Salverson, Julie. "Change on Whose Terms? Testimony and an Erotics of Injury." *Theater* 31.3 (2001): 119–25.

———. "Performing Emergency: Witnessing, Popular Theatre, and the Lie of the Literal." *Theatre Topics* 6. 2 (1996): 181–91.

Winterson, Jeanette. *Art Objects: Essays on Ecstasy and Effrontery.* New York: Knopf, 1996.

Practicing Responsible Arts:
The Downtown Eastside Community Play

by Savannah Walling

In the fall of 2003, my company, Vancouver Moving Theatre, produced a community play for Vancouver's Downtown Eastside. Although we've created interdisciplinary and community-related performing arts for over twenty years, this was our first experience creating this type of community play. The responsibilities turned out to be daunting yet inspiring.

Located on a spit of land in Burrard Inlet, the Downtown Eastside is culturally rich and culturally diverse. First Nations people have lived here for over two thousand years. It's been an entry point for immigrants for more than a century. It's the birthplace of the city of Vancouver. For over a hundred years, people have gathered at the Carnegie Building on Hastings and Main to find lost friends, catch up on the news, and connect with the community.

Our Downtown Eastside home is a unique mixed income community of families and singles, housing and industry, shops and parks: distinctive, fluidly shifting, overlapping mini-communities include Gastown, Main and Hastings, Chinatown, and Strathcona. Each street is like walking in a different neighbourhood, filled with people from different walks of life and circumstances. Lots of interesting people doing different things make them interesting blocks to live in. Residents value their heritage and their socio-economic and cultural diversity.

But although it is tremendously strong and united in some ways, the Downtown Eastside is fractured and alienated in others: it's been a divided community whose groups don't readily interact because of mistrust, fear, and indifference that stem from language, cultural, and socio-economic differences. An inner-city location means inner-city problems: hard times, poverty, homelessness, prostitution, and drug dealing, as well as the pressures of gentrification and urban development. Still, after years of struggle—against demolition, incompatible new construction, and being treated as a "dumping ground" for the larger city's social problems—the community survives. We love our neighborhood.

For thirty years, the Downtown Eastside has been home to me and my husband and colleague, Terry Hunter. It's the community that gave birth to our art, to our company and professional practice, and in which we gave birth to our son. Perhaps that's why fate, along with the urging of the Carnegie Community Centre, saw to it that we produce this community play for the Downtown Eastside as the culminating event of Carnegie's one-hundredth anniversary celebration.

Carnegie's vision was inspired by a form of community play discovered in Britain in the 1970s by playwright Ann Jellicoe and brought to Canada by Dale Hamilton. Canadian adaptations of the form have been produced in Saskatchewan, Manitoba, Ontario and B.C. In this kind of community play, a small core of experienced theatre artists work with community members (as many as want to participate) to create an artistic work of the highest achievable standard to express and celebrate their community—a play for and by the community. The artists are responsible for relating to the whole community, working in partnership with the existing systems, and refraining from taking sides on divisive issues. The artist's job is not tell them what to think, but to listen and learn from the community and look for opportunities for people to create art and get involved—because the more they help, the more interested they are.

We knew the task was too big, the time line too short, and the resources on hand insufficient. But we also knew the Downtown Eastside has tremendous talent. We knew the community's problems have been sensationalized in the Canadian media and its rare gifts ignored. We knew it was our turn to serve to the best of our ability. The vision was inspiring—and terrifying.

The pressures to succeed were immense. As Aboriginal community actor Stephen Lytton said, "[The] production was an enormous task, being where it's coming from. And the failure of it would have been far more damaging because of where it's come from. It was like carrying the weight of the whole community on your shoulders."[1]

Terry and I live in the Downtown Eastside. We couldn't leave after the play finished. We would have to live with the consequences: if our work fell short, the whole community would pay—not just us. What if our efforts shed an even worse light on the Downtown Eastside and its residents? We needed all the help we could get. It came slowly and in many forms. As organizing committee member Bob Eberle said, "There was tremendous collective will to make it happen. We were creating something historic that was important to the neighbourhood. It was important to hear a play that was powerful and spoke to the neighbourhood in a truthful voice."

Our community play turned into an epic, year-long event that involved over two thousand volunteers and twenty-five professional artists in every aspect: research and sharing stories; processions and skill building workshops (43 in all); building costumes, puppets, and sets; helping backstage; and performing. The project scale strained our small "mom and pop" company. It strained the play's resources. It strained our marriage. Everyone involved was over-extended and over-worked. There were so many different responsibilities, from small to enormous, that we often had to remind ourselves we were only creating a play.

Our first responsibility was to make sure that we and our co-producing partner were climbing the same mountain. (It took a month to work out the details.) We agreed to operate according to the purpose and principles outlined by the Carnegie Centre. We agreed to celebrate the Downtown Eastside community's past, portray its present in all its variety, and share visions for the future. Focusing on issues the community thinks are important and giving voice to those who live there, we were to build new connections in a shared experience that bridged the neighbourhood's diverse cultural and socio-economic groups. We agreed to hire a culturally diverse team of artists that included women (and East End residents) in leadership positions, to develop capacity in the arts, and to support the community in making art. As part of the larger purpose of improving perceptions about the neighbourhood, we were to get media and the larger community out to the play. We had to fundraise for the play and keep the project on budget and well managed. We agreed to balance process and product, and leave behind archives of the process, materials, and production.

We were also responsible for meeting the Vancouver Moving Theatre's artistic mandate. We set out to create a meaningful, accessible show that engaged people's hearts, minds, and imaginations, and to this end we had to tailor the event for this unique community. Our theatre strives to stimulate new art through the interdisciplinary and intercultural exchange of ideas. Sometimes we put student and community performers onstage with professional performers. And of course we would strive to deliver professional service, quality, and value while working with an attitude of partnership, cooperation, and respect.

The artistic goals of this particular community play gave rise to further responsibilities. Our task was to write a musical play honouring the people and history, struggles and triumphs, cultures, and art forms of the Downtown Eastside. To this end, we planned to research significant events and experiences via an outreach program that would involve hundreds of people. We would retell stories heard over and over again and make up new stories inspired by real people, and then distill the script to stories of struggle and triumph that insisted on being heard today. We needed to create a script that would remain coherent while incorporating and interweaving as many voices, stories, songs, and perspectives as possible, and build in an unlimited number of characters for up to a hundred actors. We were responsible for assembling a strong team of artists who knew the neighbourhood, were good at what they do, understood and enjoyed a collaborative process, and had experience guiding and enthusing community volunteers—all towards establishing a collaborative process for generating new material, sharing images and ideas, and crystallizing themes. On a more mundane but still challenging level, we had to convert an empty hall into a theatre and clothe over one hundred and ninety characters. And finally, overall, we were responsible for mounting the play effectively and doing our best to provide everyone involved with a positive experience.

With regard to our co-workers, Terry and I were responsible for providing an achievable plan of duties with clear priorities and goals, resources to fulfill the tasks, and follow-through on ideas and plans. We were responsible overall to admit to our mistakes and—to the best of our ability—to do no harm. We knew we had to be mindful of the consequences when we were making choices—some could help and some could harm. Decisions needed to fit our intentions, our resources, and our community. We tried to make our choices transparent, to acknowledge all help, to let things happen slowly, and when in doubt to compromise. We knew every person we met had something important to teach.

We also had responsibilities with regard to the neighbourhood. We needed to consult with the community (providing Chinese translation wherever we could) to determine subject matter, themes, music, and presentational styles, and incorporate their feedback to make sure the language and stories had the ring of truth, were culturally respectful, historically accurate, and honestly portrayed the Downtown Eastside. In all this, we had to honour the neighbourhood's unique social, historical, and physical characteristics; to witness without judgment and respect what it takes to cope and survive in hard times; and to give voice in a non-intrusive way to social issues that come up over and over again. We had, in short, to look at harsh realities without overlooking the "phoenix in the ashes." Our community needed to see and recognize itself in the play and production.

We also were responsible for hundreds of volunteers. We had to provide a safe and confidential place for sharing stories. We needed to cope respectfully with difficult issues involving security and inclusion-exclusion so we could provide a safe working environment for everyone, ensuring that everyone was treated with respect in every circumstance. We had to provide a fun, friendly, welcoming, and smoothly running environment for rehearsals and building sets and props. We were responsible for providing three months of healthy snacks on a limited budget for an unpredictable number of volunteers (some of them in great need) and bringing in tangible benefits as play resources improved (two cast suppers, four weeks of child care, complementary tickets, and an archival DVD of the show). And after the show, we had to provide transition events to close the circle on the project in a helpful way and ease the inevitable post-production letdown

The hundreds of participants were volunteers. They were unpaid, generously giving of their time and drawing on their courage to move into new territory. As professional artists in a community play, we had to be fully prepared at each rehearsal, support and speak with respect to cast members at every step of the process, and work out differences between members of the artistic team at another time and place.

The responsibilities we faced were large and multi-faceted. From the first day, the idea of a community play evoked both excitement and negativity. We faced distrust (of new money, new faces, and big budget projects) and suspicion (of "poverty pimps" and "make-work" projects). We met tensions (between cultural groups, between neighbourhoods, between "haves" and "have-nots") and resentment (toward foreign community play models that employ some and expect others to volunteer). Over the year, we stumbled onto bad memories, bad dreams, and bad feuds. We faced language, literacy, economic and cultural barriers, and issues of food, poverty, legal and illegal drugs, safety, and security. In order to make the play a familiar, welcoming, and intriguing presence in the Downtown Eastside and to build a web of support, we hired an outreach team who lived or worked in the Downtown Eastside's historical neighbourhoods and understood their concerns. We met with people and organizations to learn how we could work with them and what they could bring. We attached play-related events to existing programs and provided excellent and accessible skill-building workshops. In short, we did our best to meet distrust, suspicion, and resentment with respect and patience, and provide a safe and inviting public event where people could socialize and enjoy creative activity.

These responsibilities were enormously challenging. We drew on the experience of over thirty years of professional and community work. We learned on the job. We didn't always succeed. We worked as hard as we could for one year, but nothing we could do was enough—ever. We could have/should have/wanted to have met more people, talked to more people, and involved more people.

We worked too fast. We created a project that normally takes two to three years in just one. We took nine weeks to rehearse the kind of community play that normally takes twelve. Relationships take time to build. Trust takes time to grow. As organizing committee member Bob Eberle said, "You realized how fragile the thing was and the huge damage if it had failed."

The experience was not perfect for the participants. Some felt the volunteers should have been paid. As participant coordinator Leith Harris reported, some feelings were hurt and some people got lost along the way. Some people did not like their assigned lines, or did not understand the English, or could not read and were too shy to say. Some people misplaced their schedules or scripts. Some did not have phones and messages went astray. Some did not like the food. Others were disappointed or felt betrayed when a song was cut. Some things went missing. When security and issues of inclusion and exclusion arose, creative, respectful, effective solutions had to be found.

Nor was the experience perfect for the artists. The artistic team was over-worked and needed two more weeks of rehearsal and more staff—including a chef! Sometimes people got sick. People didn't always get along. Sometimes they did not have enough resources or experience for the task at hand, or they were not as prepared as they should have been. And sometimes their vision was bigger than the available resources.

People faced family emergencies, plumbing problems, computer crashes, accidents, deaths, robberies, evictions, alcohol and drug issues, mental health and personality issues and many economic barriers. But, as Leith Harris wrote in a a poem called "The Downtown Eastside Community Play," published in the *The Carnegie Newsletter*,

> The genuine caring
> and generous sharing
> of time, energy and knowledge
> made it all worthwhile and more.
> Plus—THE AUDIENCES LOVED IT!

When serious concerns emerged, cast members brought them to the producer as respectful petitions. Cast and artists were careful to protect the show and the rehearsal process.

Finally the miracle was accomplished: the play went up, sold out seven of eight shows, and earned standing ovations. Everything worked wonderfully well: the lights, costumes, music, choreography and script. The actors portrayed their characters with conviction, spoke with passionate understanding, and formed a strong, supportive team. I was so humbled to be in the presence of such strength and beauty, I cried for an hour after the first night.

The responses to the play, by both those on the stage and those in the audience, illustrate how overwhelming the experience was. "We met the challenge," stated Stephen Lytton, a community actor, "[W]e, as a people, came together and succeeded in that mandate of building bridges. The sweetest part was that we had worked together." Mary MacAulay, a Downtown Eastside resident, was full of praise: "*The Downtown Eastside Community Play* was powerful and humbling and magical and educational. Many of our friends, neighbours, and my daughter's classmates were in it and loved it from the inside out. We loved it from the inside in. We wanted to see it twice, but it was sold out. Bravo!" And Jo Ledingham's review in *The Vancouver Courier* was likewise enthusiastic: "*In the Heart of a City* beats with vitality and hope…. These funny and brave performers are proof that the courage and humour that kept Main and Hastings alive and kicking through the nineteenth and twentieth centuries is still around."

After the run of eight shows was finished, the aftermath arrived. Some cast members felt lost. The artistic team was exhausted. I was burnt out, emptied. Our company had no plans for the future. Who had had time to plan? We didn't know that wrapping up the play would consume one more year.

Big questions arose. When the consequences of failure are so immense, how ethical is it to commit to such an enormous project before you have the resources in place to pull it off? How ethical is it to do a big community arts project without some kind of sustaining follow-up? As organizing committee member Jil P. Weaving asked, "What do you do after the party leaves town and not everybody gets a goody bag?" Who does the follow-up? The artist? The community partners? The funding agencies? The community? But what could we do? Carnegie is a community centre, not an arts producer. The directors of Vancouver Moving Theatre are middle-aged and moving into new phases of personal practice.

This is what we've done. After the play ended, we organized a series of low-key transition events, including a thank-you party, a post-mortem workshop for participants, showings of the archival DVD, and a power-point display on the making of the play. We created an eight-panel display on *The Downtown Eastside Community Play*, which is now on permanent display at the Carnegie Community Centre. Carnegie Community Centre committed to produce a community arts festival, create a five-year community arts business plan, and research the feasibility of setting up an independent nonprofit arts organization within two years. Terry, as the executive director of Vancouver Moving Theatre, advised the community centre on these plans.

Vancouver Moving Theatre co-produced (with the Carnegie Community Centre) *The Heart of the City Festival*, which finished on October 24, 2004. Over four hundred artists (most from the Downtown Eastside) performed in sixty-two events at over twenty-five locations. This time we paid honorariums to all the artists. Festival events included a panel of community play participants, *The Downtown Eastside Play—One Year Later,* staged readings of three new original plays, and songs by local writers, *Through the People's Voice,* as well as two days of information sharing and skill building workshops for local actors, *Breaking into the Biz Forum.* From January 28 to February 6 this past winter, we associate produced (with NeWorld Theatre and PuSH International Performing Arts Festival) James Fagan Tait's adaptation of the novel *Crime and Punishment.* This project added five performers from the community play to a team of fifteen professional actors. These events are Vancouver Moving Theatre's way of saying "thank you" to the enormously talented community who supported last year's Downtown Eastside community play.

People in the Downtown Eastside are excited about the emerging community of artists and the circle of energy and hope. Community artists are excited about making and presenting all kinds of art and speaking about the community in their own voice. They are looking for training, self-employment, and job opportunities that will allow them to produce their art and live with dignity. Carnegie Community Centre hopes to make arts and culture an integral part of the economic and social renewal of the Downtown Eastside Community.

But what is next? And whose responsibility is it?

(2005)

Note

[1] All quotations unless otherwise noted are from informal interviews and conversations that took place over the course of the project and its aftermath. [The specific dates and places are unrecoverable-ed.]

Works Cited

Harris, Leith. "The Downtown Eastside Community Play." *The Carnegie Newsletter* (15 January 2004): 5.

Ledingham, Jo. "Inner city play has lots of heart." *The Vancouver Courier* (3 December 2003): 36.

The Cultural Equivalent of Daycare Workers?

by Ruth Howard

I will start with a quotation, a memory and some questions:

The quotation is from a column by Peter Harris in the Community Arts Ontario's Newsletter, *ArtsOn* in 2003. He ventures that, although we must "resist the idea that *community artists* are a special subset of artists in general, not all of us may be comfortable in the role of the cultural equivalent of daycare workers."

Over a year later I was still chuckling and bristling at this phrase, and sent this email to Amelia Potter in July 2004:

> I laughed when I read that because on one level it is so undeniably true, as anyone who has spent any time with us at DPNC will attest to. But it's also not true—or at least it's what's not true about it that makes the work worthwhile.

And now the memory, which takes us back three years to an arts drop-in at Davenport Perth Neighbourhood Centre (DPNC): the artists make tea, prepare snacks, listen, chat and lay out a variety of art activities for participants of varied ages, origins and abilities. An elderly woman arrives, whom we greet with smiles and tea but no common tongue. She has brought a pair of nylon underpants and wants to use our sewing machine to add some lace to its borders. In fact, she expects us to provide her with the lace to do so, and is mildly indignant that we don't have quite the right colour. When she has finished her sewing, she asks us for transit tickets for her round trip. All of this is within the broad continuum of our project expectations. Perhaps she will come back next week and take some interest in our activities; perhaps she did. I don't remember.

But the *lace-on-the-underwear* incident became our catch phrase for questions we were starting to ask ourselves: What, if any, is the point of connection between the desires and intentions of the artists and the participants? Do they know why we think we are doing it? Do we know why they are doing it? Does it matter if in either case the answer is "no"? Does it matter if the reasons are different, as long as both are satisfied? What does any of this have to do with "art"? In what ways aren't we "the cultural equivalent of daycare workers"? In short, should we be dismayed or delighted that people see us as an excellent opportunity to mend their underwear?

Posing these questions prompted me to conceive of an evaluative process that would examine the "relationship between artist and community members." This scheme received some funding from the Laidlaw Foundation, via Community Arts

Ontario's *In-Print Dialogue* Program. What I proposed was the documentation of four typical days in the life of our DPNC *Arts For All* drop-in at one-month intervals: recording "community participants' comments," taking photographic snapshots, and writing my own reflections in a journal: "particularly my own artistic concerns, which often have no place to be aired within a community context."

Unfortunately, after documenting for two days in this fashion, with interviews conducted by Mara Shaughnessy, a Jumblies intern at the time, most of my data was lost in a car theft. Almost a year later, in an attempt to revive the project, I hired video-grapher and researcher Amelia Potter to interview *Arts For All* artists and participants, and DPNC staff members. [1] As well, I still had one surviving set of un-transcribed audio interviews (conducted by artist Mara Shaughnessy). After yet more time passed, I hired Amelia Potter again to transcribe these disparate interviews. While doing so, she added her own commentary, which prompted an interesting e-mail dialogue. And then I got busy again, moved on to a new multi-year project, and this conversation became yet more unsifted material.

Which brings us to the present: a new article to write, the same questions of ethics and aesthetics in the air. And so I revisit these fragments of voices over a three-year period, and find them intriguing: perhaps more than they would have been at first. The questions that Mara and Amelia ask, approximately a year apart, are not identical in quality, partly because both the *Arts For All* project and my thinking about the work had moved on, and partly due to the chance differences in interviewer styles, back-grounds of interviewees, and scope of the requested task: Mara used an audio recorder, and only interviewed participants, most of whom didn't speak much English and were relatively new to the project, while Amelia used video, interviewed more long-term and English-speaking participants, and also talked to staff and artists—the latter to replace the journal idea, which I had abandoned as too self-conscious, having lost my first attempt.

I would like, nonetheless, to offer some of these comments as glimpses into what is artistically compelling in this community-engaged work, why some artists would actively seek to do it, and how one can stray and play in the space of this "cultural day-care," and still remain in the realm of "art."

What I was prepared to discover from the interviews was a verification of the *lace-on-the-underwear* theory: that the participants and the artists' sense of what they were doing and why they were doing it didn't necessarily correlate. What I had expected provocatively to propose was that this disjoint in perspective was not incompatible with art-making as I wanted to extend its definition.

In fact, the participants do indeed express a variety of reasons that have nothing to do with art for coming to our project in the first place:

> …mainly I come to give me something to do with my days. A lot of my time is pretty well free 'cause I'm on disability and I'm not working, and I really can't hold a full time job 'cause of what happened to me in the past, and I reminisce about that a lot, so I just keep busy with hobbies.

> I come because I need to have Canadian experience—for job, for everything. But now I can't speak English well, so I need to do something and to learn something for future…

> …basically I was trained a lot in my country, and when I came here I asked about what kind of volunteer section they have: they told me they have places for art or working in the kitchen. Then I choose art and I like it.

This awareness of these non-artistic motives can be disorienting for the artist:

> For me at first it was interesting because I didn't realize that people participating in this had quite different motivations. So, as that's become clear, my ability to work with the diverse groups we have has become stronger—or, I wouldn't necessarily say stronger, but maybe clearer. Because people are coming here for volunteer hours and very specific personal reasons in terms of their own goals. And recognizing that what I'm doing with them if I'm running a drama workshop is part of their participation, and it might mean that they're going to be involved in the play; or it may mean that they're just logging their hours as is required. That for me was a big realization. I did start to think "Well who am I then?" (Varrick Grimes)

What, more surprisingly, the transcripts also indicate, backed up now by observations over several years, is that over time the DPNC participants, whatever their original impetus, begin to talk about art and the aims and value of our arts project with growing ease, subtlety, depth of understanding and personal investment. This change doesn't take long to become apparent: the following comment was made by a woman on her third visit to our drop-in:

> That is a good pass-time and you have a good school for your talent, and it is open and you can do something good and creative, which you like. When your piece is done it's like giving birth to a new art! When I came here the organizers gave me the things. They cut it for me, and they said, "you have to do something—whatever you like—it depends upon your creation." So, they give me some ideas and I gave some ideas of mine and these are working together.

Another young woman involved with *Arts For All* for three months, when asked why she keeps coming, says:

> Because it's art, because people need to learn everything I think. I like to learn everything because it's better I think for life, for mind—everything!

And a participant for almost two years says:

> Before I used to think when I was making something that I had to copy things—that's what I was supposed to do. But I have learned from you

> that I can pull ideas out of my mind and make with them something new.

How different are these sentiments from my own?

> I guess what I'm really trying to accomplish here is to create a really beautiful, interesting, powerful piece of art—piece of theatre, which at the same time involves everyone who comes in and wants to be part of it in a way that's meaningful for them. (Ruth Howard)

By the time our large-scale 2004 performance of *Once A Shoreline* was approaching, many participants, despite barriers of ability and language, could comfortably explain the imagistic and logistical complexities of the piece:

> Yeah it is a story of some long long time ago here on Davenport Road and after the lake was no more water here—and the first immigrants in Canada they came and stayed here in Toronto and lived in the district of Davenport and I remember that 'cause I was one of them myself.... The play is going to be very big.

> You gotta have 8, maybe 10 puppeteers, maybe 15 people doing the boats, choirs, a few other people, the main characters, winds, voices, so maybe 30, maybe 50, maybe a little bit more, maybe a little less.

> We're supposed to do what our imagination would tell us it was like if we were trying to survive on a faraway island and what we do to return home.

The gulf that I was prepared to defend does not, in fact, seem to exist in any enduring way. The lace-sewing seems to fall into the same category as the tea-drinking: a conducive context—and this I will come back to later on—for our artistic desires and aims.

When we turn to the artists, it is clear that this acquisition on the part of the participants of a language and understanding of art is not just the product of a one-sided facilitation by artist-service providers, but part of a reciprocal process that is a central artistic ingredient of our community-engaged artwork. The artist's point of view sometimes remains in the shadows in aesthetic frameworks that shed light on the experiences of participants/performers and public/audience. Theatre scholars, for example, have talked about an aesthetics of "emergence" in shows involving untrained actors (Fancy, Little). Our artists' transcripts point to what might be seen as another distinctive aesthetic factor: one that has to do with lack of control:

> ...EVERYTHING that you propose has to be reconsidered. Never at any point in time do I feel I'm bending everybody to my will, which is sometimes the perception that you're feeling in other theatre... but here there are MASSIVE variables. (Varrick Grimes)

> ...you have this artistic idea and are sharing with other people and it's not quite how one expects: they don't quite do what you expect.... And

it's about playing with that and seeing what you can do under those cir-cumstances, which in some ways is what theatre's all about anyway, but here it's much more so…. All these people, do they even know I expect them to come and perform? Or, even if I have said that, are people going to do it? Why would I think they're going to come? I've seen in past experience that people will do that and like to do that but I don't know if these people will—so there's everyone carrying their rafts, but are they going to do that in front of an audience? Or, do people even know there's going to be an audience? (Ruth Howard)

There is an overall sense from the artists that the work is about doing what you can, then going along with what happens…. (Amelia Potter)

In explaining the work that I do in artistic terms, I have often described it as my pre-ferred *box of crayons*. But it suddenly strikes me how peculiar these crayons are: they can walk away at any moment, or start drawing something else on their own if they feel like it, which once again raises questions. What kind of art comes out of such an unstable and recalcitrant medium? What, if anything, can be done better this way, in terms of artistic outcome? It is, at any rate, interesting to view this non-coercive dynamic as an aesthetic quality rather than simply an unavoidable nuisance. It cer-tainly places an imperative on interlinking process and product, which leads us to another common theme amongst the artists interviewed: their immersion in rela-tionships with the participants.

I think the thing that has amazed me the most is the relationships that I've had with people. There are so many worlds I've been introduced to—just incredible…. And, as an actor, writer you're mining, always try-ing to find stories all the time, here people just tell them to you! If you sit with them for half a minute you've got a wicked story, and it's such a privilege!… The whole subtext is just these relationships with people who I care about. And that's great. You don't find that often in profes-sional theatre. (Mara Shaughnessy)

…Getting to make my own art alongside of people—here I get to do this. I get to have these conversations with Al, like about his puppet designs and awesome cardboard boat designs and that kind of stuff. And being inspired by people and inspiring people…. (Noah Kenneally)

My relationship to the community has been a really interesting and fun experience… through that process I feel like I've gotten to know people. It's kind of funny to say, but them enacting another character sort of brings out amazing things in people that you don't get to see when you're just chit chatting. And, it's very exciting. (Wende Bartley)

I would say that this experience on the part of the artists of receiving a gift of artistic value from the participants—the setting up of the conditions under which this can happen—is one of the necessary ingredients for a process of community-engaged arts creation, as distinct from the more detached function of the daycare worker, social service programmer or art teacher. Rachael Van Fossen talks about the community artist as "an agent of change in herself" (4). Putting ourselves in situations where this change can happen and impact on our artistic practice is the counterpart to the equally important but better-documented transformative power of community arts for its participants, and locates the artist, as well as the participant and audience, within the aesthetic of "emergence."

> …Just as for everyone else who walks in the door to take part—and I have to find a way for them to have it be worthwhile and meaningful so that they can grow creatively and so on—I need to allow the same thing for myself… and so I have to be out pushed into a scary place—to an exciting kind of challenging place—where I'm doing stuff that I haven't done before just like all the other participants are. (Ruth Howard)

* * *

The importance of this transformative interchange is highlighted by the difference in the way the artists and the staff talk about *Arts For All*:

> The artists and DPNC staff seem to have a really different conception of what the work is about… this is reflected in how they talk about the community at the centre. The artists tend to call them "participants," while the staff members tend to call them "clients" and to speak a lot more about the problems the clients might be coming to the centre for. (Amelia Potter)

The staff members also favour the word "program" over "process," "project" or "production" and tend to speak in the third person:

> I just think it's a terrific program. There should be more like it in other centers. And I honestly believe that the volunteers truly love and are proud of the program…. That's what DPNC is about: our clients, and respect.

> *Arts for All* is a great program because it includes all the different programs, the youth, the adults, the seniors. The seniors have been able to explore their ideas and use their skills through art.

Notably, the staff member interviewed who had been most engaged herself in our activities, at one points makes a sudden switch from third to first person: from the external service provider to someone within the artistic relationship:

> *Arts for All* is bringing happiness to all the programs. So, we're able to exchange: to participate with youth, children, seniors, like we're all more integrated through *Arts for All*.

We can now contemplate the snacks, tea-drinking and chatting—not to forget the underwear sewing—as more than chores of the cultural daycare, and also more than "outreach strategies," but rather as the water in which we all, artist and participant, dip our paint brushes:

...It's really amazing how much discussion happens, like how much chatting gets done, at the same time as this.... (Mara Shaughnessy)

...It involves a lot of drinking of tea and snacks too, which isn't necessarily a bad thing. (Varrick Grimes)

...When I came in I was tired and cold. I had a beautiful lovely tea, which made me refreshed, yes, and warm. (*Arts For All* Participant)

I heard myself in a recent conversation say cheerfully that I was "inclined to think of most things as art," and I do increasingly feel that the created social context and relationships are part of the "art" and not just the means of achieving it. This does not, however, in any way diminish the importance of the artistic thing we are creating in whatever media. In one message to Amelia Potter I say that the distinctive feature of community art, as opposed to anthropological research, is:

...that with art we are making something together. The learning, changes and reflections are by-products. It's the actual making of the art, in however expanded a way one defines that, which is the main thing.

I believe that the best of our work occurs when we can hold these ideas together as one: the ideas of *transformative exchange* and of *making something together*: process and product, if you like, but at the point where they become indistinguishable. Certainly in *community arts*—and to some extent, I would venture, in any artistic endeavor—the process (which can include "most things") and the product (the *thing* that we are "making together") are contexts and pretexts for each other. And it is with this awareness that we can best speak as artists about what we are doing:

I don't think there is a separation for me (between "art that consciously takes inspiration from life" and "other art").... Well, with music, it's a very abstract art form and I've always struggled with that. I've always tried to find a way in through something that was not about music.... So, I guess that's what I mean when I say, "there's never been a separation." (Wende Bartley)

It's interesting for me personally because at first I was kind of frustrated... but then after a while you realize that these circumstances provide a really interesting opportunity for things that I can do as director living in Toronto that I would never be able to do even with a massive budget... so basically there are fabulous, fabulous opportunities available in this context.... That is certainly my personal stake in it all. It's not necessarily the reason I started doing it: it's actually probably a better reason than the reason. (Varrick Grimes)

...So I'm very focused on what my vision of this show's going to be or this whole process but you have to kind of negotiate that—but I'm also very focused on making everybody happy, you know? So some of what I'm trying to accomplish is to allow those two things to happen simultaneously and enhance each other instead of jostle and detract from each other. It's just not easy, sometimes there's a real contradiction in that, and sometimes it works. (Ruth Howard)

When it works, it's not just the participants who care about the tea, conversation and personal needs, and it's not just the artists who care about the things we are making. As one participant exclaims, covering aesthetics, participant emergence and audience response all in one breath, as the production approaches:

> I want this to come out really good. I am very excited just talking about it. I hope all the people come and see the play.

* * *

I don't want to romanticize, or gloss over the real "frustration" mentioned earlier: the days we feel like we're "only here to make tea and wash dishes" (Noah Kenneally), and a "scrambling around kind of feeling" (Ruth Howard), which makes it:

> ...quite hard to keep a grip on what I'm trying to accomplish because it's where a certain aspect of what I'm trying to accomplish bumps right up against another aspect of the work.... Like today one of the things I was trying to accomplish was to get straight strips of fabric cut for textured costumes which I thought was a good task for lots of people to join in... but we didn't have any sharp scissors, which makes it hard to cut, and it's one of those things that you would think is easier than it is... so that's why it's hard to think of the big picture when this last little while what I've been trying to accomplish is not get all my fabric ripped into little shreds. (Ruth Howard)

In fact, and in my very own words: *"It's so much to keep everyone going that sometimes you just feel like you're, not exactly running a daycare centre, but something like that...."*

Nonetheless and essentially, it is about something else entirely: something to do with the serious wanting and "striving" in these deliberately mingled categories of artist, participant, partner and audience, which stirs in with our tea and weaves into the things and events we are making. And the mingling and wanting and making combined is what makes it "come out really good" when it does: and the coming out *really good* is what we are all changed by and end up able to talk about, and what draws us to putting together the ideas of "community" and "art", in a society where this isn't a pairing so obvious that it needn't be mentioned.

(2006)

Notes

[1] This documentation by Amelia Potter became the basis of my short documentary *Those Dreaded Dichotomies*, made at Vancouver's Documenting Engagement Institute in 2004, and produced as part of a suite of videos about community artists by Pacific Cinemateque.

Works Cited

Fancy, David. "Prometheus Performed: the aesthetics of the untrained actor in emancipatory theatre practice." Paper presented to the Canadian Assocation for Theatre Research. Halifax, 2003.

Harris, Peter. "A Word from the Front Lines: Community Arts Guest Editorial." *ArtsOn* (Community Arts Ontario) Newsletter (Fall 2003): 8.

Howard, Ruth. "Those Dreaded Dichotomies." *Docmenting Engagement* video suite. Vancouver: Pacific Cinemateque and Roundhouse Community Centre, 2004.

Little, Edward. "Towards a Poetics of Popular and Community-engaged Theatre." *Directing and Authorship in Western Drama*. Ed. Anna Migliarisi. NY/Ottawa/Toronto: Legas, 2006. 153–70.

Van Fossen, Rachael. "The Artist as Agent of Change in Herself." Keynote address. Artists as Agents of Social Change symposium. Common/Weal/CARFAC. Saskatchewan Cultural Exchange Society: Regina, October 2002.

The Politics of Play:
Welfare State's Swan Song

by Clarke Mackey

> As a twelve-year-old I could draw like Raphael,
> but it has taken me my whole life to learn to paint like a child.
>
> Pablo Picasso [1]

Growing up, the kids in my family dressed in homemade costumes and built struc-tures we could inhabit and destroy, improvising elaborate narratives for days on end. These narratives were a bricolage of current books, movies, and TV shows put through the blender of our collective imaginations. In the backyard, forts, spaceships, schooners, castles—all were fashioned from overturned garden furniture, musty old blankets, and discarded lumber. Later, when I worked as a daycare teacher, I came to realize that children—all children as far as I could tell—want to move, sing, imagine themselves as someone else, paint, speak in rhymes, and fashion three-dimensional objects with magic powers. This is the origin of art, and the desire to make art comes naturally to all human beings. Like talking, we just did it, without having to take lessons. Somewhere along the way, however, most children are told that only a few people have talent and the rest of us don't. By the time they're in grade six or seven they've abandoned those childish games and learned to enjoy prepackaged art and entertainment. But the fundamental desire to imagine and make things is still there and expresses itself daily: cooking, gardening, hobbies, family celebrations and musi-cal jam sessions. I've come to call these unofficial, homemade activities *vernacular* culture.

Vernacular culture was very much on my mind last year as I sat in the bleachers of an enormous circus tent near Ulverston, a market town in England's Lake District, bundled up against the uncommonly cold winter, waiting for *Longline: The Carnival Opera* to begin. As the last of the three hundred audience members—children, old hippies, townspeople, and intellectuals—streamed in, I could feel the weight of the moment in the air. It was to be Welfare State International's last show. This loosely organized gang of "makers" and performers started putting on "events" far removed from any form of legitimate theatre or art gallery way back in the late 1960s. Unlike most of their counter-culture compatriots, however, they didn't turn into respectable doctors, TV producers, or academics. The founders of Welfare State remained authen-tic anarchists, continuing to practice a community-based celebratory theatre into the new century. In the process, along with the Bread and Puppet Theatre in Vermont, they became the inspiration for scores of political theatre groups and events around the world. Companies like Shadowland in Toronto and Public Dreams Society in

Vancouver owe their origins to Welfare State International, as do the lantern processions for AIDS and Hiroshima Day now held in many cities.

Longline was their "exit rite of passage" according to Welfare State's founder John Fox.[2] Billed as an ecological fable, the opera was the culmination of a three-year "community residency." Working out of a renovated architectural marvel called Lanternhouse on one of the town's main streets, Welfare State artists lived and worked in the community of Ulverston recording oral history, songs, and stories; creating rites of passage, exhibitions, installations, performances, and concerts; organizing workshops, lectures, meetings; and producing CDs and DVDs. The purpose of *Longline* was to tie all these strands together into a final celebration within the community. Two weeks later, on April Fool's Day 2006, Welfare State International ceased to exist, and the two people who were its driving force, John Fox and Sue Gill, became freelance artists once again.

The circus ring stage was surrounded on three sides by audience. The five-piece band inhabited the back quarter and, above them, a collection of circular and rectangular screens projected the slides and videos that ran as a kind of chorus through the show's two hours. Using wall-to-wall music and a menagerie of carnival and circus techniques, *Longline* told the story of a rock in neighbouring Morecambe Bay from a million years ago into the future. Four other characters witnessed the changes of time and progress along with the rock: Jack, a fisherman; Gladys, "the dreamer"; and the ghosts of Sam, an immigrant slave from the West Indies, and the Blue Orphan girl, so named because she was covered in blue dye from a Victorian factory where she laboured making laundry soap. As the story progressed, the rock was swallowed up by rising levels of sea and sand caused by climate change. The other characters were subdued by the war-making institutions of global capitalism. In the end, as must happen in all celebratory pageants, the evils were dramatically vanquished and the humble characters triumphed—in this case, the rock transformed into a space ship. Jack, Gladys, Sam, and the Blue Orphan Girl all took off into outer space in search of a new life. The decision to make exiting the planet the only choice available for our meek victims of environmental and social collapse was just one example of the dark heart beating at the centre of this ambitious work.

How does one evaluate a performance like this? The visual images (moving sculptures is one way of imagining them) were astonishing. It was Welfare State's métier to create brilliant, heart-crushing, unsentimental images using the detritus of consumer civilization. There were moments of great theatrical power—for instance, when the Jack and Gladys puppets hold hands and "sing" a duet of friendship, their puppeteers and singers tenderly surrounding them. The score by Tim Fleming was exceptional in the way it spanned such a range of musical styles and emotional states, stepping a fine line between pop sentimentality and inaccessible avant-gardism, but never succumbing to either.

If I were to apply the shopworn standards used by critics to assess professional musical theatre, however, there were a few things about this production that wouldn't pass muster. For one thing, it was difficult to follow the plot, such as there was, especially toward the end. The characters didn't really have relationships beyond the most rudimentary, and the conflicts were black and white, with obvious heroes and villains. In addition, the pace of the show was very slow. There were many examples of what French critics call "*longeurs*," when the action stopped so that particularly important sets of visual images could be laid out for the audience to contemplate. The narrator, the one potentially integrating agent in the mishmash of performance styles and modes of address, lacked the charisma to enforce unity.

To apply these standards to *Longline*, however, is to completely miss the point. Welfare State International developed a new collective artistic process that founder John Fox has called "applied vernacular culture." Its goals were directly opposed to the aims of professional theatre and the international art scene. Rather than focusing on producing "great" artistic products that could be repeated, reproduced, and sold to a global audience, Welfare State International was committed to encouraging non-professionals, non-artists, people from all classes and backgrounds to not just enjoy or consume art but actually make it themselves under the guidance of professionals. The empowering of ordinary people to tell their own stories and express their own aspirations had a distinctly political dimension, as John Fox explained to me in 1985:

> The aims are to release creativity. This is done through working with individuals who join in community events with us. But it's also to release creativity in society at large. People have been saying this for years. Sadly the situation is still there. There is the same hidden curriculum both in school and in the whole society, which does not allow people to generate their own ceremonies, to create their own art, to believe that they can create for themselves. Once people start to have control over their own lives and over their own creativity, then they will not tolerate a repressive political nor any other kind of regime which stops them doing that.

These goals were partly achieved by giving people permission to play, because it is often in the safety of play that people can risk revealing their deepest fears and dreams. Process thus became as important as product. Under these circumstances, it would have been counterproductive to attempt conventional musical theatre. Imposing those standards on non-professionals would have dampened all the risk-taking, truth-telling, and spontaneity that Welfare State was trying to tap. New goals required new standards, and any evaluation of a Welfare State event must ask how well their own stated goals were met.

Homemade

Children plagiarize promiscuously from their immediate material and cultural environment, creating props, characters, and story twists from what is readily at hand. Similarly, *Longline* was a strange amalgam of seemingly incompatible styles and techniques: sand painting, clowning, magic acts, trapeze artists and acrobats, puppets of all shapes and sizes, a shadow play, fireworks, dance numbers, a community choir, pantomimes, monologues, and television animations that looked like the work of an anti-social six-year-old. The materials used to make the images, puppets, and props came, for the most part, from the garbage dump. In one deeply moving scene, a crippled, deformed cow made out of plastic bleach bottles hobbled in slow motion across the stage in the aftermath of environmental devastation.

Near the middle of the second act, the cosmic clowns attempted to dramatize a thunderstorm using homemade noisemakers. While it was supposed to be a serious, climactic moment, they hammed it up with that slightly over-the-top, I'm-having-a-good-time-up-here posture reminiscent of adolescent role playing. This playful approach was also apparent in many of the other performances. And after a while it didn't matter that the narrator, cast from the local youth theatre group, lacked the authority of a professional. It was more appropriate in this context that a recognizably ordinary person should be the story's mouthpiece.

Doing away with the spectator

When children play, there are no spectators. To watch others playing is to be excluded. Welfare State International was always committed to crossing and dissolving the boundary between spectator and performer. The band and lead singers were experienced performers, but the bulk of the large cast—the community choir, the teenage dancers, the elementary school kids, the brass band—were all local enthusiasts working as volunteers. The benefits for those on stage were obvious, but there was another benefit as well. For those in the bleachers, the medium was the message. Their children, relatives, and neighbours were onstage, all contributing to this community celebration. The message said, you too, you who have no "talent," can make your own art right here in the town. You don't have to always buy entertainment made elsewhere.

The performers transgressed the boundaries between stage and spectator in other ways. On one occasion the clowns embroiled the audience in a dispute, dividing the room in two and getting each side to compete by making louder and louder bird sounds. On another occasion, Tyndale Thomas, an inspiring gospel singer from Manchester, taught the audience two different back-up parts to a song and then, Pete Seeger style, sang the melody over top.

Never the same twice

Children engrossed in dramatic play shape the narrative spontaneously based on their responses to each other and the flow of their imaginations. So too was *Longline* a constantly evolving process with no fixed text. In the same way that improvising musicians use a simple repeating pattern of chords to play their riffs against, Welfare State used an elementary fall and redemption narrative as the skeleton to support the rich procession of images, songs, and performances that evolved within the various communities. The cosmic clowns and other performers were encouraged to improvise their parts based on audience response. The day after each show, the company would meet and hash out yet more changes. Some were significant. For example, after open-ing night, the performers decided to take their bows *before* the dramatic coda, where the audience was to process outside the tent for the final send-off scene, rather than at the end of the show. "We have to separate the theatre from the ritual," John Fox said. This unconventional approach, discovered through the experience of performing in front of others, was much more effective.

On the third night, John Fox and the clowns learned that one of acrobats was turning fifteen that day. They quickly revised one scene to include a funky rendition of *Happy Birthday* while the unsuspecting youth was presented with a junkyard cake. The audience enjoyed the genuine surprise on the acrobat's face and were, at the same time, reminded of the ever-evolving nature of this kind of live performance. For most professionals, trained in the careful shaping of performances in rehearsal, this constant altering of the text can be nerve-racking; for Welfare State International, however, it was a necessary part of their creation process.

Coda

Welfare State's experiments in process, form, and context have gone further than any others in pointing the way to a more empowering, embodied, and democratic model for cultural performance in the new century, especially among those who have been disenfranchised because of class, gender or ethnicity. No one can say for sure what effect *Longline* had on those who made it or who shared in the experience from the bleachers. One thing is certain, however. There were a lot of people in Ulverston that week who didn't sit watching slickly produced American television shows or play vio-lent hyper-real video games or go shopping at the mall. Instead, they joined together in a collective storytelling ritual that connected with their pasts and with the rivers of the future.

On the third night, I happened to turn around at one point in the coda. We were standing outside in a petrified forest, the moon almost completely hidden by unset-tled clouds. An enormous papier-mâché vessel had just taken off into the heavens in a fiery blast of fireworks. In the quiet that followed, a delicate cradle of stars, conjured up through magic at the beginning of the show, slowly descended to muddy earth. People around me were openly weeping. Several couples were holding each other in their arms. I realized I too had tears in my eyes. What were we crying about? The beau-tiful lullaby sung by Tyndale Thomas: "The world's not upside down/Follow the plough/to the pole star held forever still"? The fact that Welfare State International was coming to an end? Or were we crying because of how far all of us had travelled from our playful, empowered, hope-filled childhood passions?

(2007)

Notes

1. Quotation on the wall of the Picasso Museum in Barcelona; allegedly said by Picasso in 1956 in a school classroom.

2. All quotations from John Fox are from personal interviews between 1985 and 2006, the precise dates and places of which are unrecoverable—ed.

Works Cited

Coult, Tony and Baz Kershaw, eds. *Engineers of the Imagination: The Welfare State Handbook.* Second Edition. Methuen, 1999.

Performing an Asylum:
Tripping Through Time and *La Pazzia*

by Kirsty Johnston

> O! Visitor to Toronto "La Belle" standing by the city Hall,
> Walk due west 'long Queen street, 'till you come to a high stone wall;
> Within the walls is a palace, extending right and left,
> This dear visitor is the home, for people of sense bereft,
> There are illusions and delusions, around you by the score
>
> But on this point, I'll not say much, being sensitive and sore;
> This, you must remember, that patients here within,
> Are here, because we all were born into a world of sin...
> Now come inside the building, and enter into the halls,
> You will see many patients, whose sorrow for pity calls.
>
> Graeme L. patient at the Hospital for the Insane, Toronto, 1907
> (qtd. in Reaume 1)

The "high stone wall" noted by patient Graeme L. still marks the site of a Toronto mental health care facility. Although it is now called the Centre for Addiction and Mental Health, Queen Street Division, and the original asylum buildings first erected there in 1850 have been demolished and replaced by concrete buildings more formally akin to 1960s institutional modernism, the same stone walls continue to mark the site's eastern and western borders. Within the walls the site has undergone many changes, each connected to shifting visions of the asylum, its role within the city, and the effective provision of mental health care.

This essay considers two theatrical productions performed by the Workman Theatre Project (WTP), an integrated theatre company that involves people with mental illness experience and seeks to challenge stigma. Both *Tripping Through Time* (1993) and *La Pazzia* (1999) built upon the particular institutional space of the mental hospital and former asylum grounds to provide audiences with different reminders of the social history and contemporary resonance of asylum life. In *Tripping Through Time*, audience members were diagnosed randomly and individually, labeled as inpatients, and employed in patient's work. *La Pazzia* positioned the audience as medical clinicians engaged in a psychiatric postmortem. Explicit references in each to the site's asylum history and geography connected the diegetic space with the actual environment surrounding both audiences and performers. The two productions played with specific spatial and historical features of the institutional site to open discussion of how people diagnosed with mental illness have experienced the highly stigmatized institutional space over time.

Whereas *Tripping Through Time* sought to build bridges to the broader community without, *La Pazzia* aimed to remind the medical professional community within of its responsibility to guard the dignity of patients. *Tripping Through Time* was produced as part of a larger public exploration of the asylum's history, while *La Pazzia* was produced for the site's clinicians and administrators as they marked the beginning of a new administration. The first drew newcomers into the space, received critical praise, and became one of the company's most requested productions; the second attracted protest and challenged its audience to rethink divisions between onsite communities and their own connections to past and present psychiatric practices. What shaped these different outcomes? How did each production use the institutional space to further the company's aims?

Since 1989, the walls noted by Graeme L. have also contained the Workman Theatre Project (WTP), a performing arts company with its own board and independent mandate that operates out of the institution's Joseph L. Workman Auditorium. The company is dedicated to artistically training and integrating people who have received mental health services with professional theatre artists. Founded in 1989 by former psychiatric nurse Lisa Brown, the company has since created over 20 theatrical productions, each focused on bringing an aspect of mental illness experience to public attention, and each aimed at challenging stigma about such experiences. The company's productions have toured locally across Ontario and Manitoba, and internationally to Germany.[1] It is important to note that the company is not involved in drama therapy or psychodrama; rather, it aims to foster artistic achievement by providing professional theatre training to its members. Company members, now numbering over 400, are defined as individuals with interests in the arts who have received mental health services at some point during their lives. Members are active at all levels of the company, and, following its mandate, each production has been created with an equal number of theatre professionals and company members. Unlike Graeme L., WTP members do not invite audiences onsite simply to engender pity; rather, the WTP uses theatre to engage audiences in re-imagining mental illness experiences, and to feature artistic voices with such experiences.

My association with this theatre company began as a doctoral student seeking to understand one theatre's approach to community engagement by challenging stereotypes about mental illness. After having attended a striking performance of Terry Watada's *Vincent*, a formally innovative play that took up the real-life story of a Toronto man diagnosed with schizophrenia who was shot dead in a violent encounter with police, I approached the WTP to investigate its history and attempts to explore mental illness theatrically. In due course, I volunteered in productions, examined the company's archives, and served as its research and education coordinator for the inaugural Madness and Arts World Festival, held in Toronto in 2003. Interacting with and interviewing company members over a period of several years, reading about past productions, and viewing tapes of performances as well as observing the process involved in creating new works, I was struck by how often the company relied on innovations in form to break from longstanding and stigmatizing patterns of mental illness representation. This had certainly been the case with *Vincent* in which the central character was never seen onstage, but appeared in voiceovers and through the descriptive dialogue of other characters. These choices aimed to undermine visual clichés of schizophrenia representation and forced audiences to confront their own assumptions about how schizophrenia is commonly understood. In *Tale of a Mask*, an earlier WTP production also written by Watada, the juxtaposition of different formal traditions, including Noh drama and a cinematic detective narrative, helped audiences to experience how depression is read differently by different cultures. The company's largest-scale production to date, *Joy. A Musical. About Depression* played with preconceptions about depression and offered a kaleidoscope of colors and different musical selections. With a book by Maja Ardal and lyrics by Joey Miller, the musical ranged from somber beats to upbeat tempos and destabilized the performance of depression while raising questions about its ultimate knowability.

Experimenting with form, I learned, importantly shaped the WTP's practice; to understand this theatre company's innovative work required close attention to its formal choices and to its exploration of their possibilities and limits. Company members wished not only to address mental illness stereotypes in their work, but also to reconfigure the ways in which we imagined the lived experience of mental illness by unsettling our understandings of its performance. More particularly, WTP artistic director Lisa Brown explained that the company has worked to counter representations that insist on marking the person who has a mental illness as visibly different.

Although the company has formed its mandate and arguments independently, its work has aligned it with cultural theorist Sander Gilman, who has investigated representations of the mentally ill in medical iconography and broader aspects of visual culture and has discovered a historically persistent adherence to visual and somatic expressions of mental disease.[2] Art, he argues, has tended to quote art rather than any historically specific experience (*Picturing* 41). Petra Kuppers has similarly argued in this journal [*Theatre Topics*] that the bodies of people who have received mental health services are often "violently read for clues to their 'abnormal' minds" (130). Adherence to such visual stereotypes and "clues" over time is all the more striking in the face of changing social, medical, psychiatric, and cultural contexts. For artists at the WTP, the overwhelming persistence of the kinds of dehumanizing and misleading visual stereotypes outlined by Kuppers and Gilman is a key factor in the stigma against the mental illness experience—a stigma that many people who receive mental health services in Canada cite as being worse than the illness itself (Simmie and Nunes 294). By emphasizing nonstereotypical, contextualized, historically specific lived experiences of mental illness, the company hopes to combat popular and persistent misconceptions. *Tripping Through Time* and *La Pazzia* both attended to the particular history and contemporary context of the institution out of which the company operates.

The WTP's regular performance site, the Joseph L. Workman Auditorium, is attached to the Queen Street Division of the Centre for Addiction and Mental Health. The entrance to the theatre is in the foyer of the mental health center, thus the connection between the two sites is immediately apparent upon arrival at the theatre. One could argue that, at some level, each WTP production brings the audience into the space of the institution, and thus provides them with a lived experience of institutional space. However, not all WTP productions have challenged or sought to highlight the institutional connections of the space. What distinguishes *Tripping Through Time* and *La Pazzia* from other WTP productions is their use of theatrical techniques to encourage audiences to experience the institutional setting explicitly.

Both *Tripping Through Time* and *La Pazzia* were first produced in conjunction with larger celebrations and explorations of the mental health centre's particular history. *Tripping Through Time* was commissioned by the WTP to be presented as part of City and the Asylum: Perspectives in Art, Culture and History of Mental Health in Toronto, a program produced by Brown that ran during 22–27 June 1993 at the Queen Street Mental Health Centre. The week-long series of free cultural events for the general public sought to probe "the history of Toronto's mental health institution," and, by promoting community outreach and understanding of mental health issues, "build new bridges for the purpose of social change" ("City and the Asylum").

The broader community audience targeted by the "City and the Asylum" coordinators contrasts with the internal audience organized for *La Pazzia* six years later. *La Pazzia* was commissioned by the newly formed Centre for Addiction and Mental Health to help celebrate its amalgamation of the Queen Street Mental Health Centre with one other psychiatric hospital, the Clarke Institute, and two addiction agencies, the Donwood Institute and the Addiction Research Foundation.[3] Two afternoon performances were scheduled for 14–15 January 1999.[4] While an internally circulated flyer encouraged patients, staff, and volunteers to attend the second performance, the first was by invitation only. This invitational event sought to foster recognition by hospital staff, administrators, mental health professionals, and Ministry of Health officials of the "Queen Street Mental Health Centre's long-standing contribution as a Provincial Psychiatric Hospital caring for people with mental illness" (1001 Reflections Invitation). The exclusivity of the event, however, drew criticism, because people who had received mental health services were excluded.

By examining the production choices that shaped *Tripping Through Time* and *La Pazzia*, the emphasis on patients' perspectives and the role of the institutional space in the company's performances come into better focus.

Tripping Through Time

On the afternoon of 22 June 1993 a large facade with a door in the middle of it stood on the Queen Street Mental Health Centre west lawn near the site's original high stone wall. The facade consisted of ten connected flats painted to resemble the site's original 1850 buildings—those of Ontario's first provincial lunatic asylum. Before this frontage, the first audience of *Tripping Through Time* assembled. After a ribbon-cutting ceremony at the facade's entrance and a scene showing the first inmates being admitted to the hospital, an attendant began to usher audience members through the door. As they entered, an actor playing the asylum's first medical superintendent, Dr. Joseph Workman, ticked off their "diagnoses": "epileptic, senile, exceedingly violent, masturbation, homeless, idiocy, epileptic, criminally insane, homeless, paresis [as the last of the audience is entering], homeless" (Barrie 7).

As audience members continued to move around the mental health centre's grounds to watch further scenes about the asylum's history, they were invited to help fold the hospital laundry and wind inmates' wool, follow a psychiatrist demonstrating therapeutic techniques, and, finally, discuss with the performers what they were witnessing. Thus, along with the performers, audiences participated in simulated hospital admission, diagnostic labelling, and inpatient labour. From these moments, we can sense the production's attempts to collapse history and elide the distinction between audience and performer, asylum inmate and theatre participant.

The WTP sought to reach a broad audience with *Tripping Through Time*. Since part of the aim of the show was to challenge audiences' preconceptions about the location, which had become closely associated with stigma surrounding psychiatric care, it was important to draw in new audiences who knew the site only by reputation. Afternoon and evening performances were free. A press release (1993) targeting local media extended the company's appeal beyond its regular mailing list and word-of-mouth of its members. Further, its connection to the broader arts initiative "City and the Asylum" increased its visibility and made its outreach aspect explicit. Articles in *Now Magazine*, Toronto's major alternative arts weekly, and the *Toronto Star*, the largest city daily, announced the performances in their arts sections. The show drew steady attendance through its run of 12 performances and was subsequently discussed in Bird and Nyman's article in *Canadian Theatre Review*, Canada's primary theatre periodical. Although the company kept no systematic account of its audiences, casual recollections and the imprecise evidence of photographs taken by members suggest a large and diverse group.

Tripping Through Time was commissioned in part to draw connections between the institution's past and present. Prior to its commission, Brown and director Lloy Coutts had imagined a production that would use the many architectural layers of the site;[5] they had hoped to incorporate the different buildings constructed in different phases of the site's development to provide a history of the space (Coutts 2001). As the project evolved, however, the company was drawn to focus less on architecture and more on the changing onsite health care practices and patient experiences over time. More specifically, and in keeping with the company's primary aim to attend to voices of people with mental illness experience, the production turned its attention to how patients experienced the space over time. This focus lead it to the most open and flexible institutional space—the outdoor grounds, framed by the original asylum walls on the one side and the modern facility on the other.

Coutts and Brown approached playwright Shirley Barrie to research the history of the space and its relationship with mental health care. In *Tripping Through Time*, Barrie sought to give voice to patients' experiences of the Queen Street Mental Health Centre from 1850 to the present. Researching the center's history, she noticed an absence in the documentation of such experience: "There were lots of official documents in the public archives but very little about the patient's experience. The patient's voice was very limited. The play tries to redress that" (Barrie, qtd. in Bird and Nyman 9). Barrie's strategy for redress was to use the institutional environment in ways that aligned audiences with a series of patients' perspectives on life within the walls of the institution.

The play consisted of ten scenes suggesting various historical stages and events in the history of the Queen Street site. The scenes covered periods from 1850, when it was the Provincial Lunatic Asylum, to the present, and all but the last introduced significantly different characters, action, and situation. Barrie's script moved chronologically from the erection of the asylum in 1850 and its early operations under Medical Superintendent Workman, to the final scene where Workman's ghost listens to a contemporary homeless man singing the song "All I Want is a Room Somewhere" in the doorway of the Queen Street Mental Health Centre. Drawing a connection between the original asylum and the contemporary centre, the playwright concluded the play with an excerpt from one of Workman's actual speeches:

> The absence of adequate legislative provision for the support of the poor in this Province, has led to the introduction into this Asylum of many destitute and harmless people, who might have been more economically supported in their own localities; and some of them indeed might, with a sufficient outdoor allowance, have been permitted the continuance of that most prized of all human privileges, personal liberty. (*Pause*) Dr. Joseph Workman. Do you remember me? I first made that speech over a hundred and twenty-five years ago. It seems that in all the intervening years, this province has stumbled from crisis to crisis never committing itself to a coherent mental health care policy. (*Pause*) Is it ever going to be any different? (Barrie 46)

Barrie's script used a variety of dramatic structures and styles to demonstrate these 125 years of crisis. Coutts noted a paradox in *Tripping Through Time*: "Despite the script's chronological ordering of events and documentary elements concerning the history of the space, its mise en scène demands are pointedly unnaturalistic, unrealistic, highly stylized and diverse" (2001). This diversity challenged Coutts, scenographer Sue LePage, and the company performers to find a range of staging techniques that would allow them to achieve their primary goals of connecting the past and present, reconfiguring the understanding of the lived experience of mental illness, blurring the lines between audience and patient to challenge the stigma associated with mental illness, and drawing connections between the performance and the history of the site itself.

The beginning of the production and its early scenes demonstrate how the space was variously configured to accomplish these goals. The production immediately invited audiences to connect the past and present by placing them in front of flats painted to look like the original asylum buildings, while the contemporary institution loomed large nearby. After passing through the facade as Workman ticked off their individual "diagnoses," audience members found the lines blurred between spectator and mentally ill resident. Stepping through the doorway, audiences confronted the facade from the opposite direction as though they were historical inpatients. Painted to resemble the brick interior of the early asylum, this side suggested a day-room for women inpatients. Several such women, all of whom were costumed in nineteenth-century patient dress, mingled with the audience in this scene. Beyond the facade to the south was an exterior garden scene in which similarly historically costumed male patients were working. Entering between these two spaces, some audience members were conscripted into helping the women fold sheets or wind wool, while the rest watched both this activity and the men hoeing and planting on the grounds to the south of them. Distinctions between audience and inpatient, past and present were blurred again in these instances, particularly for those who laboured with the women.

Subsequent scenes connected the performance with another kind of audience experience of the site drawn from the institution's history. As the performers continued with the inpatient labour, dialogue shifted the focus back to the facade's doorway as Susanna Moodie, a well-known Canadian pioneer and author who had toured and written about the asylum not long after it was built, entered the space. The scene continued with a focus on her interactions with the female inmates. The audience then followed Moodie and Workman as they walked about the grounds and engaged with a number of patients. Just as Moodie had toured the asylum, audiences also strolled from patient to patient; unlike her, however, they did so after first being diagnosed and identified as inpatients. This challenged the safe distance they might have felt when encountering characters drawn from the institution's annals. Audiences followed, for example, as Moodie and Workman passed a lone female figure isolated and restrained in a wheelchair to the west of the other performers. Workman warned Moodie that the woman was most safely observed from a distance. Seeing Moodie and the audience pass by her, the inmate shouted until she exhausted herself: "I can go home! I know the way!! Let me out! [Focusing on Moodie] Take me home. I know the way" (Barrie 12).

In this moment, we can see how the production used the shared space to provide audiences with a number of competing focal points: Workman and Moodie; the woman in the wheelchair; and the audience itself as it was directly addressed by the woman, yet led by Workman's advice to ignore and move away from her. Directing her pleas to the audience, the woman indicated that she shared their space and time. Beyond Workman, Moodie, and this lone patient, the continued work of the female inmates in the day-room and the men in the background also provided competing focal points throughout the scene. Thus, the audience was surrounded by several frames of action, all of which contributed to a shared sense of space and time between audience and performer. This encouraged audiences to draw connections between the performance and the history of the site while highlighting historical patient experiences.

The WTP was careful to incorporate the remaining original asylum site walls into the performance as a means of connecting past and present. The wall itself was explicitly mentioned in scene 5, "Into the Twentieth Century," when the audience sat near it on wooden benches to listen to the arguments of two of the site's former medical superintendents, Dr. Daniel Clark (appointed in 1876) and Dr. C.K. Clarke (appointed in 1905):

> Clarke: *(To audience)* And [Dr. Clark] constructed this prison-like wall around the asylum, cutting patients off from the community.
>
> Clark: Yes I did. But only to protect them from the too curious gaze of the passers-by. (Barrie 16)

Inside the wall, the performance invited the curious gaze of the audience as it encountered the performance sites. However, the distance associated with gazing was frequently subverted by the production's many attempts to provide the audience with opportunities to participate in or observe simulated patient experiences of the institutional space. For Coutts, such scenes in which character and audience experiences were elided provided moments where "realities clashed and we went beyond them" (2001).

Other scenes in the production were less concerned with blurring the distinction between audience and performer than with providing visceral demonstrations of patients' lived experiences of mental health care associated with the institution's past and present. For example, in one scene that positioned the audience more traditionally as spectators in front of a medical demonstration, several treatments were explained and demonstrated on a single patient: metrazol convulsive therapy, insulin coma therapy, lobotomy, and electroconvulsive shock therapy. By contrast, a subsequent scene titled "Deinstitutionalization" offered strikingly different and competing frames of action. This scene examined the period from 1955 to 1975 by showing an elaborate soccer game played by characters on another part of the grounds who wore various jerseys upon which were written "Neuroleptics," "Anti-Depressants," "Ontario Hospital," "Psychiatric Units," "Community," "Federal Dollars," or "Homes for Special Care." During the game, a coach directed the play, cheerleaders mingled with the audience, and the ghost of a patient who had died in scene 4, Susan Gilbert, reacted in pain to each kick of the ball.

The flats of the facade were also used in several different configurations to suggest key aspects of patient experience. In scene 8, "The Old Hospital Disappears, 1968–1975," the actors tore down the facade of the asylum to make way for the Queen Street Mental Health Centre, the actual buildings of which were immediately indicated and highlighted for audiences. In scene 9, "The Rise of the Consumer Survivor," the actors ran in and out of the facade's one remaining doorframe after the razing to demonstrate physically the revolving-door syndrome of mentally ill patients who are released, but driven back to the centre because of inadequate support outside the institution. As these examples suggest, each of the ten scenes introduced new characters, physical actions, historical periods, and, importantly, audience and performer spatial relationships.

In *Tripping Through Time*, the staging offered competing interpretations of spatial cues and clashes of spatial reality. The play's scattered staging, explicit references to the asylum wall, and competing foci of action drew audience and performer together in the explicitly institutional space. Barrie's strategy of privileging patient voices in her historical dramatization was therefore complemented by LePage's scenography and Coutts's exploitation of the multiple focal points within the space: all sought to implicate audiences in patients' experiences of the asylum, and all sought to draw audiences inside the institution's walls to challenge their current perceptions about the history of the space.

La Pazzia

Six years after *Tripping Through Time*, the WTP mounted a new production with a different emphasis and target audience that would also play on the found spaces of the site. On 14 January 1999, an audience of hospital staff, administrators, and government representatives gathered in the same mental health centre's cafeteria, all attending by invitation to mark the transition of the Queen Street Mental Health Centre into the newly amalgamated Centre for Addiction and Mental Health. Between the greetings and cake cutting ceremony, the audience gathered below the steps leading into the cafeteria to witness a woman slowly descend toward them. As she descended, four slide screens on the walls behind and beside her displayed different images related to the history of mental illness, psychiatry, and the particular institutional space in which the crowd was gathered.

The woman, called La Pazzia, told the peculiar story of her own postmortem at the hands of the asylum's medical staff and interns; as an immortal being, she was able to describe her conscious feelings and impressions after the event. Halfway down the stairs, she stood beside a screen bearing the projected image of a nineteenth-century postmortem amphitheatre.[6] After looking at the image, she turned to the audience below and said:

> Now began a strange exhibition. All around, on the seats of an amphitheatre, were stretched a hundred young fellows, some of whom were near to me, and you, dear Professor, were among these; the others were higher up and more distant. Oh! how many eyes were fixed on my members, which I through all my life had so modestly guarded, excepting on occasions in which I was rather indiscreet. How many complimentary epigrams did I hear! (34)[7]

Deitre Courchesne's performance as La Pazzia gesturally drew the connection between the diegetic amphitheatre audience and the production's audience. Looking directly at audience members and sweeping her arm to indicate that they formed the audience of "a hundred young fellows," she included them within her story world. Further, as she removed a layer of the cotton garments in which she was swathed, she shielded herself from the audience's eyes as though they were the "many eyes" in her monologue. Her gestures implied a connection between the diegetic postmortem audience and the audience gathered to celebrate the asylum's past (*La Pazzia* video). Thus, as in *Tripping Through Time*, the production used gestures and the performance environment to elide the distinction between audience and performer and institutional postmortem witness and theatrical spectator.

Outside of this event, however, the performance drew jeering and faced difficult questions. Protesters stood at the entrance to the celebration and handed out flyers. "And they didn't invite us," the sheets ran:

> People who live at Queen Street, *the patients*, were not invited to "1001 Reflections." Was it because:
>
> 1. More than $15,000 tax money was spent to throw the party?
> 2. The Minister of Health and other eminent people were invited?
> 3. Patients are not thought "good enough" to sit with the Minister or $15,000?
>
> If you said yes to any of these, we invite you to come out of Reflecting and meet people at Queen Street! We won't bite. We have a lot to say about health care, the past and future, living and surviving! We're ready to share—are you? (Protest flyer)

Thus as the audience assembled to see *La Pazzia* it was confronted by the exclusivity of the occasion and the frustration of those who felt marginalized by this community-building event. Given that WTP members are committed to empowering patients and giving voice to patient experiences, at first glance it seems unusual that the company was involved in this exclusive event. Further analysis of the production choices, however, helps to explain how they used the particular features of the audience, the occasion, and the site to work within their mandate and reorient mental illness representation traditions.

Compared with the *Tripping Through Time* audience, those who gathered for *La Pazzia* were less diverse and tended to have more familiarity with the institution from a professional rather than from a patient perspective. *La Pazzia*'s director, Anne Steacy, understood though was not entirely comfortable with the narrow and controversial features of this intended audience. However, she also recognized that the project's aim with the production was to remind attendees to respect the dignity of patients. The *La Pazzia* script was based on the article, "A Wonderful Post-Mortem," in *The Canada Lancet*'s October 1889 issue. This article for the monthly journal of medical and surgical science, criticism and news was Joseph Workman's translation of the concluding chapter of *Ragione e pazzia* (1884) by Professor Augusto Tebaldi of the University of Padua (Tebaldi). Both Tebaldi's original chapter and Workman's translation aimed to remind medical professionals that patients are human beings whose dignity must be protected. Driven by a similar impulse, Steacy aimed to connect her contemporary audience with medical professionals of the site's past. Although *La Pazzia* was performed as part of the center's celebration of its new amalgamation, it also marked a difficult period in the site's history. The celebration brought together various professionals from the original pre-amalgamation institutions, some of whom had experienced the institutional merging as painful and confusing. Some professionals felt, for example, that the methods of care and issues of concern for addiction treatment were incompatible with those of mental health; there was some fear that this new mixing of mental health patients with addiction patients would impede and confuse the respective treatments of both. Further, many professionals quit the centre in protest over the proposed changes, leaving behind a smaller team whose members were expected to celebrate the process of amalgamation even as they were still smarting from its losses and changes. Aware of this background influencing her audience, Steacy's directorial choices sought to remind it of its primary responsibility: the respectful care of patients. They also reminded the audience of its place in the evolving history of onsite mental health care.

Many of Steacy's directorial choices linked the institution's former psychiatric practitioners with the professional audience. At the end of the performance, for example, after disappearing behind a screen at the bottom of the stairs, Courchesne changed quickly into a contemporary, formal black-velvet dress, high-heeled shoes, and a beaded necklace. Thus, when she emerged to take a bow in front of the audience, she was formally and festively dressed like the invited guests. In a personal interview with the author Steacy explained that this choice worked to blur the distinctions between audience and performer and past and present as well as between illness and health.

In "A Wonderful Post-Mortem," Workman emphasized the relevance of Augusto Tebaldi's work for his professional contemporaries: "It is manifestly but a parting *jeu d'esprit* of a good-natured author, but it may be read by that class of young men for whom, no doubt, it was mainly intended, with some profit" (33). In the production, an unseen male voiceover provided these introductory words prior to La Pazzia's entrance. An image of Workman, which would have been familiar to most of the audience from his bust in the centre's foyer, was projected on one of the slide screens during this reading. Beyond the obvious connection of Workman's involvement as the translator of the text and his position as both the founding superintendent of the asylum and the namesake of the theatre venue, the production linked the spatial cues of the diegesis with the institutional performance site.

As we saw in the opening example from *La Pazzia*, it is the reference to the amphitheatre that is the production's primary means of implicating the audience in the diegesis. The narrative of both the production and the article focuses on a dozing alienist physician, a term Workman and his contemporaries used to refer to what we now call a psychiatrist. The physician awakes at his desk to discover a strange letter, his reading of which then forms the rest of the text. The letter is from La Pazzia, who offers the story of her own postmortem. She describes her experience of uncomfortable psychiatric treatments and her sudden relief at being considered dead. In the

WTP production, as La Pazzia described her experiences under the medical gaze, she demonstrated gesturally and with the aid of a projected archival image of the institution's postmortem amphitheatre that she was similarly under the gaze of the audience.

Beyond such gestures, textual references, and slides, the emphasis placed on the institution's history by the occasion would also have made the audience aware that they were witnessing a performance in the Queen Street Mental Health Centre/Centre for Addiction and Mental Health, an institution in which such postmortems have occurred. The three-hour event surrounding the production began with greetings and remarks from representatives of the Ministry of Health, the Community Advisory Board, and the former Queen Street Mental Health Centre administration. After these, *La Pazzia* was performed. Celebratory remarks and thanks followed. All aspects of the celebration were thus organized to highlight the historical legacy and future of the institutional space.

The director, Steacy, has described her organization of the slides in the production as deliberately subversive. Along with the images of the postmortem amphitheatre and Joseph Workman, she included many others from the mental health centre's history: photographs that displayed the initial exterior of the Provincial Lunatic Asylum, interior images of early patient cells, asylum staircases and amphitheatres, and the outer wall demarcating the asylum. Also included were images of a variety of doctors and nurses from the institution's history. Knowing the professional composition of the intended audience and the controversial exclusivity of it, she sought to subvert simple and traditional distinctions between madness and reason, patient and physician, past and present. As an example of this subversion, she cited the series of images showing some of the more harrowing treatments administered to mental patients: trepanning, hydrotherapy, and electroconvulsive, or shock, therapy. These were shown as La Pazzia spoke the following lines: "You have now, my dear Professor, the story of the postmortem of a living woman. You may be grateful to me for the secret as I am to you for all the kindness lavished on me by you, and for all the experiments made on my body both in life and supposed death" (*La Pazzia*, unpublished script 15). On the word "kindness," each of the screens showed an image of one of the above-mentioned treatments to subvert La Pazzia's suggestion of gratitude and kindness with images of inhumane medical treatment.

The subversive quality of the images in relation to the text also suggests the extent to which the company's choices undermined the primacy of the text in performance. The production was thus not merely the retelling of Workman's translation of Tebaldi, but a performance event guided by the WTP mandate to disorient commonplace understandings and representations of the lived experience of mental illness. In adapting Workman's translation for the stage, the WTP produced an embodied, multilayered, and disorienting enactment of the text in which several production choices undermined or challenged institutional authority. The constant flow of images provided by the slides created several competing focalization points throughout the production and threw into question the authority of any particular viewpoint.

Courchesne's direct implications of the audience in the diegetic space and her mingling with them as a colleague and celebrant at the performance's end introduced nonfrontal staging techniques. The specific features of the performance space were also highlighted by the historical slides of the institution that ranged from its earliest days to its most contemporary, its key figures, and an array of former psychiatric-care techniques used on the premises. In these ways, Steacy connected the event's gathered professionals with those of the institution's past. Apart from these elements, however, the production maintained a more traditionally frontal relationship with the audience. This allowed the director to draw parallels between the diegetic postmortem spectators and the actual audience members attending the production. Like the student doctors at the post-mortem, the contemporary audience members looked at LaPazzia from a distance. Maintaining this distance through the bulk of the performance also made La Pazzia's final demolition of this separating frame—the moment when she emerged newly costumed and indistinguishable from the audience itself—all the more striking for its collapse of space and time, historical patient and contemporary clinician.

Conclusions

Like Graeme L. in 1907, WTP artists have invited spectators to come within the institutional walls and reflect upon patients' lives. In the cases of *Tripping Through Time* and *La Pazzia*, however, the artists chose to structure this reflection through specific theatre techniques aimed at helping audiences experience the site from patients' perspectives. Aware of an imbalance in historical accounts of the institution that ignored these perspectives, playwright Shirley Barrie was careful to include scenes informed by such common patient experiences as being diagnosed and labeled when admitted or taking up various work duties assigned to inpatients. The company's production of *La Pazzia* took a text translated by a historical figure from the institution's past and presented it in a nontraditional theatre space that highlighted the institutional setting and drew connections between patient experiences of the past and present and blurred the boundaries between patients and clinicians. Both Coutts's and Steacy's directorial choices exploited the cues of the institution, animating its spatial features through performance. As always at the WTP, both productions invited audiences to re-imagine mental illness experiences in ways that both featured and attended to the specific and contextualized voices of people with mental illness experiences. Reacting against the kinds of representational patterns outlined by Gilman and Kuppers, the company's artistic choices aimed to challenge homogenizing, ahistorical, generic, and visually clichéd representations of mental illness. In place of these, they offered vivid accounts of particular lived experiences of mental illness, and sought to blur the categories that would denigrate and distance such experiences.

Site-specific techniques in these two productions, however, did not lead to the same outcome. Although both sought to create a level of sympathy between audiences and past patient experiences as a way of informing contemporary understandings, they were executed for different reasons, involved different audiences, and produced different effects. One production succeeded in opening the site to a wide public audience and raising critical questions about the space and stigma associated with it, while the other effectively engaged an internal audience at an important moment of institutional change to focus on respectful patient care.

If these forms offered different possibilities for the WTP in these two productions, they proved nevertheless similarly adept at creating particular experiences for audiences that unsettled common notions about the institutional space and challenged traditional patterns for representing mental illness. In other WTP productions, which also sought to question and destabilize mental illness stereotypes, innovations in form tended to focus on changing audience perceptions of the mad character. In *Vincent*, the character diagnosed with schizophrenia was never present onstage so as to avoid visual clichés—and thereby to pose questions about visual clichés; in *Tale of a Mask*, a mask served as a focal point to underscore the cross-cultural understandings of mental illness in a diverse, multicultural society; and in *Joy*, an excess of visual display and contrasting musical performances as well as embodied characterizations of such symptoms as anxiety, headache, and despair led to a hyper-embodied representation of depression. In all of these cases, the innovations in form focused on the representation of illness by actors in performance. In *Tripping Through Time* and *La Pazzia*, however, audiences were thrust into a new role, not only in the space of the theatre, but also on the grounds of the institution in the participatory actions of patients. The effect of this shift in audience perspective was to offer some of the more radical destabilizations of audiences' understandings of mental illness that the WTP has offered to date.

The work accomplished by site-specific, nonfrontal staging in the context of these WTP 1990s productions raises the question of whether these approaches have something particular to offer theatre companies working in disability arts or community theatre more generally. In both *Tripping Through Time* and *La Pazzia*, site-specific, nonfrontal staging allowed the company to implicate audience members in the respective productions' action, upsetting the comfortable distance that a more traditional fourth-wall framing might have provided. After all, the mere invitation to view theatre in an asylum space is not in and of itself new, nor does the mingling of theatre and asylum space necessarily challenge stigma or unsettle stigmatizing patterns for representing mental illness. One can think, for example, of the nineteenth-century practice in Ontario and elsewhere of inviting the public to view asylum patients perform in amateur theatricals (see Miron). During such moments, traditional framing patterns kept spectators and patients distinct and did not seek to highlight the specific cues of the institutional space. By contrast, by empowering artists with mental illness experiences to make choices about how such experiences are represented, the WTP productions attended to specific historical and material aspects of the environment itself, moving away from framings that would allow audiences to feel a safe distance from patients' perspectives of the space.

The WTP artists are not generally frustrated by a lack of mental illness representations; indeed, mental illness has long been a favorite theme, trope, and device in theatre. Instead, like other disability theatre practitioners, these artists aim to challenge the more stigmatizing aspects of these longstanding performance traditions. If site-specific, nonfrontal staging techniques are employed in ways that upset commonplace or stigmatizing distinctions between people with mental illness experiences and those without them, if the techniques aim to suggest a specific, historically contextualized, lived experience of mental illness rather than an ahistorical, generic artistic representation, then the possibilities that site-specific, nonfrontal staging hold for further disability theatre practice will be generative.

(2008)

Acknowledgements

For their helpful responses to earlier drafts of this article the author wishes to thank Professors Deborah Levine, Robert Nunn, Domenic Pietropaolo, Richard Plant and Matthew Evenden as well as Lisa Brown, Richard Ingram, Jonathan Chambers and the other editors and reviewers of *Theatre Topics*.

Notes

[1] In 2006, the company toured its production of Terry Watada's play *Vincent* to the "Madness and Arts World Festival II" in Münster, Germany. The play's narrative is based on the real-life shooting of a man diagnosed with schizophrenia by Toronto police officers. The Workman Theatre Project founded and produced the first "Madness and Arts World Festival," which ran for ten days in 2003 at Toronto's Harbourfront Centre. The festival hosted over a hundred artists from ten countries and included theatre, dance, visual art, comedy, and improvisation. More information on the festival can be found at www.madnessandarts.com; see also Johnston.

[2] Chief among these are Sander Gilman's *Disease and Representation* and *Picturing Health and Illness*. Both use madness as a "test case" or focal example to study disease representation. In the first work, Gilman stresses the value of studying representations of madness in visual art, literature, medical illustration, and iconography in order to promote a broader understanding of the cultural perception and social practice of medicine and illness in history and society. He builds his arguments by investigating a broad historical and cultural range of visual mental

illness representations in high and popular art, the art of the insane, and medical iconography.

3 A *Toronto Star* article differentiated the mandates of the institutions involved in the amalgamation: "The Clarke Institute is a psychiatric hospital that specializes in research. The Donwood Institute is a centre that treats a growing range of addictions from alcohol to smoking to gambling, and the Addiction Research Foundation focuses primarily on research although there is a treatment component"; see Vincent and Boyle.

4 My analysis will focus on this first controversial performance.

5 Coutts had already worked with the company as a director on several projects. She would later direct the WTP's *Tale of a Mask*.

6 These details are drawn from my review of a video of the performance of *La Pazzia* (1999).

7 A note on the translation of the terms "professor" and "doctor." The classroom element implied in English by the use of "professor," as opposed to "doctor," differs from the Italian usage of similar terms. In Italian, "professore" may refer both to a university teacher and/or a doctor in charge of residents or interns—a doctor at the top of the hierarchy in the particular area of specialization. I am grateful to University of Toronto Professor Domenico Pietropaolo for making me aware of these distinctions.

Works Cited

1001 Reflections Invitation. Centre for Addiction and Mental Health Internal Flyer. January 1999. Workman Theatre Project Archives.

Ardal, Maja (book), and Joey Miller (music). *Joy. A Musical. About Depression.* Unpublished manuscript, 2000.

Barrie, Shirley. *Tripping Through Time.* Unpublished play, 1993.

Bird, Kym and Ed Nyman. "Quipping against the Pricks: Comedy, Community and Popular Theatre." *Canadian Theatre Review* 77 (1993): 8–12.

Brown, Lisa. Personal interview. 12 May 1999.

"City and the Asylum: Perspectives in Art, Culture and History of Mental Health in Toronto." Press release, 1993.

Coutts, Lloy. Personal interview. 21 May 2001.

Gilman, Sander L. *Disease and Representation: Images of Illness from Madness to AIDS.* Ithaca, NY: Cornell UP, 1988.

———. *Picturing Health and Illness: Images of Identity and Difference.* Baltimore: Johns Hopkins UP, 1995.

Johnston, Kirsty. "Staging Schizophrenia: The Workman Theatre Project and Terry Watada's *Vincent.*" *Modern Drama* 47.1 (2004): 114–32.

Kuppers, Petra. "Towards the Unknown Body: Silence, Stillness, and Space in Mental Health Settings." *Theatre Topics* 10.2 (2000): 129–43.

La Pazzia. Unpublished play. Workman Theatre Project. 1999.

La Pazzia. Video recording of the WTP production at the Centre for Addiction and Mental Health Queen Street site. 14 January 1999. Producer: Michael Flynn for the Instructional Media Centre, Ontario Ministry of Health.

Miron, Janet. "'Open to the Public': Asylum Visiting in Nineteenth-Century Ontario." *Mental Health in Canada: Historical Perspectives.* Ed. James Moran and David Wright. Montreal: McGill-Queen's UP, 2006. 19–48.

Protest flyer in response to the 1001 Reflections Centre for Addiction and Mental Health celebration. (Copy Supplied by Anne Steacy).

Reaume, Geoffrey. *Remembrance of Patients Past: Patient Life at the Toronto Hospital for the Insane, 1870–1940.* Don Mills, ON: Oxford UP Canada, 2000.

Simmie, Scott and Julia Nunes. *The Last Taboo: A Survival Guide to Mental Health Care in Canada.* Toronto: McClelland & Stewart, 2001.

Steacy, Anne. Personal interview. 17 November 1999.

Tebaldi, Augusto. From *Ragione e Pazzia* (1884). "A Wonderful Post-Mortem." Trans. Joseph Workman. *The Canada Lancet: A Monthly Journal of Medical and Surgical Science, Criticism and News* 22.2 (1889): 33–36.

Vincent, Donovan, and Theresa Boyle. "Merger Must Protect Mentally Ill: Activist." *Toronto Star,* 15 January 1998.

Watada, Terry. *Tale of a Mask. Canadian Mosaic: 6 Plays.* Ed. Aviva Ravel. Toronto: Simon & Pierre, 1995. 43–85.

———. *Vincent.* Unpublished play, 1997.

Workman Theatre Project (WTP). *Tripping Through Time.* Press release. 17 May 1993.

www.workmanarts.com. 20 December 2007. http://www.workmanarts.com.

They Don't Get Us
and We Don't Get Them

by David S. Craig

The title of this reflection comes from Philip Akin, the Artistic Director of Obsidian Theatre. We were in rehearsal and I was going over the list of concerns that educators had with Joseph Jomo Pierre's stage play *Born Ready*. My theatre and his, with Theatre Passe Muraille, produced the play as a double bill with my play *Smokescreen*, but it's *Born Ready* that has educators nervous. The situation was grim. We had budgeted four out of eight performances for school groups. The York Region School Board was refusing to allow students to attend, the Separate School Board did not approve students attending and the Toronto District School Board, while not refusing to allow students to attend, were struggling to come to terms with, what they perceived as, problem passages in the text. The play would go on to receive a coveted four out of four star review from the *Toronto Star* and fulsome praise from the few young people who did see the play. But the goal of engaging 2,400 young people in a discussion on risk never happened.

How did this happen? What was it about *Born Ready* that we, as theatre artists, were so excited to present and educators found so challenging? It's hard to gauge in the case of the York Region School Board. No reason was given. Teachers who had made bookings were told to cancel them. But for the most part, the educators involved were committed, progressive and arts friendly people who were trying to engage with our idea, but couldn't. They wanted theatre, but they didn't want this theatre.

The first problem, the use of profanity, I was ready for. Or I thought I was. Most schools are struggling to create a respectful learning environment and frown on students swearing. When my theatre performs in schools we respect that value. That's why we programmed *Born Ready* in a theatre. But the profanity actually wasn't the problem. Everyone seeing the play, including educators, agreed that these specific characters would speak exactly as they are portrayed. Their concern was that if they allowed students to attend a play with profanity it might be construed as approval and they could be open to complaints from parents. We had two teachers who told us they could lose their jobs if they brought students to *Born Ready*. I had another teacher who was afraid students might blackmail her by threatening to tell their parents that the play had bad words.

I have spent my working life trying to get the attention of principals. I want them to book my show. When I became a parent I was astonished to find that I could walk into my child's school, unannounced, and within fifteen minutes be speaking to the boss. A considerable amount of power has been ceded, released, granted or grabbed by parents. The result is a kind of chaos. Educators have to placate ultra-conservative parents who won't allow their children to sing in music class and ultra-liberal parents who resent being told that their kid is stoned in class. They are trying to appeal to everyone and they can't because (a) parents have different values and (b) parents feel empowered to complain when their values aren't reflected.

As a dramatist, ironically, I am caught in a similar conundrum. How do I write a story that will appeal to everyone in Toronto? Currently we are producing plays for specific audiences. Obsidian is a Black theatre. Fu-gen is an Asian theatre. Buddies is a gay theatre. Nightwood is a feminist theatre. Stratford is a classical, musical theatre. Divide and attract. A Toronto story would require the character mix of a Dickens novel, the resources of a Broadway musical, eight hours of playing time and simultaneous translation. "Nicholas Nickleby 416/905." Without those resources, the successful playwright does what successful playwrights have always done—get specific—which brings me back to *Born Ready*. The play explores Black gun violence. This is immediately controversial because the media has created a negative stereotype that equates Black men with gangstas. This is serious stuff and the Black community, justifiably, want positive roles models like Nelson Mandela and Martin Luther King. This is all well and good but pointing up to the light is incomplete unless you also explore the appeal of the dark. This is what *Born Ready* does. It is a tragedy. It shows the downward spiral of the characters with authenticity, complexity and feeling. There is violence but it is not glorified. The play shows that poverty makes guns attractive and guns lead to death. As a pedagogical message, I can't imagine a clearer one. But unfortunately, and ironically, the fear of being accused of cultural stereotyping has stopped young people from seeing the work of a talented Black playwright produced by Toronto's largest Black theatre which explores a subject that is of critical importance to us all.

Of all the three School Boards, the one that tried hardest to engage with *Born Ready* was the Toronto District School Board and their comments were the most difficult to receive. *Born Ready* is the story of two Black youth growing up in Toronto in conditions of poverty and neglect that are shocking. The first time these young men like what they see in the mirror is when they pick up a gun. The gun means food, clothing and, most of all, self respect. *The gun is portrayed by a woman.* Now when I say this to a theatre artist they immediately go "Whoah." They see that portraying the sensual attraction of a weapon by personifying it as a woman is a theatrical idea full of meaning and resonance. Here's what the Equity department of Toronto District School Board said after carefully examining the script:

> There are elements of dehumanization/objectification of women in this play that must be addressed with students. The term misogyny should be discussed and deconstructed for students as part of a continuum in a discussion of sexism in this play.

You see immediately how the virtue of a theatrical idea, one that illuminates our understanding of human behaviour (i.e. why young men are attracted to guns) has been viewed through a completely different lens. Far from exploring the roots of gun violence, the focus is on sexual stereotyping and the dehumanizing of women. How did this happen? One factor was that the playwright didn't make the metaphor crystal clear and thus the female character's "subservience to her man" was misunderstood. There was fear that young people would not be mature enough to appreciate the dramatic irony of the play although we saw no signs of that from the youth audiences we were able to attract. Some young men view woman as sexual objects. That behaviour was dramatized on stage for all to see, and women, young and old, judged it harshly. I think sexism and objectification is more subtly, insidiously and deliberately fostered in *Ms. Magazine*, but I'm not an expert. My point is that these concerns missed the point.

2005 was declared the Year of the Gun in part because a Black teenager was shot dead outside a church and a White teenager was shot dead shopping on Boxing Day. In 2007 the numbers got worse. The tragedy of bullets randomly killing innocent civilians is putting a chill on the whole city. Young Jordan Manners was executed in his high school. The Falconer Report found that he died of "pure neglect." That's exactly the point made in *Born Ready.* Joseph has taken his reality, his specific experience, his truth, funnelled it through the theatrical imagination and come to exactly the same conclusion as the provincial report. Surely educators, the gatekeepers of our audience, would be happy to have the opportunity to discuss these issues with their students. If we are not helping them to confront this truth, in the safe environment of a theatre, with their teachers at their sides, in the hands of award-winning artists, when WILL we tell them?

Questions. It's something theatre does very well. As a playwright, I am not trying to say anything. If I say nothing perfectly, I will have said everything. American playwright David Mamet says that "religious films"—and by extension plays—(by which I think he means work that attempts to improve the audience) "have as much chance of increasing humane behaviour as *Porgy and Bess* has of ending segregation." I'm not sure he's right. I prefer British playwright Tom Stoppard's take. He doesn't think theatre can change specific public policy but he thinks it can change the social atmosphere out of which public policy might be changed; what he calls "the moral matrix from which we draw our values" (qtd. in Gussow 20). It achieves this, as Shakespeare famously said, by holding "a mirror up to nature." By showing, as opposed to instructing, we invite young people to make up their own minds. This gives theatre enormous credibility. Their response to *Born Ready* is that it is "real." It is a reality many of them are living and they are enormously grateful and appreciative to see it portrayed onstage. When they see *Smokescreen*, they say, "Thank you for treating us like adults." Mission accomplished! Yet the lack of a clear-cut, unambiguous "message" creates problems for educators trained to deliver clearly defined learning outcomes. That's fine but there is another way to educate and develop the kind of high level thinking we will need to solve the problems of our age. Expose young people to something really stimulating, something that has direct relevance to their lives and then help them unpack that experience into meaning.

Arts-in-Education is my métier and I have been able to make the hyphens hold these two words together for over thirty years. *Smokescreen*, although controversial to some, has successfully toured high schools and been translated into four other languages. Recently, the Ministry of Education through the Elementary Teachers Association financed a ten week tour of my play, *Danny, King of the Basement*, about child poverty. Educators are my colleagues and friends. But co-producing *Born Ready* has cast us as adversaries. I hear their concerns. To reach my audience I must and I will. Because I believe my 3,000-year-old art form has the capacity to powerfully engage young people by revealing their world. "The play's the thing to catch the conscience of a King." Word.

(2008)

Works Cited

Gusow, Melvyn. *Conversations with Stoppard*. New York: First Grove, 1996.

Mamet, David. *Bambi Versus Godzilla: On the Nature, Purpose and Practice of the Movie Business*. Toronto: Random House of Canada, 2007.

Of, For, By

by Yvette Nolan

There is an argument to be made that theatre that is created of, for and by a community must be community-based work. If that is the case, then all the work that Native Earth Performing Arts has developed and produced in its twenty-eight year history is community-based. The company was founded specifically to give voice to Aboriginal artists, to provide a forum for the artistic expression of the Aboriginal experience in this country.

Most theatres in this country could make the same argument, then—purporting to express the values, interests and concerns of the communities in which they are situated—but few do. There is still the whiff of the amateur about community-based work, the scent of Popular Theatre, and as one colleague sniffed at me early in my career, "You know, there are those who say that Popular Theatre is neither."

Nevertheless, Native Earth has for many years provided Native artists a place to work together, producing professionally such plays as Tomson Highway's *The Rez Sisters*, Marie Clements's *The Unnatural and Accidental Women*, Tara Beagan's *Dreary and Izzy* and the Aboriginal adaptation of *Julius Caesar, Death of a Chief*. In recent years, the company has developed a program specifically in response to requests from the community—or communities—for work that addresses their immediate concerns.

Native Earth's Made To Order program arrived like most newborns, nameless. In 2004, a forward-thinking community justice organization thought to offer a topic-specific theatre performance to its conference attendees. The organizer contacted Native Earth and asked for a piece that would illuminate some of the issues around Aboriginal conflict resolution. She didn't want answers, she said, she wanted the piece, or pieces, to end "up in the air" so that the assembly could then discuss possible solutions and outcomes.

I come from Popular Theatre. My mother was a member of Nellie McClung Theatre in Winnipeg, I interned at Popular Theatre Alliance of Manitoba under Artistic Director Margo Charlton, or rather, beside, since PTAM was feminist and fair. I honed my playwriting skills by writing Made To Order pieces for advocacy groups for Persons Living With Aids, for co-op housing groups, for grassroots groups that wanted to *Up Your Funding*.

For the Aboriginal Conflict Resolution conference, I wrote four scenes that animated various potential conflicts, both within and outside Aboriginal communities;

each scenario suspended at the moment of crisis. We sent the text to our contact, and set to work rehearsing the piece. To our surprise, when we got to the conference in Kitchener-Waterloo, we discovered that the theatre piece—sadly still unnamed—was the backbone of the day. The organizers had looked at our piece and shaped the day around the performance.

Nina Lee Aquino, who at that time was working at Native Earth as the Marketing Coordinator, had directed the piece for the conference, and pushed to formalize the program. We called it Made To Order, homage to the PTAM program where I cut my teeth, and began to promote it.

These community-commissioned pieces occasionally take on a life far beyond the one-off they were intended to be. I knew this from *Everybody's Business*, a musical comedy about HIV/AIDS that I was a part of back at PTAM in the 1990s. Originally collectively created for a conference on Women and AIDS, the show got picked up for a run at the Museum of Man and Nature as part of a plague exhibit. I revised it for the Museum, and again for two tours of Manitoba, Saskatchewan and Northwestern Ontario. The last time I remember doing *Everybody's Business* was at the West End Cultural Centre in Winnipeg as a part of Pride celebrations.

Native Earth's *Savage* was also created as a one-off. In 2007, a teacher at Fort Frances High School contacted us. The school was struggling with racism, homophobia and intolerance, and this teacher thought that theatre would be a way to open up the discussion. He knew the company from Native Earth's tour of *Tales of An Urban Indian*, which had played in the high school the year before.

Savage tells the story of Gary, a young Native man, who is bullied and beaten because he is gay and Native. He is protected by Fiona, a young Native woman, who keeps him from running away to the city long enough to finish high school. Nine hundred students saw *Savage* in its first iteration.

The Attorney-General of Ontario's Victim Services Secretariat picked up the play to tour to five more rural communities. Once again, we revised the text, adding in a fourth scene that addressed poverty issues, and took to the road. Since then, *Savage* has played to more than 5,624 people in 18 communities, in schools, universities, in cafeterias and conferences. The script will be published in an anthology of Made To Order work next season.

The Made To Order program puts Native Earth right into a community, in front of an audience that may never set foot in a theatre. *Strong Medicine*, our play about tobacco use in Aboriginal communities, played to health professionals gathered from across Ontario.

One of our most challenging commissions was for the Canadian Aboriginal Minerals Association; how do you make consultation active and theatrical? *Stakes* featured a dancing moose who refers to both *Hinterland Who's Who* and John Ralston Saul's *A Fair Country*, a young woman who undergoes a makeover from buckskin clad forest nymph to hard-hatted, work-booted, chain-saw-toting prospector, and a rap that wraps up the whole extravaganza, complete with cards a la Bob Dylan. Most of the executives from across Canada who gathered at the Palais Royale for dinner and entertainment would never get a chance to see a play by Native Earth, much less one that spoke directly to them about the issues with which they grapple on a daily basis.

The communities Native Earth engages through the MTO program vary widely, often shifting within the life of the project. *Takin' Pride* was commissioned by an Aboriginal Education centre to address the logo issue in schools and played first in a school that was in the throes of a heated debate about changing its teams' warrior logo, a school where the student body believed itself to be absolutely without Aboriginal students. In the year since its debut, *Takin' Pride* has played to 1350 people: students, school boards, to teachers and an Annual General Meeting.

In most cases, Made To Orders are commissioned by one representative of a community who envisions a dialogue within her community that will be facilitated by the animation of an issue, or issues: *Savage* was commissioned by a teacher who could see the intolerance in his school; *Strong Medicine* by a health care professional who dealt with the effects of tobacco; *Takin' Pride* by an educator in charge of a large multicultural population; *Stake* by a mining professional looking for a meatier entertainment than a stand-up comedian and a band.

The most recent request for a Made To Order piece came from a new community. The Graduate Law Students Association at Osgoode Hall was organizing their annual conference. Their chair contacted Native Earth and asked for a piece that would illuminate some of the issues around Aboriginal people and justice. She says they know the law, she and her colleagues, but she wants to reframe the discussion in a way to make them, to make us all, think about the intersection of law and First Nations, about the reality of the justice system in the lives of Aboriginal people.

Created with these objectives in mind, *The Road Forward* is a different kind of community-commissioned piece, weaving together excerpts from extant works, works about disappearing Aboriginal people, about the historically problematic relationship with police, about the Indian Residential School Settlement, about the Burnt Church confrontations over the lobster fishery. The piece ends with a song—"The Road Forward" by Jennifer Kreisberg—accompanied by a series of projections, quotations from the Royal Commission On Aboriginal Peoples, and a host of contemporary Aboriginal public figures, writers, actors, singers, lawyers, educators.

This engagement with a community of lawyers has given us occasion to examine the Made To Order program. On the one hand, there is a pleasing circularity in the fact that seven years on from its first commission, the program is once again engaged in a discussion with a community about resolving differences in fair and inclusive ways, but the makeup of the community is surprisingly different from the 2004 conference. As far as we can tell, there was not a single Aboriginal lawyer in the GLSA audience; if there was, she did not self-identify.

This is not the first time Native Earth has been called upon to offer a Native perspective to a non-Native audience. We are in fact so often asked to educate about

Native issues that we are in the process of creating a piece that we call (in-house) *Indian 101*. However, the request from GLSA seems to be more about empowering its members to make change in their own practices, to examine their own responsibility in relationship to a community with which they will engage. Ironically, this contract seems to exemplify the values of Popular Theatre, which seeks to empower members of a community to identify, analyze and address issues affecting it. All these years later, Popular Theatre is insinuating itself back into my life, cleverly disguised as community engagement. Indeed, the principles of Popular Theatre appear to be becoming more valued in the cultural world. Arts Councils are articulating a need for community engagement, creating programs that strengthen connections between artists and communities, rewarding organizations that demonstrate an authentic relationship with a targeted population.

The Made To Order program continues to evolve within the Company, enriching the programming by creating more opportunities for artists to work on more pieces more often, to practice their craft as actors, playwrights, designers and directors, at the same time growing a community that may never have considered attending Native theatre before. The work that comes out of Native Earth continues to be of, for and by Aboriginal artists, but the audience that receives it, the communities with which it engages, continues to diversify.

(2011)

The Give-Back of the Giving Profession

by Kelley Aitken

I'm coming up the stairs from the subway at King station. Less than a metre from the top step sits a tall, skinny woman. Hair the colour and texture of straw pokes out from under her floppy deerstalker hat. She's panhandling. I tap her on the shoulder and smile.

> "Hey, Bossy Lady!" Jeanie holds her hand to the side of her wide grin and *sotto voce,* adds, "I shouldn't be here."

Jeanie usually lays claim to another corner. She has regular patrons who buy her paintings, swiftly executed swirls of acrylic on canvas board. She tells me it takes her a couple of hours or more to garner the $30 or so it takes to get her through the day. Jeanie's needs are direct and simple: wine-cut-with-water, a nice little steak or chop from the St Lawrence Market, potatoes, onions, maybe a bit of veg. Lately, I've been extolling the virtues of broccoli.

> "You need greens in your diet."

> "Okay, Bossy Lady."

The nickname is embarrassingly apt. Jeanie coined it after just one session in the art program at the Adelaide Resource Centre for Women. While the other instructors are uber-positive in their approach, my teaching style can be characterized by three words: No! Don't! Stop! Jeanie's ability to observe, name and tease me for this tendency in one fell swoop is evidence of a survival instinct honed in the ravines and under the bridges of our fair city. Though housed now in a subsidized apartment, she was living rough when she first came to the program.

> "No matter how cold it is," she explained recently, "you never get *inside* the sleeping bag, 'cause you might need to get the hell outta there." One night, she awoke to voices in the parking lot near her bivouac. "Three, four guys—they were coming for me. I threw off my covers, grabbed two empty beer bottles and smashed the ends off them, then went whooping across the parking lot like a crazy lady. They just turned and ran."

Jeanie makes the trek downtown on a daily basis, returning to her old panhandling spot. Does she feel a loss of liberty, I ask? Yes and no, she says. Making a home is hard after years of constant migration within the city limits, carrying only her sleeping roll and clothing. The building has seen violence: a month ago, a woman two floors above her was killed. But what's really getting to her is the ennui of the other residents. "I keep telling them about this program," she says. "But they won't come."

* * *

What I get from this work—teaching art twice a week at a women's centre—is anchoring, odd eh, given that it's a program for homeless women, or women whose housing needs are barely met. They live in shelters or in government housing and so, not surprisingly, are territorial (about their stuff and where they want to sit, about how long they've been in the program, about and around the sink and the coffee urn). If art is essentially a reflection of belonging or identity, then the craving to be involved in artistic practice could be described as a psychic "going home," or "being at home." Certain projects (the less demanding ones that focus on pattern and colour) produce, in the room, a kind of low hum of contentment, a homey feeling.

The Women's Art Afternoon is a community art program facilitated by Toronto's Regent Park Community Health Centre. It is housed in the Adelaide Resource Centre for Women, an un-bedded shelter that offers a variety of day programs and services for women experiencing long-term poverty. The program provides a safe and inclusive environment where women can participate in creative expression.

I've been teaching there since 2001. Along with my colleague Camille Winchester, I co-teach a smaller, more independent group with dedicated enrollment on Mondays, and on Thursdays, I alternate every three weeks with another instructor for the larger drop-in program. The instructors come up with the projects, many of which build individual components into a collaborative piece. We offer instruction in acrylic and watercolour painting; drawing using a variety of media and techniques; collage and assemblage; printmaking; encaustic; hand-building in clay; mosaic; plasticine animation, etc. On Thursdays, I am joined by a team that includes three social workers, students on placement and, occasionally, volunteers. We have a decent budget for supplies. Every week a few of the women earn honorariums by assisting with set up and clean up. (Jeanie, for example, plunges the perpetually clogged sink.)

Some of my recent projects have involved a slightly theatrical approach: mask- and hat-making using recycled papers, a communal skirt sewn together from individually designed panels, which we stepped into and sort of shuffle-danced in. Another instructor is an actor/artist/therapist who begins the class with movement: stretches and vocalizations. Given what some of the women can *say* to us and each other, the fact that this makes them shy is rather sweet. Movement makes us notice each other fully, head to toe, front to back—uncertainty gives way to smiles. In life-drawing sessions the women have taken turns posing for one another.

I get a sense of myself offering something real, and that has less to do with art— although that's the reason we're all there in the same place, with me giving my dorky little demonstrations—than with showing up as myself. Art is a way of life and being in the world, a commitment to absorbency. Those women have tough lives. They don't put on a façade, they don't wear the mask the rest of us don, reflecting our socialization, adaptability and cooperation, in short, manners. Those women don't cooperate, at least not in that middle of the road, middle-class way; they demand and beg and grab, they compete for things, ask for "presents" and want things outright: my time, supplies, praise, to sell their work. This certainty and directness saves a lot of time.

Perhaps in a setting like that I enjoy a certain paradox: I can stretch myself into a more honest shape while enjoying the theatricality. It's a big room, I have to speak in a loud voice and tell jokes and little anecdotes to snag and keep their attention if only for the few minutes of my demonstrations, inserted throughout the class. But in that moment I am also establishing something I think of as central to teaching. I'm saying to them: we're equals. Of course in many ways, we're not equal: I get paid and they don't; I have art training and they don't; and I am more or less free of mental health issues, at least the permanently disabling kind. Yet this feeling of being on a level playing field persists. Our equality is a commitment of faith on both sides. That's the genius of the program: creativity is paradoxically a blissful melting pot and an opportunity for individuals to shine. Art reaches across the centuries and says: you exist; this reflects you; your feelings are real. It dissolves the boundaries.

These women have experienced deprivation, addiction, emotional, physical and sexual abuse. They have dissociating tendencies, mental health concerns, developmental delays. It's hard for a lot of them to learn new skills. And because of that, I've had to develop a kind of full-on body involvement in my teaching: lots of demonstration followed by one-on-one attention and both of those incorporate cajoling; teasing; encouragement; acting out a process; and finally, giving up what I think of as a good result and going with the flow.

The women's art afternoon is community theatre. Sometimes it's calm. Sometimes, it's not. Mental health is a pendulum; no one is exempt and rarely is our position stationary. Much has been written about the proximity of madness and intense creativity. I am getting somewhere with this, so bear with me. It's not just that "the gloves are off" with this group, some of the women have outbursts, spark off each other in anger or frustration, speak out of turn, out of line. In the more extreme ends of their schizophrenic spectrum, the fact that some women get there at all is an achievement. But when they're experiencing equilibrium—man, oh man (woman, oh woman!)—I'd kill to draw like that, to *see* like that. It's so true to who they are; the channel to the psyche is wide open and pumping. Moira, a participant, says, and I paraphrase, "If the choice is between medication and art, I'll choose art." Some of the women in the program are walking one-act plays, emitting bulletins from the subconscious. It's a Janet Cardiff soundscape, a splintered, stratified jam session, to put it mildly, a lively place.

Forced by circumstances to compete for space, these women are by turns exhibitionist and larger than life, or capable of creating a force-field around themselves and their work. They mug for my camera; they display their work with pride; they give me back far more than the idea and materials I brought into the room.

How does this benefit my practice? That begs the question; what is my practice? Not just the in-studio creation but the way I am in the world. Teaching is a form of communicative art. It's a way to establish intimacy, community; it's an acceptable and widely used form of therapy. Teaching is service and it's an act of engagement. Like fiction writing, it touches on what Amos Oz refers to as a moral incept, curiosity about others, imagining what it's like to be in that skin, that body, that life.

Last but not least: There but for the grace of God. Their lives are so much harder than mine. I need the reminder to get out of the poor-me-unrecognized-artist whine. And when I stop teaching there, which I will eventually, I am gonna miss it like mad.

(2011)

Works Cited

Oz, Amos. Interview with Eleanor Wachtel. *Writers and Company.* CBC radio. 19 September 2010.

Suggested Further Reading

Journal Issues

Belliveau, George and Francine Chaîne, eds. *Theatre Research in Canada* 28 (2007).

Filewod, Alan, ed. *Theatre and Labour. Canadian Theatre Review* 99 (1999).

Gilbert, Helen and Sophie Nield, eds. *Performance and Asylum: Embodiment, Ethics and Community. Research in Drama Education* 13.2 (2008).

Graham, Catherine, ed. *Activist Theatre. Canadian Theatre Review* 117 (2004).

Herrington, Joan, ed. *Theatre Topics* 15:1 (2005).

Howard, Ruth, ed. *Dispatches from Artists on the Loose. Out of Place* 1 (2010).

Solomon, Alisa, ed. *Theater and Social Change. Theater* 31.3 (2001).

Stephenson, Jenn, Kim Renders, and Julie Salverson, eds. *Artists In Communities. Canadian Theatre Review*, 148 (2011).

Thompson, James, ed. *Social Theatre. The Drama Review* T183 (2004).

Wallace, Robert, ed. *Theatre and Community. Canadian Theatre Review* 37 (1983).

Audio

Cayley, David. *Puppet Uprising: Peter Schumann's The Bread and Puppet Theatre.* Four Audio CDs. Toronto: Canadian Broadcasting Corporation, 2003.

Websites

Community Arts Network (defunct but has reading room and archives): http://www.communityarts.net/.

Links to Ontario organizations and initiatives: http://artbridges.wordpress.com/.

Neighbourhood Arts Network (Toronto Arts Council and Toronto Arts Foundation): http://www.torontoartsfoundation.org/Our-Programs/Neighbourhood-Arts.

Articles, Essays, and Books

Augaitis, Daina, Lorne Falk, Sylvie Gilbert and Mary Anne Moser, eds. *Questions of Community: Artists, Audiences, Coalitions.* Banff: Banff Centre Press, 1995.

Banting, Sarah. "Courting Audiences across the Neighbourhood Divide: *Bruce—The Musical* in the Downtown Eastside." *alt.theatre: cultural diversity and the stage* 7.3 (2010): 16–23.

Barndt, Deborah. *Naming the Moment: Political Analysis for Action: A Manual for Community Groups.* Toronto: Jesuit Centre, 1989.

Barton, Bruce, ed. *Collective Creation, Collaboration and Devising.* Toronto: Playwrights Canada, 2008.

Berger, Maurice, ed. *The Crisis of Criticism.* New York: New Press, 1998.

Byrd, Kim and Ed Nyman. "Quipping Against the Pricks." *Canadian Theatre Review* 77 (1993): 8–12.

Boal, Augusto. *Games for Actors and Non-Actors.* 2nd ed. Trans. Adrian Jackson. New York: Routledge, 1992.

———. *Legislative Theatre.* Trans. Adrian Jackson. London: Routledge, 1998.

———. *Theatre of the Oppressed.* (1979) Trans. Charles A. McBride and Maria-Odilia Leal McBride. New York: Theatre Communications Group, 1985.

Boon, Richard and Jane Plastow, eds. *Theatre and Empowerment: Community Drama on the World Stage.* Cambridge: Cambridge UP, 2004.

Bouzak, Don. "Industrials for the Social Services." *Canadian Theatre Review* 99 (2001): 10–15.

Brookes, Chris. *A Public Nuisance: A History of the Mummers Troupe.* St. John's: Institute of Social and Economic Research, Memorial University of Newfoundland, 1988.

Carniol, Ben. *Challenging Social Services in Canada.* 3rd edn. Toronto: Between the Lines, 1995.

Caruth, Cathy, ed. *Trauma: Explorations in Memory.* Baltimore: John Hopkins UP, 1995.

Cohen-Cruz, Jan. *Engaging Performance: Theatre As Call And Response.* New York: Routledge, 2010.

Cohen-Cruz, Jan and Mady Schutzman, eds. *A Boal Companion: Dialogues on theatre and cultural politics.* New York: Routledge, 2006.

Cole, Catherine M. "The Rewind Cantata: South Africa's Truth and Reconciliation in Repertoire." *Theater* 38.3 (2008): 85–109.

Coult, Tony and Baz Kershaw. *Engineers of the Imagination: The Welfare State Handbook*. London: Methuen, 1983.

Court, Tony and Baz Kershaw, eds. *Engineers of the Imagination: The Welfare State Handbook*. London: Methuen, 1983.

————. *Local Acts: Community-based Performance in The United States*. New Brunswick, NJ: Rutgers UP, 2005.

————. *Radical Street Performance: An International Anthology*. New York: Routledge, 1998.

Cullis-Suzuki, Severn, Kris Frederickson, Ahmed Kaysii and Cynthia Mackenzie with Daniel Aldana Cohen, eds. *Young Activists: A Generation Stands Up For Change*. Vancouver: Greystone, 2007.

Deavere Smith, Anna. *Fires in the Mirror*. New York: Doubleday, 1993.

Diamond, David. *Theatre for Living: The Art and Science of Community-based Dialogue*. Victoria, BC: Trafford, 2007.

DiLiberto, Lisa. "Can't We Just Laugh Instead?" *Out of Place* 2 (2011): forthcoming.

Doolittle, Lisa and Troy Emery Twigg. "*Iitaohkanao'pi: The Meeting Place*: An Intercultural, Interdisciplinary Performance." *alt.theatre: cultural divcersity and the stage* 4.2–3 (2006): 25–27.

Filewod, Alan. *Collective Encounters: Documentary Theatre in English Canada*. Toronto: U of Toronto P, 1987.

Filewod, Alan and David Watt. *Worker's Playtime: Theatre and the Labour Movement Since 1970*. Sydney: Currency, 2001.

Freire, Paulo. *Pedagogy of Hope*. New York: Continuum, 1994.

————. *Pedagogy of the Oppressed*. New rev. 20th-Anniversary ed. New York: Continuum, 1993.

Fusco, Coco. "The Other History of Intercultural Performance." *Re-Direction: A Theoretical and Practical Guide*. Ed. Rebecca Schneider and Gabrielle Cody. London: Routledge, 2002. 266–80.

Gallagher, Kathleen and David Booth, ed. *How Theatre Educates: Convergences & Counterpoints*. Toronto: U of Toronto P, 2003.

Gill, Sue and John Fox. *The Dead Good Funerals Book*. Ulverston, Cumbria: Engineers of the Imagination, 1996.

Godin, Nadine. "Acadian Parlance on Stage." *Canadian Theatre Review* 75 (1993): 12–15.

Grace, Sherrill. "Representations of the Inuit: From Other to Self." *Theatre Research in Canada* 21 (2000): 38–48.

Graham, Catherine. "Performing Community in English Canada and Quebec." *Theatre Topics* 10:2 (2000): 101–11.

Heron, Barbara. *Desire for Development: Whiteness, Gender and the Helping Imperative.* Waterloo: Wilfrid Laurier UP, 2007.

Holden, Joan. "In Praise of Melodrama." *ReImagining America: The Arts of Social Change.* Ed. Mark O'Brian and Craig Little. Santa Cruz: New Society Publishers, 1990. 278–84.

Howard, Ruth. "Holding On and Letting Go: Designing the Community Play." *Canadian Theatre Review* 90 (1997): 15–18.

Jellicoe, Ann. *Community Plays: How to Put Them On.* London, Methuen, 1987.

Kaplan, Ellen W. "Going the Distance: Trauma, Social Rupture, and the Work of Repair." *Theatre Topics,* 15.2 (2005): 171–84.

Kershaw, Baz. *The Politics of Performance: Radical Theatre as Cultural Intervention.* London: Routledge, 1992.

Kidd, Ross. "Theatre for Development: Diary of a Zimbabwe Workshop." *New Theatre Quarterly* 1.2: 179–204.

Knowles, Ric. *The Theatre Of Form and The Production of Meaning: Contemporary Canadian Dramaturgies.* Toronto: ECW, 1999.

Knutson, Susan. "Through Pain to Release: Japanese and Canadian Artists Collaborate on a British Columbian Ghost Noh Drama." *alt.theatre: cultural diversity and the stage* 6.1 (2008): 8–17.

Little, Edward. "Avoiding The Missionary Position: Ethics, Efficacy, and the Other in a New Undergraduate Theatre Program." *alt.theatre: cultural diversity and the stage* 1.4 (2000): 8–10.

———. "Taking it to the Streets: The Reading Hebron Community Project." *alt.theatre: cultural diversity and the stage* 1.4 (2000): 6–7.

Mabala, Richard and Karen B. Allen. "Participatory Action Research on HIV/AIDS through a Popular Theatre Approach in Tanzania." *Evaluation and Program Planning* 25 (2002): 333–39.

Mackey, Clarke. *Random Acts of Culture: Reclaiming Art and Community in the 21st Century.* Toronto: Between The Lines, 2010.

McGrath, John. *The Bone Won't Break: On Theatre and Hope in Hard Times.* London: Methuen, 1990.

———. *A Good Night Out: Popular Theatre: Audience, Class, Form.* London: Nick Hern, 1991.

Nadeau, Denise. *Counting Our Victories: A Training Guide on Popular Education and Organizing.* Vancouver: Repeal the Deal Productions, Media Resources for Mobilization, 2001.

Nogueira, Marcia Pompêo. "Theatre for Development: An Overview." *Research in Drama Education.* 7.1 (2002): 103–07.

O'Donnell, Darren. *Social Acupuncture.* Toronto: Coach House, 2006.

Perlmutar, Lorne. "Aids On Stage: How Theatre is Living With AIDS." *Theatrum* 19 (1990): 16–22.

Prentki, Tim and Sheila Preston, eds. *The Applied Theatre Reader.* Routledge, 2008.

Sajnani, Nisha and Denise Nadeau. "Creating Safer Spaces for Immigrant Women of Colour; Performing the Politics of Possibility." *Canadian Women Studies* 25:1–2 (2006): 45–53.

Salverson, Julie, ed. *Popular Political Theatre and Performance.* Toronto: Playwrights Canada, 2010.

———. "Taking Liberties: A Theatre Class of Foolish Witnesses." *Research in Drama Eduction* 13.2 (2008): 245–55.

———. "Transgressive Storytelling or an Aesthetic of Injury: Performance, Pedagogy and Ethics." *"Ethnic," Multicultural, and Intercultural Theatre.* Ed. Ric Knowles and Ingrid Mundel. Toronto: Playwrights Canada, 2009. 54–67.

Schutzman, Mady and Jan Cohen-Cruz, eds. *Playing Boal: Theatre, therapy, activism.* London: Routledge, 1994.

Shalson, Lara. "Creating Community, Constructing Criticism: The Women's One World Festival 1980–1981." *Theatre Topics* 15:2 (2005): 221–39.

Smith, Dorothy. "Researching the Everyday World as Problematic." *The Everyday World as Problematic.* Toronto: U of Toronto P, 1987. 181–207.

Snell, Peter. "Behind Bars: Serving Theatre in Prisons." *Theatrum* 19 (1990): 11–15.

Taylor, Philip. *Applied Theatre: Creating Transformative Encounters in the Community.* Portsmouth, NH: Heinemann, 2003.

Thompson, James. *Applied Theatre: Bewilderment and Beyond.* Oxford: Peter Lang, 2003.

———. *Digging Up Stories: Applied Theatre, Performance and War.* Manchester: Manchester UP, 2005.

Weigler, Will. *Strategies for Playbuilding: Helping Groups Translate Issues into Theatre.* Portsmouth, NH: Heinemann, 2001.

Winterson, Jeanette. *Art Objects: Essays on Ecstasy and Effrontery.* New York: Alfred A Knopf, 1995.

Notes on Contributors

Kelley Aitken's collection of short stories *Love in a Warm Climate* (The Porcupine's Quill, 1998) was nominated for the Commonwealth Prize, Best First Book, Canadian Caribbean Region. She is a visual artist, writer, and instructor. She teaches art at the Adelaide Resource Centre for Women, and drawing in the collections at the Art Gallery of Ontario. She makes her home in Toronto with her partner, the teacher and environmentalist Frank de Jong. View her work at www.kelleyaitken.ca.

Don Bouzek is the Artistic Director of GROUND ZERO PRODUCTIONS, a twenty-five-year-old company which creates theatre on a variety of social issues. Since 2000 he has been working with Banner Theatre from Birmingham, UK to produce a series of Video Ballads about globalization. The latest, *With Eyes Wide Open*, is currently on tour in England. He has also worked with Alberta artists to create shows about the GWG jeans plant in Edmonton and the Black Pioneers. Mr. Bouzek also creates videos. He has done a number of web based projects, of which the RAM GWG site is the latest example. He has completed two documentaries for Athabasca U and Access TV. Mr. Bouzek has won two awards from the Canadian Association of Labour Media for his work with unions, including the Canadian Labour Congress, the Communications, Energy and Paperworkers, and the United Nurses of Alberta. Mr. Bouzek is the recipient of an Alberta Centennial Medal for his work in the arts.

Steven Bush is a Senior Lecturer in Performance at University College Drama Program, University of Toronto. He has over forty years of experience in professional theatre as an actor, director, dramaturge, teacher, and Artistic Director. He is co-author of *Richard Thirdtime*, *Available Targets*, and *Life on the Line*. He performed in Modern Times Stage Company's *Hallaj* in 2009. His *Beating the Bushes* (developed in collaboration with Richard Payne) was released by Talonbooks in October 2010, and his book of conversations with Canadian theatre pioneer George Luscombe is scheduled for publication by Mosaic Press in 2011.

David S. Craig has written more than twenty professionally produced plays including the international hit comedy *Having Hope at Home*. He has adapted *The Neverending Story* for Imagination Stage and the Seattle Children's Theatre, and *Cue for Treason* for the Lorraine Kimsa Theatre (formerly YPT). For Roseneath Theatre he has written the internationally acclaimed *Danny, King of the Basement* (Dora Mavor Moore Award for Best Production, German Children's Theatre Prize nomination) as well as *Tough Case*, *Smokescreen*, and *Rocket and the Queen of Dreams*. His one-man show *Napalm the Magnificent* (Dora Nominee—Outstanding Production & Performance Nominee) was performed extensively in Canada and at the John Houseman Theatre Centre on Theatre Row in Manhattan. For CBC Radio, David created a fifty-one part series for

Morningside based on his stage play *Booster Crane, P.M.* and for *Metro Morning*, a fifty-episode series titled *The Diamond Lane. NOW* magazine has called David S. Craig, "one of the top twenty playwrights in Canada." He is currently the Artistic Director of Roseneath Theatre (www.roseneath.ca), Ontario's largest touring theatre.

David Fancy is Chair of the Department of Dramatic Arts at Brock University, where he teaches performance and theatre as cultural practice. He writes on issues around immanence and performance, and also on performance and communications technologies.

Alan Filewod is Professor of Theatre Studies at the University of Guelph. His books include *Collective Encounters: Documentary Theatre in English Canada* (1987), *Performing "Canada": The Nation Enacted in the Imagined Theatre* (2002), and, with David Watt, *Workers' Playtime: Theatre and the Labour Movement since 1970* (2001).

Honor Ford-Smith is Associate Professor in Community and Environmental Arts in the Faculty of Environmental Studies, York University. She worked for many years as an actress, director, and producer of Caribbean theatre and is best known for her work with the Sistren Theatre Collective of Jamaica. She is editor and co-author of *Lionheart Gal: Life-Stories of Jamaican Women* (with the Sistren Theatre Collective) (Mona, Jamaica: University of the West Indies Press (2005)), and editor of the collection *3 Jamaican plays: A postcolonial collection 1977–1987* (Kingston, Jamaica: Paul Issa Publications), due out in 2011. Her anthology of poems *My mother's last dance* is available through the University of Toronto Press.

Sarah B. Hood has served as editor of three national Canadian magazines about the performing arts and published hundreds of articles about theatre in a wide variety of periodicals. A former president of the Canadian Theatre Critics Association, she has been shortlisted for the National Magazine Awards. She lectures on writing, arts, and culture in the Centre for Arts and Design at Toronto's George Brown College.

Ruth Howard is the founding Artistic Director of Jumblies Theatre, a company that makes art with, for, and about the people and places of Toronto. Theatre creations include *Oy Di Velt Vet Vern Yinger* at Camp Naivelt, Brampton (remounted for Toronto's 2009 Mayworks Festival); *Bridge of One Hair* in Etobicoke (premiered at Harbourfront Centre's New World Stage in 2007); and an adaptation of Shakespeare's *Winter's Tale* mixed with local stories in Scarborough (final production in 2011). Ruth also has several decades experience as set and costume designer at professional theatres across Canada and large-scale community plays in Canada and the UK. Awards and distinctions include: 2005 *Vital People* award, Toronto Community Foundation; 2007 Dora Nomination for costume design, *Bridge of One Hair*; Ontario Trillium Great Grants award to Jumblies for the Etobicoke residency and production.

Kirsty Johnston is an Assistant Professor in the Dept. of Theatre and Film at the University of British Columbia. Her current research is focused on intersections of disability, impairment, health, and theatre and has been published in such journals as *Text and Performance Quarterly, Theatre Topics, Theatre Research in Canada, The*

Journal of Canadian Studies, *Modern Drama*, and *The Journal of Medical of Humanities*. She is currently preparing a book on Canadian disability theatres.

After his release from Matsqui Penitentiary, **Patrick Keating** studied at Simon Fraser University and completed his BA. He is presently living in Vancouver and working as an actor in theatre, television, and film. He was nominated for a Jessie Richardson Award in 2009–10 for the role of Darryl in Shawn MacDonald's *Demon Voice* for Touchstone Theatre and just completed Sam Shepard's *A Lie of the Mind* with Main Street Theatre. He likes open spaces and back stories.

Bruce Kirkley is a full-time faculty member and currently Head of the Theatre Department at the University of the Fraser Valley. He teaches acting, voice, theatre history and theory, and Shakespeare in performance, and has also directed many productions for the department's theatre season. His research interests include the actor's creative process, and issues of media and performance. His articles have been published in *Modern Drama*, *Canadian Theatre Review*, *Encyclopedia of Canadian Literature*, *Theatre Research in Canada*, and *Theatre and Television*. He is currently co-editing, with Bruce Barton, a special issue on *Theatre and Intermediality* for *Theatre Research in Canada*.

Ric Knowles is Professor of Theatre Studies at the University of Guelph. He is the former editor of *Canadian Theatre Review* and *Modern Drama*, author of five books on theatre and performance and editor of fifteen, and is General Editor of Critical Perspectives on Canadian Theatre in English and of New Essays on Canadian Theatre. In 2009 he won the Exellence in Editing: Sustained Achievement award from the Association for Theatre in Higher Education. His most recent book is *Theatre & Interculturalism* (Palgrave 2010). He is a practicing professional dramaturge.

Professor **Edward Little** coordinates and teaches in the Theatre and Development Specialization in the Department of Theatre at Concordia University. He is also Editor-in-Chief of *alt.theatre: cultural diversity and the stage* and Associate Artistic Director of Teesri Duniya Theatre. His current research projects include serving as a member of the coordinating committee for the project Life Stories of Montrealers Displaced by War, Genocide, and Other Human Rights Violations, and as Leader of the Oral History and Performance team—one of seven research clusters comprising the Life Stories project.

Denyse Lynde is a Professor at Memorial University of Newfoundland and Labrador where she teaches theatre and drama. Her research interests lie in the theatre and drama of Newfoundland and she has been published in *Canadian Theatre Review*, *Theatre Research in Canada*, and elsewhere.

Clarke Mackey has taught in the Department of Film and Media at Queen's University since 1988. His feature films, television shows, and documentaries on social justice issues have won awards and garnered much critical praise over the last forty years. Mackey's book *Random Acts of Culture: Reclaiming Art and Community in the 21st Century* was released in the fall of 2010 by Between the Lines Press.

Yvette Nolan is a playwright, dramaturg, director, and educator. Her plays include *BLADE, Job's Wife, Video, Annie Mae's Movement, Two Old Women*, the libretto *Hilda Blake*, and the radio play *Owen*. She is the editor of *Beyond the Pale: Dramatic Writing from First Nations Writers and Writers of Colour*, and of the upcoming *Refractions: Solo*, with Donna-Michelle St Bernard. Directing credits include *Salt Baby*, *A Very Polite Genocide, Death of a Chief, Tales of An Urban Indian, The Unnatural and Accidental Women, Annie Mae's Movement* (Native Earth), *The Ecstasy of Rita Joe* (Western Canada Theatre/National Arts Centre), *The Only Good Indian…*, and *The Triple Truth* (Turtle Gals). As a dramaturg, she works across Canada, most recently at Saskatchewan Playwrights Centre Spring Festival of New Plays. In 2007, she received the Maggie Bassett Award for service to the theatre community. She has been the president of the Playwrights Union of Canada (1998–2001), of Playwrights Canada Press (2003–2005), and of the Indigenous Performing Arts Alliance (2007–2008). In 2007–2008 she was the National Arts Centre's Playwright-In-Residence. As the artistic director of Native Earth Performing Arts from 2003–2011, she was recently awarded the City of Toronto's Aboriginal Affairs Award.

Richard Payne (1949–2010) was a dedicated interdisciplinary artist, who trained with Lawren P. Harris. He was a skilled and passionate painter, an inventive scenic designer, a witty cartoonist of great insight and as a playwright, he created such works as *The Yellow House at Arles: Gauguin/van Gogh* (with Dennis Hayes). Richard was a member of the acting company at Toronto Workshop Productions for three seasons where his work with theatre pioneer George Luscombe included *Ten Lost Years*. With his own Downsize Theatre Company, Richard took the TWP mandate to organized labour and social justice venues. He also taught students and community actors all across Canada in universities, high schools, and torchlit cornfields. At TWP Richard met Steven Bush, with whom he later collaborated on many projects including *Beating the Bushes*. And it was at Matsqui Institution that Richard met Patrick Keating; there they collaborated on *Boss Ubu*.

Sherene H. Razack is Professor, Sociology and Equity Studies in Education, the Ontario Institute for Studies in Education of the University of Toronto. Her research and teaching interests lie in the area of race and gender issues in the law. Her courses include: "Race, Space and Citizenship;" "Race and Knowledge Production," and "Racial Violence and the Law." Books include: *States of Race* (Co-editor with Malinda Smith and Sunera Thobani); *Casting Out: Race and the Eviction of Muslims From Western Law and Politics*; *Dark Threats and White Knights: The Somalia Affair, Peacekeeping and the New Imperialism*; *Race, Space and the Law: Unmapping a white settler society* (editor); *Looking white people in the eye: gender, race and culture in court-rooms and classrooms*; *Canadian feminism and the law: The women's legal education and action fund and the pursuit of equality*.

Nisha Sajnani, Ph.D., RDT, is a multidisciplinary artist, drama therapist, and educator. She is the President-Elect of the National Association for Drama Therapy and on faculty at the Institutes for the Arts in Psychotherapy (NYC) and at Yale University (New Haven) where she teaches a course entitled "Applied Theatre, Trauma, and

Cultural Intervention." Nisha is the director of Creative Alternatives, an international community-engaged arts network with a local focus in Montreal. Creative Alternatives is a project partner in the Montreal Life Stories project which seeks to collect, archive, and represent the oral histories of five-hundred Montrealers who have been displaced by war, genocide, and other human rights violations. She is also the director of Project A.L.I.V.E, a trauma informed, arts-based approach to facilitating student engagement in collaboration with the Metropolitan Business Academy and the Foundation for the Arts and Trauma. Nisha is currently affiliated with the Harvard Refugee Trauma Program as a collaborator within the Global Trauma and Recovery initiative.

Playwright, librettist, and essayist, **Julie Salverson** has published, spoken and taught extensively about the artist as witness and the relationship between historical memory, politics, ethics, and the imagination. Librettist for *Shelter,* a clown opera about the atomic bomb (Tapestry New Opera, composer Juliet Palmer), she was shortlisted in 2009 for the Canadian Broadcasting Corporation Literary Award in Creative Nonfiction. She has been a participant in the Banff Centre for the Arts Writing Studio and Literary Journalism Programs. Associate Professor of Drama at Queen's University, her essay "An Atomic Elegy" is the cover story for *Maisonneuve Magazine,* Summer 2011. She is working on the nonfiction book *Atomic Elegy: Finding Community in Haunted Places.*

Sarah Stanley was born and raised in Montréal, studied at Queen's University, École Jacques Lecoq, The Vancouver Film School, and other places whenever possible. An award-winning director, Sarah has focused her attention on new plays and playwrights. Claudia Dey, Greg McArthur, Ned Dickens, Mitch Miyagawa and Tara Beagan are just a few of the many writers Sarah worked with at outset of their professional writing lives. She has also worked with established writers on their new plays, including Linda Griffiths, Susan Coyne, Robin Fulford, George Rideout and Berni Stapleton. Sarah co-founded The Baby Grand in Kingston, Ontario, in 1985, Women Making Scenes in Montreal in 1992, and Die in Debt that produced (and for which she directed) massive and celebrated productions of *Romeo and Juliet* (Under the Bathurst Street Bridge), *Oedipus* (under the Gardiner Expressway and written by Ned Dickens), and *Megatropolis.* Sarah served as the only female Artistic Director of Buddies in Bad Times Theatre, and was the inaugural Associate Artist at The Magnetic North Theatre Festival. She continues to teach, direct, and co-create. *The Book of Judith* is her latest adventure into theatre that makes her heart work better.

Rachael Van Fossen is a theatre artist, teacher, and arts consultant whose focus is the development, production, and promotion of engaged community arts. Her current research and creative interests include context-specific performance, performance of multiple identities, and rendering authorial presence visible in engaged art practices. Affiliations: Faculty, MFA in Interdisciplinary Arts Program, Goddard College; Part-time Faculty, Theatre and Development, Concordia University; Founding Artistic Director, Common Weal Community Arts (1992–1999); Artistic Director, Black

Theatre Workshop, 2001–2005; and Associate Artistic Director, Collectif MOYO (2007–2010).

A theatre artist and writer trained in dance, mime, and music, **Savannah Walling** is the artistic director of Vancouver Moving Theatre, a professional interdisciplinary arts company she co-founded twenty-three years ago in Vancouver's Downtown Eastside with executive producer and husband Terry Hunter. The small company creates repertoire in collaboration with artists from many genres, techniques, and cultural traditions; produces the annual Downtown Eastside Heart of the City Festival; and develops educational resources. The award-winning company currently focuses on community-engaged arts projects with and for their Downtown Eastside inner-city home.